I0810075

HIDDEN HISTORY *of* QUEENS

HIDDEN HISTORY *of* QUEENS

Richard Panchyk

THE History PRESS

Published by The History Press
Charleston, SC
www.historypress.com

Copyright © 2018 by Richard Panchyk
All rights reserved

Front cover: Library of Congress.
Back cover, top: Library of Congress; *bottom*: Library of Congress.

First published 2018

Manufactured in the United States

ISBN 9781467138536

Library of Congress Control Number: 2018936079

Notice: The information in this book is true and complete to the best of our knowledge. It is offered without guarantee on the part of the author or The History Press. The author and The History Press disclaim all liability in connection with the use of this book.

All rights reserved. No part of this book may be reproduced or transmitted in any form whatsoever without prior written permission from the publisher except in the case of brief quotations embodied in critical articles and reviews.

This book is dedicated to Grand Avenue in Elmhurst and Maspeth, a corridor of such central importance in my life. I have so many fond memories of the people and places I encountered along the avenue over the years. Along Grand were my favorite pizza places, the library where I'd eagerly browse for new books and records, the variety store where I bought my baseball cards, the Met Food where my grandmother took me shopping, the pool hall where I sometimes played and my junior high school. Grand was my home, and still is. Even today, as I walk along Grand, I feel that perfect combination of excited and yet cozy and comforting. I feel the connection of the past to the present to the future. Thanks, Grand! I love ya!

Contents

Acknowledgements

Thanks to all who encouraged me during my epic Queens journey. Special thanks to George Maharis, Ray Duke, Katherine Panchyk and James Sheehan for talking to me and helping shine light on some cool hidden history. Also thanks to Banks Smither and Rick Delaney at The History Press for their support.

Introduction

As I sat in my elementary school classroom in my native Elmhurst, listening to my teacher talk about the battles of the Revolutionary War, it all seemed so distant to me. Oh, sure, it was naturally fascinating to a young nerd such as myself, but it was distant, far removed from my reality in the moment. Little could I have known then that the very spot where PS 102 stood on a hill two blocks south of Queens Boulevard was once part of a massive encampment of British soldiers in 1776. I could not have dreamed that on the street where my friend and I ran around playing cops and robbers with our toy guns, soldiers cleaned their muskets and shined their bayonets two hundred years before.

And neither could I have imagined as I thumbed past the 45 single for "Love Is a Battlefield" in the Crazy Eddie's on Fifty-Seventh Street and Queens Boulevard that I was standing exactly where General William Howe sat at a desk in September 1776, happily echoing the same thought as Pat Benatar after the important British win at the Battle of Long Island and penning his official report about the battle for the bigwigs (literally) back home in England.

Hidden History of Queens is a celebration of the rich history of this diverse and wondrous borough. It's filled with the secrets of the past uncovered, recovered and discovered. As I researched the book, my travels took me to every corner of Queens, looking for history's remnants from Astoria to the Glen Oaks, from College Point to the Rockaways. These far-ranging Queens adventures were filled with fun and surprises, as I saw familiar places through a new lens—the lens of the past. I learned so much of the borough's hidden history, and I'm excited to share all of these stories with you. Join me as we discover new reasons to love Queens.

Chapter 1

Apples and Creeks and Parks, Oh My!

Queens has it all—beaches and wetlands, hills and meadows, creeks and coves, forests and parks. The borough is large and geographically diverse, with ample swaths of preserved nature alongside some of the most densely populated places in the country. That is part of the beauty of Queens—there is so much history hidden in the most unexpected places. In this chapter you'll read about a grove of ancient trees, the birthplace of the world's most beloved apple, the only inhabited island in Queens and other really cool (and occasionally stinky) places.

The Alley Pond Giant

When I found out that the oldest and tallest tree in New York City resides in a hidden corner of Alley Pond Park, I knew I had to go and see for myself. I read about how to locate the tree, and it sounded pretty complicated, as if the tree was deep in the heart of a dense forest. Well, this only steeled my determination to find the Alley Pond Giant, though I was not terribly hopeful. I was not even sure where I could enter the park to begin my trek to the site.

It was easier than I thought. The tree is located just west of the intersection of the Cross Island Parkway and the Long Island Expressway

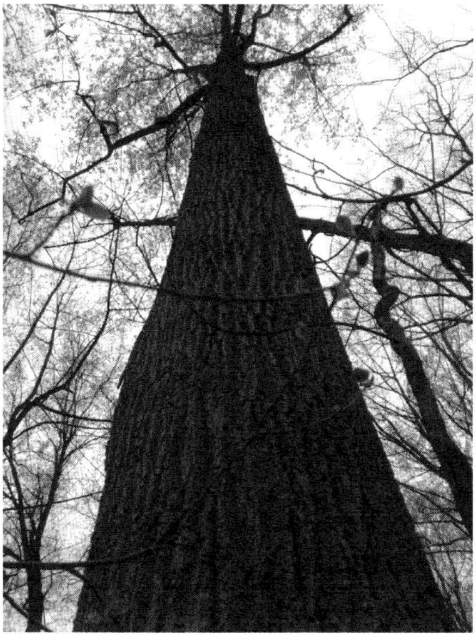

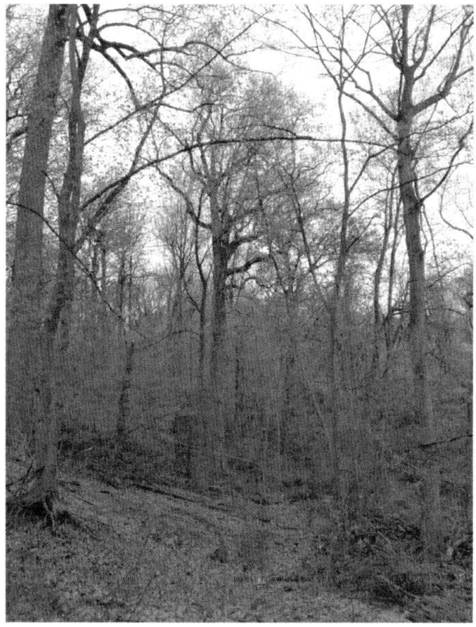

Left: Many of the tulip trees in Alley Pond Park's untouched corner of forest are giants that are hundreds of years old. *Author's collection.*

Right: The Alley Pond Giant is the city's oldest and tallest tree. *Author's collection.*

(LIE). I parked on one of the side streets off East Hampton Boulevard and walked south. An encouraging sign was, well, an encouraging sign that had been placed just outside the park by the New York City Department of Parks and Recreation describing the tree. There, I found an entrance to the park and a winding trail that led northeast, along a ridge, encircling a valley. You'd never know you were right next to a major highway (except for the glimpses of cars you can see as the trail gets to within a mere few feet of the LIE). The Alley Pond Giant sits at the bottom of the valley, which makes its height when seen from atop the ridge somewhat deceiving. But along the trail and near it are other tulip trees of tremendous height and age, so you quickly get the idea—this feels like a preserved piece of primordial forest. I read that to spot the Giant, you have to look for the chain-link fence that surrounds it. And there it was, rising up from below, a 134-foot-tall tree that is said to be more than 350 years old, dating to at least the 1660s, the Dutch era of New York. To get a better feel for its true size, I ambled down along some rocks to the forest floor. Among the giants down there I realized just how amazing it was that such a swath of ancient trees had been preserved.

All things must pass, but for now, the future looks bright for this middle-aged tree, as tulip trees can live up to six hundred years!

THE BIG APPLE'S APPLE

New York City's moniker "The Big Apple" dates only to the 1920s, but in fact, apples played a big role in the city's history going back more than three hundred years. As the story goes, sometime around 1700, the seed of an ordinary apple tree bordering on the swamp on Gershom Moore's property in Newtown, fell into the ground and germinated. (Gershom was the son of English immigrant Reverend John Moore and relative of Clement Clarke Moore, the Christmas poem author.) This type of thing presumably happened fairly often, but the result was unique. The seedling that grew developed into a mature apple tree whose fruit was quite different from the rest. Once the Moores realized the apples from this tree were different and better, they used the original tree to propagate more trees and develop an orchard full of them. Thus was born the Newtown Pippin (also known as the Gershom Moore Pippin in the early days).

The apple's popularity spread as more people tasted it. The Newtown Pippin was a great apple for eating raw, but also for cooking; the crisp fruit has the perfect combination of sweetness and tartness. It also tasted better as it aged off the tree and reached a peak of flavor toward the end of winter, with a life of up to nine months after picking! The earliest printed reference I could find to the Newtown Pippin was in a 1776 magazine article describing the province of New York; it was the only locally grown fruit mentioned by name. An 1844 book described the apple as a "large, flat fruit of a bright yellow color, with a faint blush next to the sun; the flesh breaking, juicy, agreeably acid, and fine-flavored." The Newtown Pippin had a reputation as the finest apple grown in America.

By the mid-eighteenth century, the apple was getting praise from some very notable people. Benjamin Franklin had Pippins shipped to him when he was a diplomat on assignment in London in 1759. The Newtown Pippin also was the apple of other famous eighteenth-century eyes, including George Washington and Thomas Jefferson. By 1768, it was being cultivated in England. And in 1778, Jefferson received cuttings and began growing the Pippin in Virginia. (This variety eventually became known as the Albemarle Pippin.)

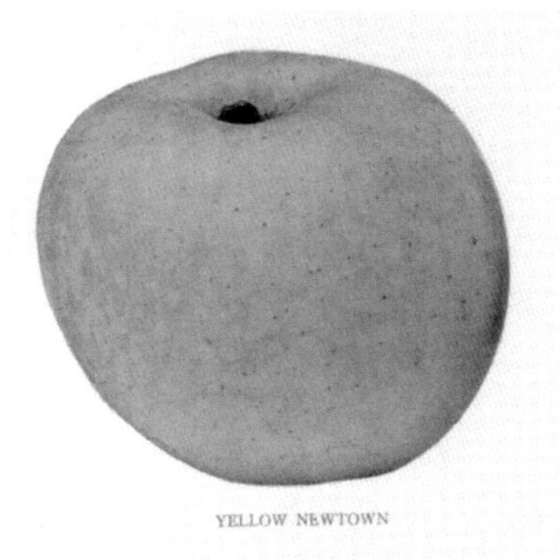

The Newtown Pippin. *Author's collection.*

The original Newtown Pippin seedling lived until 1805, when it died from excessive cuttings. (As one early twentieth-century newspaper article said, it "died for the cause, being literally cut to pieces.") In 1831, a three-hundred-acre estate in Westchester was put up for sale, with 1,500 Newtown Pippins growing on the property.

During the late 1830s at the start of her reign, Queen Victoria was given Newtown Pippins and loved them. In 1845, the imported Newtown Pippin sold in London for an incredible twenty-one dollars a barrel. In 1851, the Pippin was deemed the finest apple at the London Exposition. Though the Newtown Pippin was grown in England, people agreed that the English-grown fruit did not taste quite as good as the original New York version, likely due to soil and climate conditions. The Pippin was considered the hardiest and most long-lasting of any American apple, and that was another reason it was a popular choice to ship overseas—it could withstand the voyage (which in those days was weeks long) very well.

Though the Newtown Pippin continued to grow in the place of its origin for more than 150 years, it was not long before the bulk of its sales were attained through orchards elsewhere—first and foremost the Hudson Valley and, in the nineteenth and twentieth centuries, Pennsylvania, California and the Pacific Northwest. Newtown Pippins are used in Martinelli's brand apple juice, which gets its apples from the West Coast.

By the mid-nineteenth century, the apples were being exported from the Hudson Valley, where they grew well and in large quantities. In the 1850s, there were twenty thousand Newtown Pippin trees growing on the property of Robert Livingston Pell in Dutchess County.

Was Pippin quality consistent over the years? No, according to at least one apple connoisseur. A 1905 letter from an Englishman to the *Garden* magazine said that even though the Newtown Pippin was better than any apple in England, it was woefully worse than the Pippins that had been imported during his youth in the 1820s, proclaiming that the "Newtown Pippin of to-day is a downright fraud. All the comparative trash now received from the States is dubbed a Newtown Pippin, and is as inferior as chalk is to cheese."

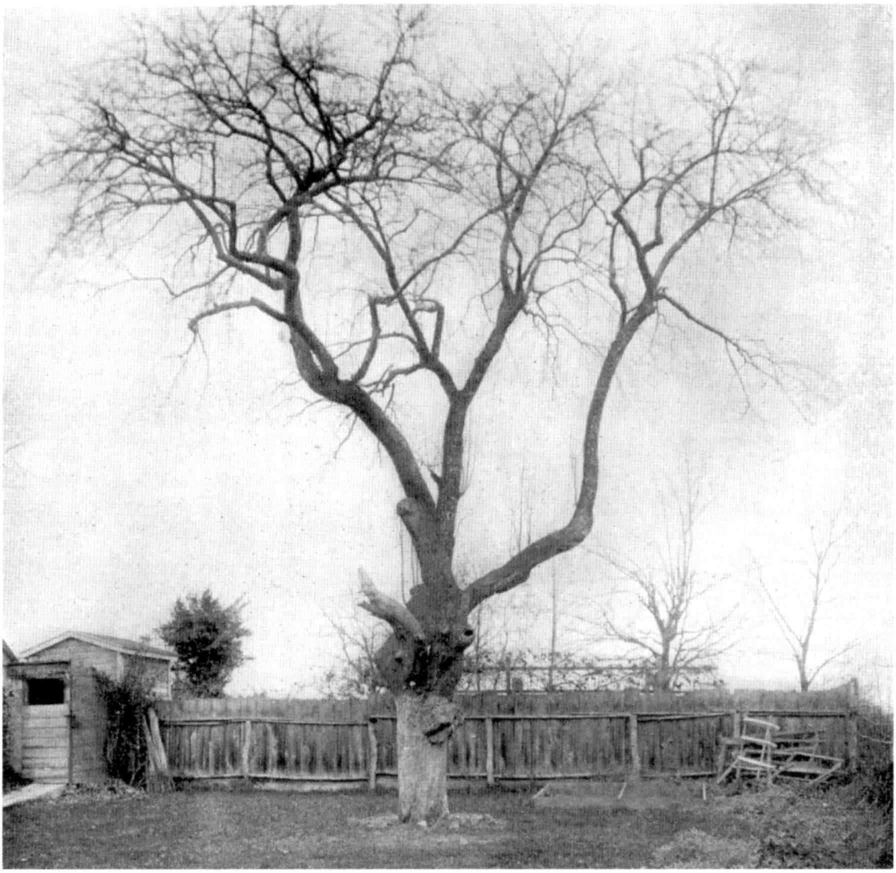

This was one of the last of the surviving eighteenth-century Newtown Pippin trees, photographed in 1902 in Elmhurst. *Author's collection.*

As Queens continued to develop and grow, there was less and less room for groves of fruit trees, though a few here and there continued to survive. By 1925, there were scant few Pippin trees left in the New York City area. About six of them still clung to life on Grand Avenue in Maspeth, near the home of DeWitt Clinton. There was also an old Pippin tree on the Riker farm in North Beach (near today's LaGuardia Airport). The headline of a 1935 article in the *New York Times* said it all: "Newtown Loses Its Pippins"—the last of the Newtown Pippin trees on Long Island died off from bugs and disease around 1935 at an orchard attached to a cider mill in Huntington (Suffolk County).

There was a general decline in Newtown Pippin consumption through the twentieth century as other apple varieties came to the market, including the Granny Smith. More recently, the Pippin has seen a resurgence in its popularity. In 2002, two trees were planted at the First Presbyterian Church on Queens Boulevard at Fifty-Fourth Avenue in Elmhurst in celebration of the congregation's 350th anniversary. Trees were also planted at Maspeth Federal Savings Bank in Maspeth and other Queens locations. The Newtown Pippin is also being grown in the Hudson Valley (though at only a fraction of its former presence) and can at times be found for sale in the autumn farmers' markets in New York City.

Hold Your Nose, We're Passing Newtown Creek

One of the most unfortunate things that has happened over time in New York and other cities is the industrial development of waterfront areas. These days, we see our waterfront areas as places for recreation and great views. And in fact, we are not pioneers in this regard. Centuries ago, almost all of the waterfront areas in what is now New York City were peaceful places with farms or mansions overlooking the water, where boating and fishing were commonplace. What happened in the meantime was the Industrial Revolution. Factories and mills required sources of water to operate, to receive raw materials and to move goods quickly onto barges for delivery, and also so they could dump their waste liquids.

Back in colonial days, what is now Long Island City was a beautiful and tranquil locale that fronted the East River. I say "what is now" because Long Island City did not exist as an entity until 1870, when Astoria and the smaller settlements of Ravenswood, Hunters Point, Blissville, Sunnyside, Dutch Kills, Steinway, Bowery Bay and Middleton were incorporated into a city. At this point, these communities were fairly bucolic, quiet places. There was no connection to Manhattan yet, other than ferry, so Long Island City was, like many places in Queens, growing slowly and steadily.

As early as the 1850s, the Hunters Point area was seen as potentially a great industrial center, due to its proximity to the ferry to Manhattan and the 3.8-mile-long, 12-foot-deep Newtown Creek, a tributary of the East River that led inland (and had itself five tributaries or arms) and was the borderline

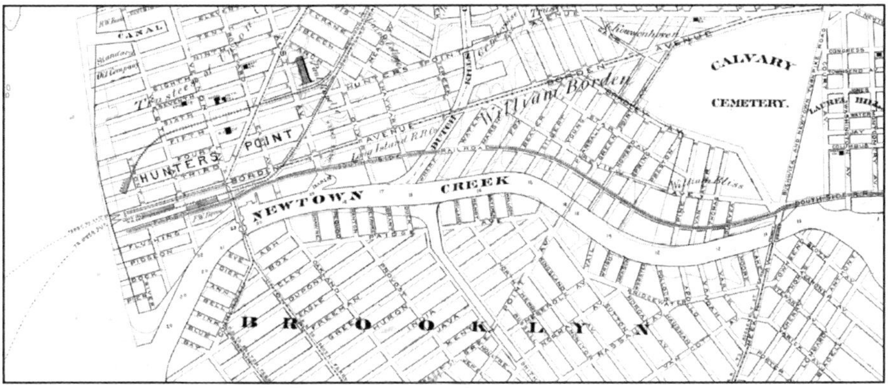

Newtown Creek, as seen on an 1874 map. *Library of Congress.*

between Queens and Brooklyn. The first kerosene refinery in the country started along Newtown Creek in 1854, followed by the first oil refinery in 1867. In those days, industry was in its infancy; the creek was still mostly, as remembered by William Smith of Elmhurst years later, "crystal clear waters abundant with fish" with boats that "frolicked along wooded banks."

But that was not to last for long. As a 1906 article in the *Brooklyn Daily Eagle* explained, establishments such as glue factories were forced to leave Manhattan and its sensitive noses for the "wilderness" of Newtown Creek, "where noses were few." The problem was, the area was becoming more and more populated, and noses were rapidly on the increase. Through the second half of the nineteenth century, petroleum refineries continued to be built along the East River and Newtown Creek. The refining process was so crude in those days that huge amounts of oil would seep into the creek, and refinery employees had to go out in boats and sop up the oil with blankets that they laid out on the water's surface.

While oil was polluting, it did not stink, unlike the byproducts of so many other industries. As early as 1881, there was an uproar about the vile smells that were emanating from Newtown Creek. Following a state board of health investigation, in 1883, Governor Grover Cleveland issued orders to thirty-two firms to abate the smells created by their factories or activities. There were many types of culprits. Even the Long Island Rail Road was asked to help by not allowing open manure-filled cars to stand on the tracks too long. The Eastern Distillery Company was ordered to remove its mash (which emanated "swill-like" odors) every twenty-four hours in the summer months. There were also pig sties and cow stables in the area. For some, the solution was easy—several firms were ordered to cover the kettles in which their noxious products such as fat and animal bones were boiled to keep the air from smelling foul. Ink manufacturers were forbidden from letting their byproducts leak into the fields adjacent to their factories. The order was backed by the threat of up to $1,000 in fines and up to one year in prison.

But even the governor's orders could not fix the situation. Fifteen years later, complaints were still pouring in about the stench of the sludge-filled, putrid waters that were wafting horrible odors to the railroad passengers on the tracks that passed directly alongside the creek. Manufacturing was not the only problem—by the turn of the twentieth century, there were six sewers that emptied human waste into the creek, three of them from Long Island City.

There was no end in sight to the growth. Some of the Long Island City establishments that existed in 1906 included the Chelsea Jute Mills, the Yellow Pine Lumber Yards and Mills, the Jacob Pfeffer Coal Yards, the American Ice Company plant and Pratt Oil Works. The planning for a bridge over the East River (what would be the Queensboro Bridge) sent people flocking to Queens, speculating that it would become a boon for manufacturing.

By 1907, lining the East River and Newtown Creek were railroad yards, steel and plaster mills, paint and dye works, oil works, chemical plants, hardware manufacturing plants, electric power and lighting and gas plants. The formerly pleasant creek's reputation continued to sink with the growing stink. It was so bad that the developer Cord Meyer, who had bought up plots of land in the village of Newtown, successfully petitioned to have its name changed to Elmhurst to avoid association with the smelly creek.

In 1929, seven million tons of coal, ore, petroleum and other materials were sent along the creek in twenty-five thousand vessels of various sizes. Despite continued media coverage of the problems, nothing was done, and industry continued to flourish along the ever-more decimated waters of the creek. In 2010, Newtown Creek was named a Superfund Site by the U.S. Environmental Protection Agency (EPA), an honor reserved for the country's most contaminated sites. Finally, there is a slow return of nature to the creek as the cleanup process begins, closely monitored by both the EPA and the Newtown Creek Alliance, which was formed in the 1990s to address the pollution. Estimates for the cleanup were in the twenty-year range and upward of $1 billion, to be paid for by both the City of New York and five polluting companies: BP America, ExxonMobil, Texaco, National Grid and Phelps Dodge Refining.

DUTCH KILLS

It's ironic that one of the foulest water bodies in all of New York City was actually one of the most desirable—one of the very first areas settled in the seventeenth century. After Willem Kieft, director-general of New Netherlands, purchased a huge tract of land that extended from the East River to the Mespatches (Maspeth) Swamp from the local Indians, a few enterprising adventurers stepped forward, requesting land upon which to build homes in the early 1640s.

The spot they chose was along a branch off of the Kill of Mespat, or Mespat Kills (today known as Newtown Creek) called Dutch Kills ("Kills" is from the Dutch for "water channel" or "stream"; it was known by the local Indians as Canapaukah Creek). This now-polluted and stagnant offshoot of the now-polluted and stagnant Newtown Creek was quite a pleasant place.

By 1643 (the date on his land patent), Richard Brutnell, an English immigrant, had settled on a one-hundred-acre farm on the east side of the Dutch Kills Creek, at the point where it met Newtown Creek. His property

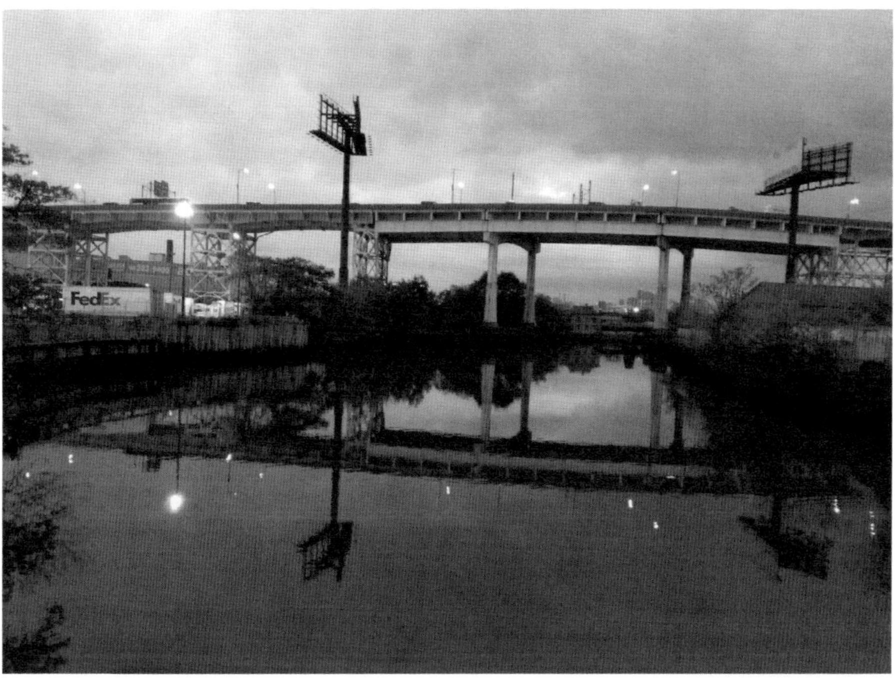

Dutch Kills today. *Author's collection.*

was directly across from the land settled by Tymen Jansen, who was a former ship's carpenter for the Dutch West India Company. North of Jansen's property was the land of Burger Jorissen, a blacksmith turned miller from Silesia, Germany, who lived there from at least 1643 until his death in 1671. By 1654, Jorissen had built a tidewater gristmill at the edge of the marshland on his property; for a while, the creek was known as Burger's or Burger Joris Kills. A man named John Hendrickson recalled in 1941 that Dutch Kills of his mid-nineteenth-century boyhood was "a fine stream and I have rowed on it and hunted on its adjacent upland within the very heart of the present Dutch Kills and Hunters Point sections of Long Island City. This creek was always maintained as a navigable stream." Burger Jorissen's mill (at what is now Forty-First Avenue and Northern Boulevard), a local landmark for two centuries, was still in operation in the early nineteenth century, but it was finally demolished in 1861 to make way for the Long Island Rail Road.

A nineteenth-century writer described the Dutch Kills as "sluggishly winding through the salt meadows of bronzed grasses." The creek was originally longer than it is today—it began just north of Northern Boulevard, but the northernmost section was filled in over the years. Even as Queens grew and developed around it, this area remained semirural until the turn of the twentieth century. By 1905, Dutch Kills was described as "a stagnant arm of Newtown Creek with very little traffic save an occasional garbage scow loaded with refuse to dump out on the meadows."

Then, change came, and it came fast. For one, there was railroad service from Manhattan through a newly build East River tunnel, as well as the new Sunnyside Yard, which opened in 1910 in Long Island City (see chapter 6). It was also about this time that the Degnon Realty and Terminal Company purchased much of the land adjacent to the Dutch Kills, intending to create an industrial center called Degnon Terminal, based around the creek and the nearby railroad tracks (to which it would construct spurs to allow the easy shipment of goods to and from factories). A 1905 article in the *Greenpoint Daily Star* was headlined "To Make Factories Grow in Swamp." Degnon was also the contractor digging the "Belmont Tunnel"—the subway extension from Manhattan to Queens—and was planning to use some of the excavated material to help fill in the marshy land near the Dutch Kills. Degnon dredged Dutch Kills to a depth of twenty-three feet to allow for the necessary barge traffic to navigate the waters and bulkheaded the end of the creek to allow for barge docking. In 1914, principal items of freight were gravel, broken stone, sand, brick and cement; this would change once the factories were built, and built they were. By 1920, there were at least thirteen

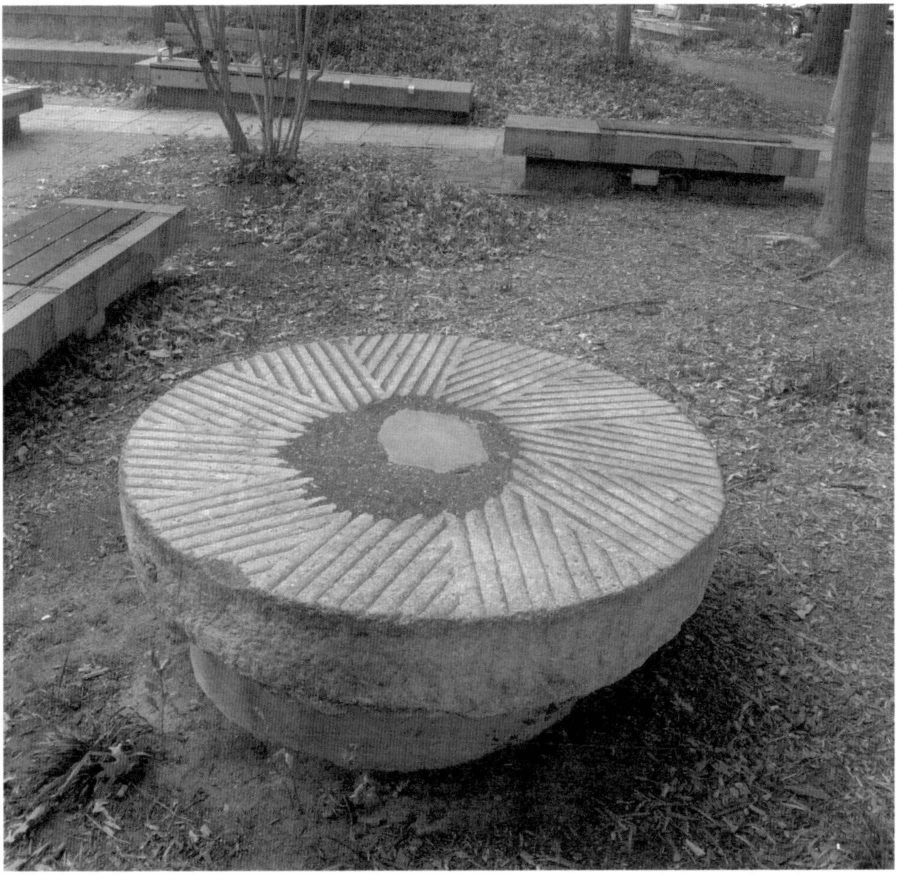

An old millstone from the mill built by Burger Jorissen in the seventeenth century. *Author's collection.*

major companies served by the Degnon Terminal shipping facilities on Dutch Kills, including the Loose Wiles Biscuit Company, the White Motor Company and the American Chicle Company.

While some of these factories date to the 1910s, one of the oldest remaining relics in the area is actually the Borden Avenue Bridge over Dutch Kills, along with the old-fashioned cottage-style bridge keeper's house—both date to 1908. Since the late nineteenth century, a movable bridge has been in this location due to the dual need for a road at that location and for boats to be able to navigate under. The bridge is a rarity for movable bridges, a "retractile" type span that can be rolled into "open" position along narrow-gage tracks to allow boats to pass through.

Though heavily polluted, as seen from the Hunterspoint Avenue Bridge and Borden Avenue Bridge, Dutch Kills offers a scenic view that, if you squint really (really) hard, you might be able to imagine was once a tranquil creek surrounded by farmland. As I stood there on Hunterspoint Avenue facing north, the end of the Kills and the skyscrapers of Long Island City, I noticed a bottle floating in the water and amused myself with the momentary fantasy that maybe it had been tossed there centuries ago and contained a message from the past.

So there it is, a creek flowing into the middle of twenty-first-century northwestern Queens, terminating just a few hundred feet from Queens Boulevard. On the surface, it may seem ironic that with all this industry and infrastructure in the area, a part of the Dutch Kills still survives. But the reality is that it survived this long precisely because of industry. Businesses located along the Dutch Kills could ship and receive goods quite easily… and cost-effectively. As late as 1985, for example, the cost for barging in freight to Dutch Kills was $0.27 per ton compared to $3.90 per ton for trucking the same load.

Thanks to the creek, there is (mostly was, but it is still occasionally referred to that way) also a neighborhood called Dutch Kills, which extended far north and east of the actual site of the creek. A new 1.5-acre park at Queens Plaza just north of Northern Boulevard, called Dutch Kills Green, opened in 2012 on the former site of a commuter railroad parking lot. One of the park's highlights is nothing less than a pair of original millstones from the old Burger Jorissen gristmill, one of which had been rescued by subsequent owners of the property and then embedded in concrete in Queens Plaza, and the other of which had been rediscovered only in the 1980s.

Kissena Park

Flushing has a storied past as the site of the country's first commercial plant nursery. Founded in 1735 by William Prince, the Prince nursery was visited by President George Washington in 1789, along with Vice President John Adams and Governor George Clinton. The Prince nursery is long gone, but remnants of another ancient Flushing nursery live on. Samuel Bowne Parsons, Quaker and member of the famous Bowne family, founded the Parsons and Company Nursery in Flushing in 1838, near present-day Rose Avenue and Parsons Boulevard. Clients of the Parsons nursery included the landscape architects Frederick Law Olmsted and Calvert Vaux, who used some of these trees in their Central and Prospect Park designs. Samuel Parsons Jr. went on to become New York City's official landscape architect. When the elder Parsons died in 1906, the nursery closed and the land went to the City of New York, which, along with other land the city had acquired and would continue to acquire, eventually became Kissena Park.

Nurseries are just that—places where young trees are grown to be purchased and replanted permanently elsewhere. When the Parsons nursery closed, though much of the nursery was cleared, dozens of saplings were left in place, a fourteen-acre grove of Parsons's trees. This grove of former tree babies is now lined with more than one hundred varieties of former nursery stock or their descendants, many of them rare and exotic. About eighty of the trees in the grove date to the nineteenth century. Interestingly, this important grove went unnoticed over the years as the trees matured, and it remained hidden history until 1981, when the trees

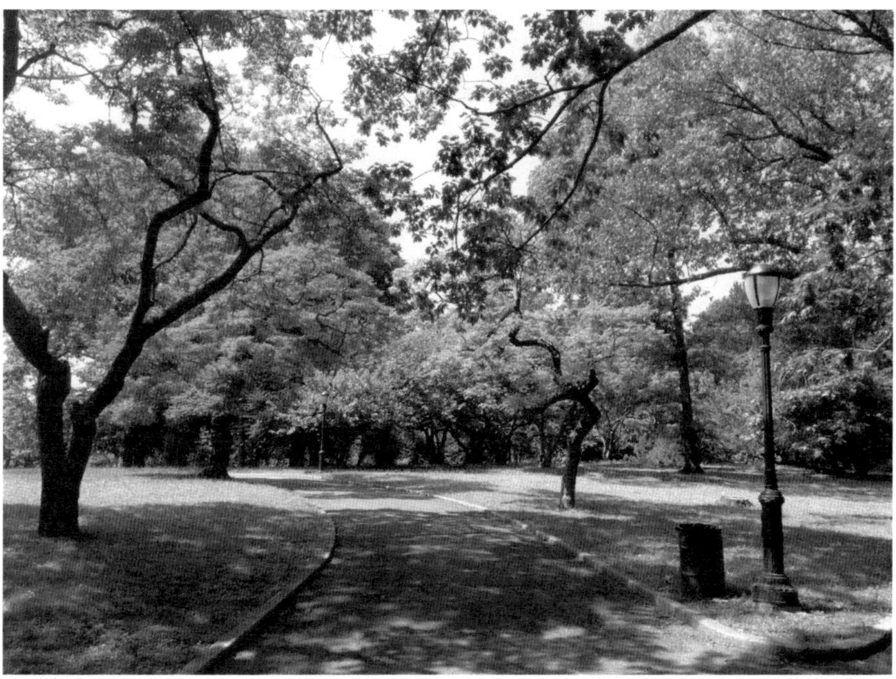

Kissena Park has a treasure trove of nineteenth-century trees. *Author's collection.*

were rediscovered by parks department employees amid an overgrown mess. Located just south of the Parsons Boulevard entrance and adjacent to the tennis courts, the venerable trees include Japanese maples (Parsons was the one who introduced them to the country), katsura and European beeches. The massive gnarled roots and sturdy wide-girth trunks are a testament to all the decades the trees have survived.

The Tiniest Parks

When city streets meet other city streets at odd angles, the circumstance can leave wasted space. If you know Queens, you know that there are lots of neighborhoods with odd-angled streets. In many cases, the parks department created little parks rather than simply leave an empty concrete wasteland. And when I say little parks, I mean very little. Fourteen of New York City's tiniest parks are located in Queens, and many of them are triangular. The smallest of the small, the tiniest park in all of New York City, is the miniscule Luke J. Lang Square off of Fresh Pond Road in Middle Village at Fifty-Ninth Road and Sixty-First Street, coming in at 1/1000th of an acre. (It's actually triangular, and the official parks department description begins with the words "This triangle…".) Like many of Queens' smallest parks, it is named after a local soldier who died in World War I. Other tiny Queens parks include Middle Burgh Triangle in Maspeth, Dwyer Square in Astoria, Dunningham Triangle in Elmhurst and Glendale Veterans Memorial Triangle.

In Long Island City, there are three small triangular parks within a few blocks of each other, thanks to Jackson Avenue cutting diagonally northeast across the east–west street grid that lies northwest of Sunnyside Yard. Two of these parks are among the smallest in the city, at 1/100th of an acre each. At Jackson Avenue and Twenty-Third Street is Albert E. Short Triangle, named after a Queens assistant district attorney and Long Island City resident. A block away at Jackson Avenue and Forty-Fifth Street is McKenna Triangle, named after Long Island City native Major James A. McKenna, who was killed in World War I. As I approached these miniparks, I wasn't even sure I was in the right place. That's how small and inconspicuous they are.

Another block north, at Jackson Avenue and Forty-Fourth Drive, is Rafferty Triangle, which was named after Captain Malcolm A. Rafferty, Spanish-American War hero of the Battle of San Juan Hill. Rafferty was in command of Company F in the Seventy-First Regiment and was known for his rallying cry of "Come on Company F!" and eventually became known as "Come on F. Rafferty." He contracted malaria in Cuba and eventually died from it in 1903. The unique feature of this park is its memorial boulder, engraved with Rafferty's name and date of death, with two embedded bronze commemorative war crosses that were vandalized in the 1970s and finally replaced in 2014.

Celtic Park

Queens is rich in parks and athletic fields that date back many decades, and outside of private-school fields, the great majority of them are owned by the City of New York and run by the parks department. However, one of the most prominent athletic complexes in Queens history was the privately owned Celtic Park, located in the part of Long Island City that is now called Sunnyside but was then known as Laurel Hill.

Celtic Park was created in 1898 when the Greater New York Irish Athletic Association bought a few acres of land for $9,000 to build an athletic complex. This was no rinky-dink kids playground—it had a two-story clubhouse with a café, private dining room, dressing rooms and dance floor; grandstands that could seat 2,500 people; a quarter-mile track; baseball, football, polo and cricket fields; and a three-hundred-foot-long rifle range.

From the very beginning, it was a popular place for athletic events. During the opening games in May 1898, the grounds were festooned with American and Irish flags, and a band played music. In October 1902, a crowd of three thousand people showed up for a big athletic meet there. Events included races, hammer throwing and long jumping. Three athletes were arrested at that event for breaking the Sabbath laws. It happened again in 1905, when a runner, a coach and a ticket seller were arrested on a Sunday, but the case was thrown out when the judge learned the complaint had been brought by the Sabbath Observance Society, which was based in Manhattan. "Let them stay over there and attend to their own business," the judge said of interference from another borough, citing that Sunday athletics were acceptable so long as they didn't disrupt the neighborhood or interfere with worship.

The complex was heavily, but not exclusively, used by Irish Americans. Among the events held at Celtic Park over the years were track-and-field

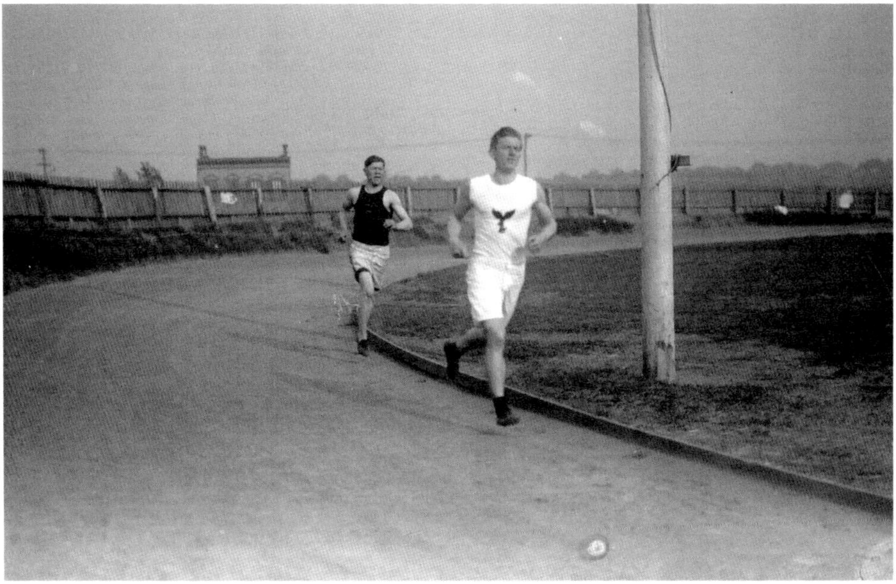

Famous athlete Jim Thorpe took part in the Amateur Athletic Union's All-Around Championship in Celtic Park in 1912. *Author's collection.*

meets, Gaelic football games, greyhound racing (despite protests from residents), elementary-school racing and a sword-and-bayonet contest. One of the highlights of Celtic Park's history was when Olympic medalist Jim Thorpe won the Amateur Athletic Union's All-Around Championship in 1912.

During Prohibition, bootleggers frequented Celtic Park with bottles of whiskey in their pockets; up to twelve were arrested every Sunday in the early 1920s. In 1922, four people at Celtic Park were shot during a riot.

In 1930, Celtic Park was sold to the City and Suburban Homes Company for $500,000, which built a housing complex on the site in 1931, known as the Celtic Park Apartments, which still stands today between Forty-Eighth and Fiftieth Avenues, from Forty-Second to Forty-Fourth Streets.

ISLAND HIDEAWAY

Technically speaking, Queens itself is part of an island, which would of course be Long Island. But there is one community in Queens that inhabits its very own island—Broad Channel, population three thousand. Located between Howard Beach and the Rockaway Peninsula, Broad Channel is a hidden treasure and the only inhabited island in Jamaica Bay.

There was no vehicular access to the island until the mid-1920s and the construction of the Cross Bay Boulevard Bridge. (The bridge from Broad Channel to the Rockaways was completed in the 1930s.) More than half of the island (the north side) is composed of the Jamaica Bay Wildlife Refuge (part of the Gateway National Recreation Area), originally created in the 1930s by Robert Moses and run by New York City. It was later transferred to the jurisdiction of the federal government. More than 330 species of birds have been spotted there, half of the entire number of bird species in the Northeast! The Jamaica Bay Wildlife Refuge is also the only wildlife refuge in the National Park System.

The southern part of the island is occupied by the community of Broad Channel, which has a very quaint early twentieth-century feel to it. The island was pretty much uninhabited until the late nineteenth century. The railroad first crossed Jamaica Bay in 1880, and hotels started to spring up near the station to cater to those who sought a fishing or crabbing holiday or simply a weekend picnic by the sea. By 1914, there were twenty-seven fishing clubs in Broad Channel.

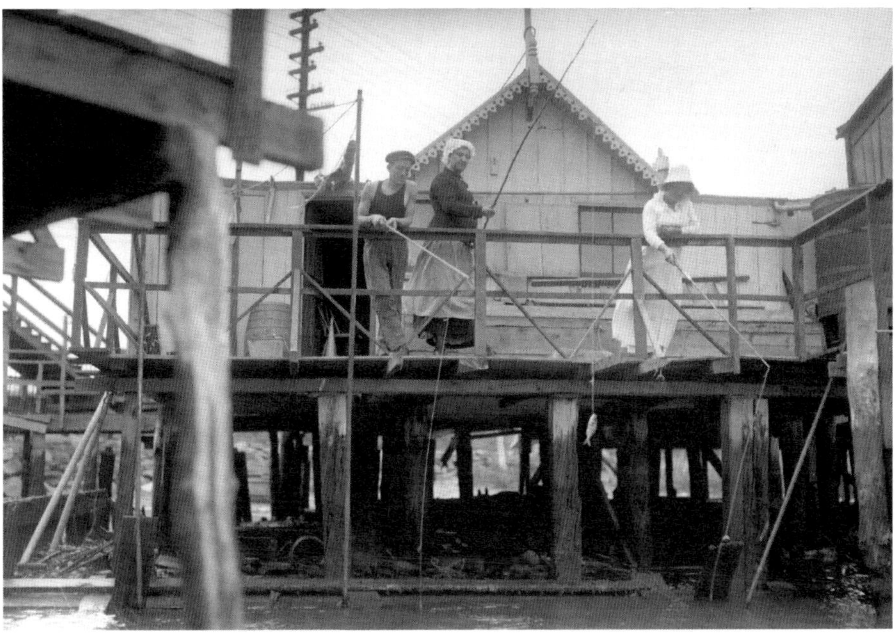

Fishing in Broad Channel, circa 1910. *Library of Congress.*

Full-scale development began in earnest in 1915, when the City of New York leased the land to Broad Channel Corporation, which started building and renting cottages, as well as streets and boardwalks and other infrastructure. Once a bridge to the mainland was built, the community grew even more popular. Still, by the mid-1920s, only about twenty-five families lived in Broad Channel year-round. It was a popular destination during Prohibition for those craving alcohol.

A trip to Broad Channel these days is a fun little adventure. Most of the buildings date to at least the 1920s, and the village retains a very seaside fishing village feel to it, with many original cottages still intact. There is a station on the A line of the IND subway, and Broad Channel has its own public library. Susceptible due to its proximity to the water and its vulnerable location, the community was damaged by flooding during Hurricane Sandy.

HIDDEN GEOGRAPHY TALES

Queens is not only a large borough, it is also a geographically fascinating one. Its shape is so jagged and uneven on its eastern border that if you were to start out on Bermuda Street in Atlantic Beach (Nassau County) and go in a straight line north, you'd pass into Far Rockaway (Queens) then into Inwood (Nassau), then into a little neighborhood just east of JFK Airport (Queens), then to North Woodmere Park (Nassau), then into Rosedale (Queens) and up through St. Albans, Queens Village and Little Neck before reaching Great Neck (Nassau).

Everyone knows that Staten Island is just a hop away from New Jersey. Oh, and Manhattan, too, and the Bronx, both just across the Hudson. But Queens is pretty far from New Jersey, right? Well, that's what I thought. Until I had a closer look at a map. Turns out that the westernmost point of the Rockaways, Breezy Point Tip, is only one and a third miles from New Jersey waters and less than six miles from the tip of Sandy Hook!

Breezy Point Tip and much of the Rockaway Peninsula are farther south than all of Brooklyn, or any other point on Long Island, for that matter.

The easternmost point in Queens, Langdale Street in Glen Oaks, is farther east than several Nassau County communities, including Elmont, Valley Stream, Inwood, Lawrence, Cedarhurst, Woodmere, Atlantic Beach, Great Neck, Lake Success and parts of New Hyde Park, Manhasset and Port Washington.

The northernmost point in Queens, in College Point, is farther north than the southernmost point in the Bronx, Port Morris.

The westernmost point in the borough, Hunters Point, is farther west than Broadway and 121st Street in Manhattan.

Highland Park is in both Brooklyn and Queens, as is Cypress Cemetery.

Queens is so expansive that to travel between the farthest-apart points in Queens (Breezy Point Tip to Ralph Demarco Park in Astoria) would take about fifty-six minutes with no traffic, a distance of twenty-seven miles.

THE NUMBER'S UP

Before Queens was part of New York City, it comprised numerous villages and towns, each with their own street naming system, and a few main roads connecting them. Come 1898 and consolidation with Manhattan, a more unified street system had to be implemented. After all, there couldn't be twenty-five Main Streets all across Queens! Around 1915, New York City began to implement a massive new system of renaming named streets to numbered streets (north–south) and avenues (east–west), with the general rule that the avenues went from low to high as you went north to south, and the streets went from low to high as you traveled west to east. I learned this early on, as I rode the local subway from Manhattan through Queens, passing 36th Street, 46th Street, 65th Street and then 74th Street/Roosevelt Avenue…if I continued to Shea Stadium, the 111th Street station was the last stop before my destination.

While the subway ride made it seem pretty straightforward, in reality, it's not so simple. While many street names may have changed to numbers, the orientation of the streets did not change. Queens' streets were not and are still not a perfect N-S-E-W grid, far from it; many streets run northeast or southwest and are interrupted by train tracks and highways, parks and cemeteries. Another complication is that, in places, like Elmhurst, numbered avenues are interspersed with numbered roads, drives or terraces in the same series. You could live in Middle Village and be at the corner of Eighty-Fifth Road and Eighty-Fifth Street, next to Eighty-Fifth Drive. You could live in Maspeth on Sixtieth Lane, between Sixtieth Avenue and Sixtieth Road, or at the corner of Sixtieth Road and Sixtieth Drive. Very confusing! How far an avenue or street continues is also somewhat arbitrary. Fifty-Fifth Avenue in Maspeth turns rather suddenly into Fifty-Fourth Avenue for no apparent reason as it approaches Principe Park. Fifty-Sixth Avenue hops and skips its way across Queens, from Maspeth through Elmhurst and then resumes past Flushing Meadows–Corona Park just before Kissena Park, continues for a while in Bayside, and then vanishes past Alley Pond Park (though Fifty-Seventh Avenue is still alive and well at that point in Little Neck).

Street names were not the only thing that changed during the twentieth century. House numbers were now completely different, too. On streets, the prefix reflected the number of the nearest avenue, and on avenues of the nearest street number. My address as a child was 80-20 Broadway in Elmhurst. Plenty of streets got to retain their old-time names—if the street was important enough or the grid in the section it was located in was too off kilter from the numbered streets around it—but the new numbering system still applied. My apartment building was between Eightieth and Eighty-First Streets, hence the 80 in the prefix. Seems simple now, but imagine the confusion and resistance among millions of Queens residents back in the day, who had to basically change their home identities. The change was drastic. If you lived at, let's say, 150 Jackson Street, you might now be 86-02 Forty-Sixth Avenue.

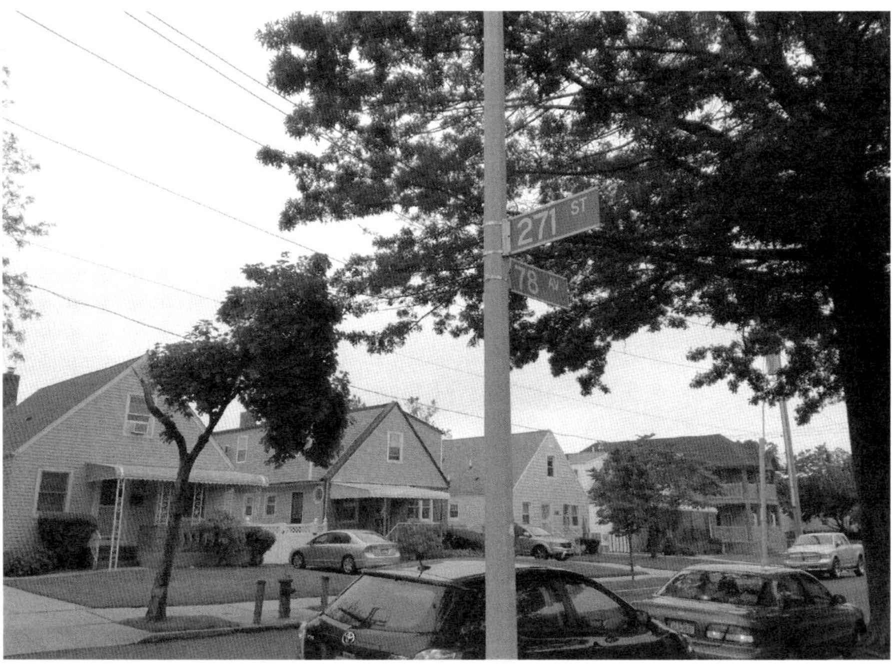

271st Street in Glen Oaks, Queens, is the highest numbered street in all of New York City. *Author's collection.*

Implementation of the new system was gradual and painful. According to a 1930 article in the *Brooklyn Daily Star*, change was slow to come:

> *Borough officials and bureaus still frequently use old street names and numbers. Real estate developers use them. Real estate brokers use them frequently, perhaps because it is easier to refer to property by addresses by which it was described previously than it is to determine what the proper addresses are. The telephone book lists a multitude of old names and street numbers furnished by subscribers. In some of the older communities of the borough, residents commonly use the old addresses in conversation and writing. Old street names are displayed far more prominently than new ones on some of the rapid transit stations.*

A twenty-five-dollar fine was threatened to anyone who did not switch to the new numbering system.

Queens is not unique; except for Staten Island, the other boroughs also have numbered streets. However, street-wise, Queens does have one distinction: the highest numbered street in New York City. Located at the eastern edge of Queens in the residential neighborhood of Glen Oaks just off Union Turnpike and right at the border of Nassau County, 271st Street is the highest number in the city. And that means the house numbers on 77th Avenue begin with the prefix 271-.

Chapter 2
Queens at War

As a kid growing up in Queens, I loved playing with my plastic toy soldiers. You know the ones, the ubiquitous green-colored figures that you could buy in a pack of fifty at the local variety store. As I lined them up on the floor in my room, I imagined the toy soldiers were taking part in some random war in some random place. Little did I realize that where my house stood there had once been British soldiers camped out in tents and huts, fresh from their victory at the Battle of Long Island in August 1776! Queens was not only a hotbed of military activity during the American Revolution; in the years that followed, Queens also served as a training ground for many soldiers heading off to war.

Loyalist Queens

As hostilities between the British and Americans reached a boiling point in 1775, the Patriots in New York were concerned about the high number of Loyalists in Queens. It was unnerving to have so many "disaffected," as they called them, living so near to such a pivotal location now that war had broken out. Accordingly, on December 12, 1775, the Provincial Congress, meeting in New York City, called out by name four men in Jamaica, seven in Newtown and one in Flushing who had "been supplied with arms and ammunition, from on board the Asia ship of war [a sixty-four-gun British navy warship that had arrived in the New York area in 1774], and are arraying themselves in military manner to oppose the measures taking by the United Colonies, for the defence of their just rights and privileges." Among these were three members of the Moore family, relatives of Clement Clarke Moore.

On January 3, 1776, the Continental Congress ordered Colonel Heard to take a force of 900 men to Queens and disarm anyone who voted against sending deputies to the Provincial Congress and to seize the men who had been called out by the congress the month before. As a result of his search of the county (which then included what is today Nassau County), Colonel Heard imposed an oath of loyalty on 471 men, disarmed 349 men, and seized almost one thousand muskets and powder and lead from those deemed at risk of using the weapons against the Patriots. They also managed to capture 19 of the 26 men who had been named by the congress, but they were released after promising not to cause any trouble.

In April 1776, twelve Jamaica men sent a petition to the Provincial Congress saying their cattle and personal effects had been plundered by a Captain Ephraim Bailey for not appearing at arms at a military drill. They explained that they could not possibly have appeared armed when Colonel Heard had taken their guns away.

In August 1776, as the British prepared for an attack on New York, some of the "disaffected" were caught by the Americans supplying vegetables and provisions to British ships that were off the south shore of Queens. Others were caught attempting to escape to the British ships.

Despite the valiant efforts of the Patriots, there were simply too many Loyalists in Queens, and time was quickly running out.

GOD SAVE US ALL

In late August 1776, the British were readying their attack on Long Island, and American general Nathaniel Woodhull was ordered to go from his home in Mastic to Jamaica, where he was to take charge of a company of militiamen and drive cattle (as well as transport grain and provisions) from western Long Island to the east, to keep this valuable livestock out of British hands. In the days that followed, Woodhull succeeded at least in sending 1,400 head of cattle to the Hempstead Plains. It was not easy, considering he was short of men, who were losing hope in the cause as the days passed.

On the same day Woodhull wrote his letter, General George Washington's troops engaged British general William Howe's troops in Brooklyn in what was known as the Battle of Long Island. The British overwhelmed the Americans, but Washington was able to evacuate most of his troops across the East River to Manhattan. Woodhull had requested reinforcements, but Washington's reply was that the men were needed to protect New York City. A couple of days later, Washington decided to give up Long Island to the British, due to the "fear of having our communication cut off from the main…and the extreme fatigue our troops were laid under in guarding such extensive lines without proper shelter from the weather."

Woodhull ordered his men to fall back to a position four miles east of Jamaica while he remained in Jamaica village to gather intelligence about the Battle of Long Island that had just taken place. Proceeding east along the turnpike on the afternoon of August 28, Woodhull intended to join his men, but a severe thunderstorm hit, causing him to take shelter at Increase Carpenter's Tavern on Jamaica Avenue in Hollis. Not long after he had hitched his horse to a post behind the tavern and taken a seat inside, the British Light Dragoons arrived. Woodhull ran toward the back door and struggled to unlatch it so he could escape their clutches. He finally managed to get outside and run toward his horse, but it was too late. He was surrounded. He was forced to surrender and give up his sword. Next comes the part that sealed Woodhull's place in American legend: Now officially a prisoner of the British, Woodhull was supposedly asked to say "God save the king" but instead calmly said "God save us all," which inspired the wrath of one of the British officers, who struck Woodhull with a sword repeatedly on his head and arm, almost severing the arm completely. Woodhull fell to the ground and was carried to a maple tree near the tavern, where he almost bled to death before being taken to the old stone Presbyterian church in Jamaica (which stood at Jamaica Avenue and Union Hall Street), where his wounds were dressed, and from there to Brooklyn, where Woodhull's arm was amputated. He died from his injuries on September 20.

The story is an intriguing one, but as with many historical Queens moments, there have been many versions of it told over the years. We may never know the exact true details of what happened that summer day in 1776, but in writing this book, I was determined to dig a little deeper into where exactly the tavern was located and what became of it.

That Woodhull stopped at the tavern (built in 1710) is not disputed, though opinions on exactly where he was struck what would prove to be fatal blows vary wildly. Some accounts said he was confronted in front of the

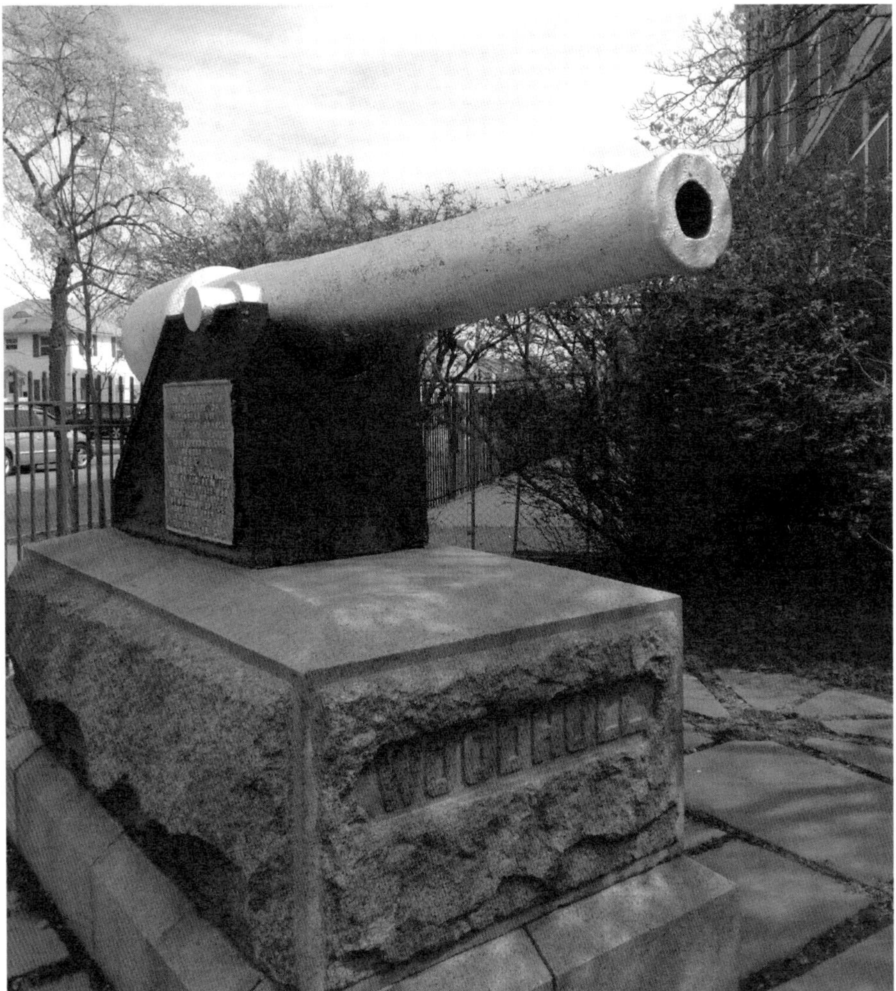

A commemorative cannon sits on the PS 35 school property in honor of the martyred General Nathaniel Woodhull, who was mortally wounded not far from the spot. *Author's collection.*

tavern; others said in back of the tavern near his horse; still others said inside the tavern (which is almost definitely not true). I have read several accounts that say the attack took place about two hundred feet east of the tavern. This seems tangible, since the general would have been trying to escape from the approaching British (coming from the west) to the east.

Accounts of the tavern's location have varied, as well. The main problem in verifying it is that most newspaper accounts of the early twentieth century didn't bother to give a location, because it was such a landmark—everyone knew where it was! From what I could determine, it was actually located between 195th Street and 196th Street on the north side of what is now Jamaica Avenue.

So what became of this famous site? It continued on as an inn and tavern for many years. During the early nineteenth century, it was owned by Samuel Mott, the sheriff of Queens. By the early years of the twentieth century, it was known as Goetz's Hollis Hotel. In 1919, the land was divided into forty-three lots, and the entire property was put up for sale and bought by a developer. Though it continued to serve as a tavern briefly, its days were numbered by the onset of Prohibition. No alcohol means no tavern. Between 1919 and 1921, there were several suggestions and attempts made to save the old landmark. Some favored creating a public park like that which had been created in Jamaica at King Manor, while others suggested a soldiers and sailors monument. Despite the pleas and suggestions of the public, the building was demolished in August 1921. After it was knocked down, a row of small business buildings was erected along Jamaica Avenue, and 195th Place was created running north–south in the middle of the property and was lined with newly built colonial homes. All these structures are still there today, and walking along the street today it is hard to envision the old roadhouse. It must have seemed very strange when the new buildings were erected, as an aerial from 1924 reveals much of the surrounding area was still undeveloped.

The spot where the sword likely fell upon General Woodhull was, by the early 1920s, on the property of an attorney named Rawdon Kelly. His home, between 196th and 197th Streets, was used as a meeting site by the Hollis Field Club, and the pear tree under which the blows were struck stood until about 1917. Once the tavern fell, there was a suggestion to preserve the site of the attack, but alas, that building was demolished soon after and apartment buildings erected on the site. There is an old tree on the former tavern site that likely coexisted with the tavern in its last years, and an old ivy-covered tree that survives on the former attack site property, but beyond that, nothing else remains from those days.

The only tangible remembrances of the martyred general are a cannon and a memorial granite block that were placed on the grounds of nearby PS 35 (90th Avenue and 191st Street in Hollis) in 1904, as well as the names "Woodhull Avenue" (which runs southwest from Jamaica Avenue at 197th Street and then loops back north to meet Jamaica Avenue again at 188th Street) and "Carpenter Avenue" (a block east).

THE OCCUPATION OF NEWTOWN

As the Revolutionary War began to heat up, both sides knew that controlling New York City (Manhattan) was critical to gaining momentum and power in the war. On August 27, 1776, ten thousand of General George Washington's men engaged twenty thousand of General William Howe's men in Brooklyn in the Battle of Long Island (aka the Battle of Brooklyn). The British overwhelmed the Americans, but Washington was able to evacuate most of his troops across the East River to Manhattan.

Following the battle, the British knew they had a good foothold in Long Island but wanted it to be a stepping-stone to taking New York City proper. Accordingly, General Howe made his temporary headquarters at the "Big House on the Bowery Bay Road," owned by Samuel Renne, supervisor of Newtown and also a magistrate and elder of the Presbyterian church. The British did not look kindly toward Presbyterians (they tore down the Presbyterian church in Newtown and used the wood to build huts to house their soldiers), but that did not stop them from using Renne's house. The house, built in 1762, was located near the intersection of Queens Boulevard and Fifty-Seventh Avenue. In 1784, when the house was being offered for sale by one Richard Lawrence, who had purchased it from Renne, the structure was described as having "eight rooms and fire-places." I am guessing that with the war recently over and the British vanquished, the fact that "General William Howe slept here" was not touted.

From this home, General Howe wrote his report on the Battle of Long Island on September 3, 1776, to be sent back to Lord George Germaine in England. (He held the position of secretary of state for the American Department in Parliament.) After describing the action of the battle, Howe wrote in closing: "The behaviour of both officers and soldiers, British and Hessians, was highly to their honour. More determined courage and steadiness in troops have never been experienced, or a greater ardour to distinguish themselves, as all those who had an opportunity have amply evinced by their actions."

And then on to the bad news:

> *In the evening of the 27th, the Army encamped in front of the enemy's works. On the 28th, at night, broke ground six hundred yards distant from a redoubt upon their left, and on the 29th, at night, the Rebels evacuated their intrenchments and Red-Hook, with the utmost silence, and quitted Governour's Island the following evening, leaving their cannon and a*

> *quantity of stores in all their works. At daybreak on the 30th, their flight was discovered, the piquets of the line took possession, and those most advanced reached the shore opposite to New-York as their rear guard was going over, and fired some shot among them. The enemy is still in possession of the town and island of New-York, in force, and making demonstration of opposing us in their works on both sides of King's Bridge.*

Aside from the house itself, what was the occupation of Newtown like? Where did the troops reside and for how long? Following the Battle of Long Island, British forces remained in the Newtown area only until September 15, when they began to cross to Manhattan in pursuit of the retreating Continental army. Howe was personally in command of the Twenty-Third Regiment, the Royal Welsh Fusiliers. The heights behind his residence (known as Nassau Heights as recently as the early twentieth century) were occupied by his troops while he was in Newtown. They built hundreds of huts, which must have dwarfed the actual settlement of Newtown itself.

Though Howe's troops left in mid-September, they were not the only ones to be stationed in the area. In his report back to England, General Howe had summed up the disposition of Long Island thusly: "The inhabitants of this Island, many of whom had been forced into rebellion, have all submitted, and are ready to take the oaths of allegiance." But Howe was not quite correct in his rather broad and reassuring statement. While Newtown itself was largely Loyalist, there were still Patriots everywhere, and they were not forced into anything. In recognition of this continuing threat to British occupation, a Loyalist militia force of about six hundred men, under the command of General Oliver Delancey, was established and stationed in Newtown in the same huts the Welsh Fusiliers had once occupied, during the winter of 1777–78. Their mission was to defend Long Island and apprehend or

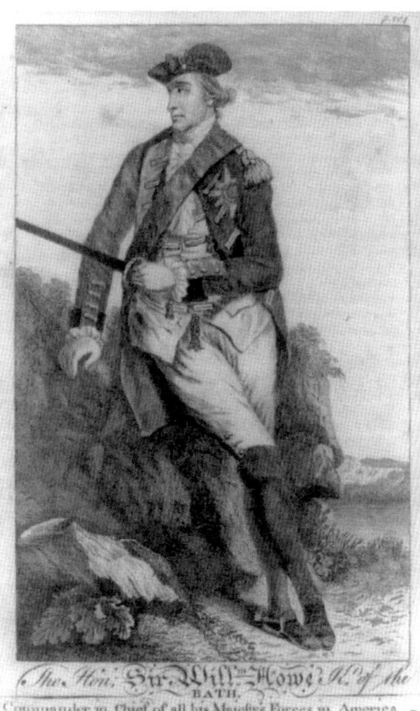

British general William Howe made his headquarters in Queens during the early part of the Revolution. *Library of Congress.*

drive off the Patriots, defending Long Island from concealed rebels. The huts on Nassau Heights were also used as a hospital for invalid soldiers. Remnants of the encampment existed until at least the 1850s, and much of the land was undeveloped until the early twentieth century, when houses such as the one I grew up in were built on the streets south from what is now Seabury Street and beyond.

So what became of the historic Renne House? It changed hands to the Bretonniere family and was known as the Bretonniere farm during the nineteenth century and beyond. By the early twentieth century, a sign had been placed at the spot to mark the building's significance. The home was demolished in 1939 by its then owner, a Cuban tobacco planter who refused to sell the house to the local government for use as a museum. This was well before the existence of the New York City Landmarks Commission, and so there was no recourse to save the building. When I was a teenager, the site of the house was occupied by a Crazy Eddie store, then later a Herman's Sporting Goods store and, more recently, a furniture store.

Other British generals were also stationed at homes in Queens, including Major General James Robertson, who made himself at home in the house of William Lawrence in what is now the village of Astoria, while an army of ten thousand men occupied tents in the near vicinity. Meanwhile, Lieutenant General Sir Henry Clinton set up shop in the home of Nathaniel Moore in Woodside, a little north of Jackson Avenue, near the Moore-Jackson family cemetery.

RIFLE RANGE IN THE WRONG PLACE

The Creedmoor Park Rifle Range was opened in the spring of 1873 on a big flat expanse of land in what is now northeastern Queens (but was then part of the much bigger, pre-consolidation Queens, which included Nassau County). Owned by New York State, the range was used for practice for National Guardsmen and also hosted competitions. The area was known as Creedmoor Park, after the original owners of the farm there, the Creed family. It is now part of Queens Village. It didn't take long for the range to become popular. In honor of the grand opening, the National Rifle Association sent a notice to all the regional National Guard regiments announcing a shooting competition (two hundred yards and five hundred yards) at the newly completed Creedmoor range, which would award a total of $300 in prizes. The meet was a success, and many more followed. A three-day meet in October 1873 drew one thousand entrants.

Back then, all of the surrounding area was farmland, and newspaper articles of the time referred to the site as "the prairie at Creedmoor" and the people living nearby as "country folk." At first, there was just a single headquarters building on the site. The first clubhouse was built in 1897 for the Seventh Regiment. It had twenty-five beds and a large dining room, three shower baths and gas lighting. Within a few years, different regiments had built their own clubhouses, which provided a place for guns to be stored and the comforts of home to the shooters. At its peak, the Creedmoor range was used by ten thousand members of the National Guard. Every year, numerous local, national and international matches were held at Creedmoor, such as the one held in 1906 when the Seventh Regiment went up against the Queen's Westminster Volunteers, who were visiting from England. Nearby streets were named accordingly—Winchester Boulevard, Musket Street and Range Street.

On paper, it seemed like an idea situation, but in reality, it wasn't. Despite the size of the range property, stray bullets were escaping the grounds and causing problems for neighboring residents. At distances of one thousand yards, the trajectory of the bullet, along with any wind, could cause the bullets to go far afield from their intended targets. In 1905, a grand jury

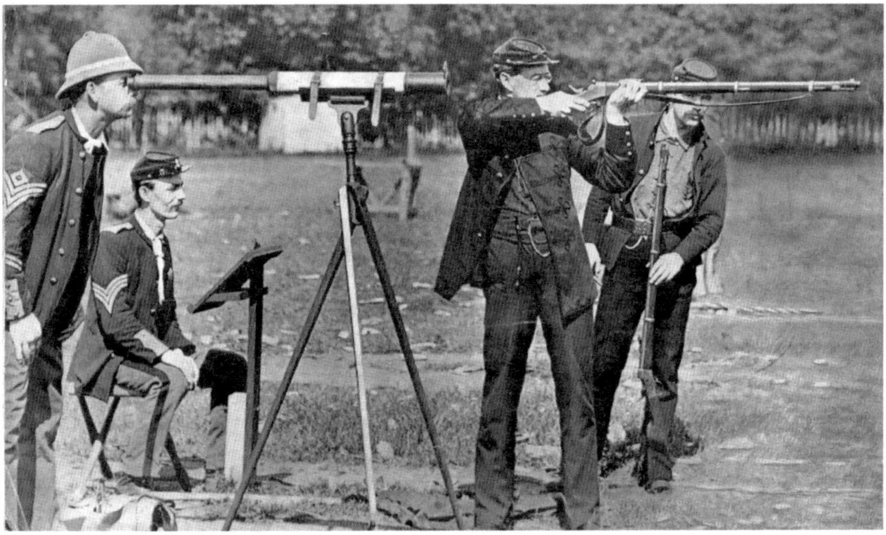

In its later years, the Creedmoor range was plagued by complaints of stray bullets flying onto neighboring properties. This image shows a scene at the range in 1888. *Author's collection.*

was formed to look into allegations of bullets landing on private property outside the range. The head of the Queens Health Department and the department's chief clerk examined the site and surrounding area and determined that it was impossible for anyone to be in jeopardy from bullets unless they trespassed onto the state property.

But the complaints from local residents kept coming. Despite the high fences and embankments, bullets sailed past regularly. In 1907, a woman spent four weeks in the hospital after being struck by a bullet. Another woman, who lived a mile and a half from the range, was fetching a pail of water in her yard when a bullet flew over her head and hit a branch on a locust tree. John Henrickson, who lived southwest of the range, had five bullets fly into his house between 1902 and 1907. Daniel Strattel, who owned a farm behind the range, gathered, along with his friends, 150 pounds of bullets that had left the range. Another farmer had a horse killed by an errant bullet. Bullets were even said to have ripped through the millionaire William K. Vanderbilt's home in Deepdale.

With rising pressure on him, Governor Charles Evans Hughes called for a new grand jury investigation. This time, the findings were definitive. The grand jury report issued on October 4, 1907, said "the lives of the farmer and those of his employees as well as his live stock are in constant danger from the said rifle range" and demanded that "the State authorities abandon the use of the Creedmoor range for the purpose of rifle practice."

Based on the findings of the grand jury, on October 8, 1907, Hughes issued an order for all shooting practice to be stopped at Creedmoor, the day before National Guardsmen were to begin their sharpshooting classes. Talk was that Peekskill could be a good site for such a rifle range.

The interesting twist on this story is that local politicians were scheming to buy the Creedmoor range land from the state, some four hundred acres of it, and develop and sell it and make a great profit. Their plans were thrown off course in 1909 for reasons that are explained in the continuation of the Creedmoor story on page 152.

Fort Totten

Just off the Cross Island Parkway in the Bay Terrace section of Queens, one exit before the Throgs Neck Bridge, is a 147-acre peninsula that is packed with 150 years of New York's military history. Because of its strategic location on the Long Island Sound, the site (then known as Willets Point) was selected for construction of a defensive fortress during the Civil War (not to be confused with Fort Totten in Washington, D.C., also Civil War vintage). Starting in 1862, part of the site was used as a recruit depot and temporary encampment for troops on their way to the battlefront. In 1864, a general thirty-seven-ward hospital was established that could hold 1,500 patients. In 1873, the fort was used as a torpedo training post for West Point graduates. Many of the old pontoon boats that had been used during the Civil War were sent to Fort Totten for use by the Engineering Battalion in military bridge building.

Robert T. Lincoln, President Lincoln's son and the secretary of war, visited Willets Point in 1884 and was so impressed that he authorized the troop strength to be raised from 200 to 450. It officially became known as Fort Totten (after a brigadier general) in 1898, when a second set of fortifications was built for the Spanish-American War. During World War I, officers stationed at Fort Totten conducted a survey of the land within a half mile of the base to look for Germans residing nearby. According to a newspaper article, "If any are found, they will be ordered to move until the war is over."

Fort Totten was very active during World War I. In 1915, one drill involved fourteen shots fired by each of the seven twelve-inch rifles, aimed at a twenty- by thirty-foot floating target anchored thirteen thousand yards (more than seven miles) away. The test was held again at night to see if the firing was as accurate in the dark. As a newspaper article explained, "Hostile fleets and hostile armies do not conform to union hours and knock off work for the day when the five o'clock whistle blows." The Coast Defense commander issued a warning to all residents within a five-mile radius that during the test all windows should be opened at least six inches and all heavy pictures and mirrors should be removed from walls to prevent breakage.

The fort had many uses over the years. It has housed the Engineer School of Application (1865–1901), Eastern Artillery District Headquarters (c. 1901), Electric Mines and Army School of Submarine Defense (1921), a prototype anti-aircraft installation (1922), the Anti-Aircraft Artillery Headquarters (1941–44), the North Atlantic Wing of the Air Transportation Command (1944), the New York–New Jersey Sub-Area Command Headquarters (1949), First Region ARADCOM for the Nike Anti-Ballistic Missile Defense System (1954) and, most recently, has served as a U.S. Army Reserve post (1974). The old fortifications are still there on the tip of the peninsula, as are numerous buildings, some of which date to the nineteenth century.

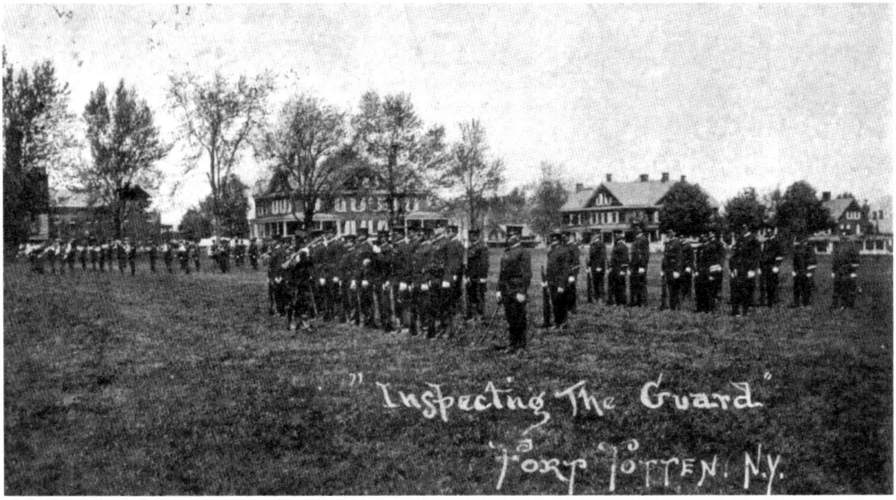

Fort Totten, circa 1909. *Author's collection.*

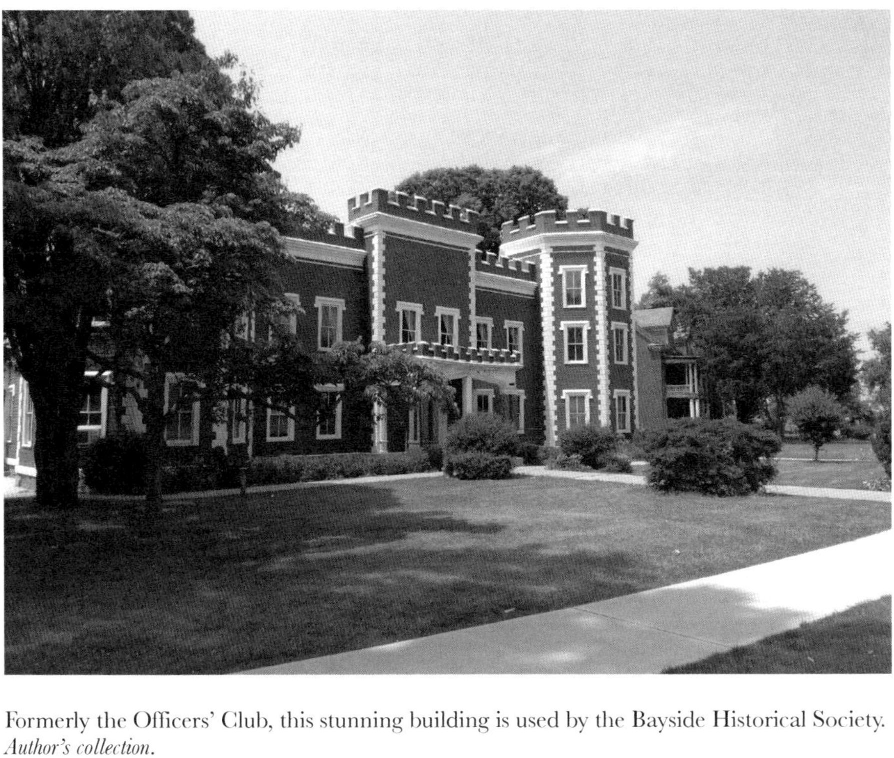

Formerly the Officers' Club, this stunning building is used by the Bayside Historical Society. *Author's collection.*

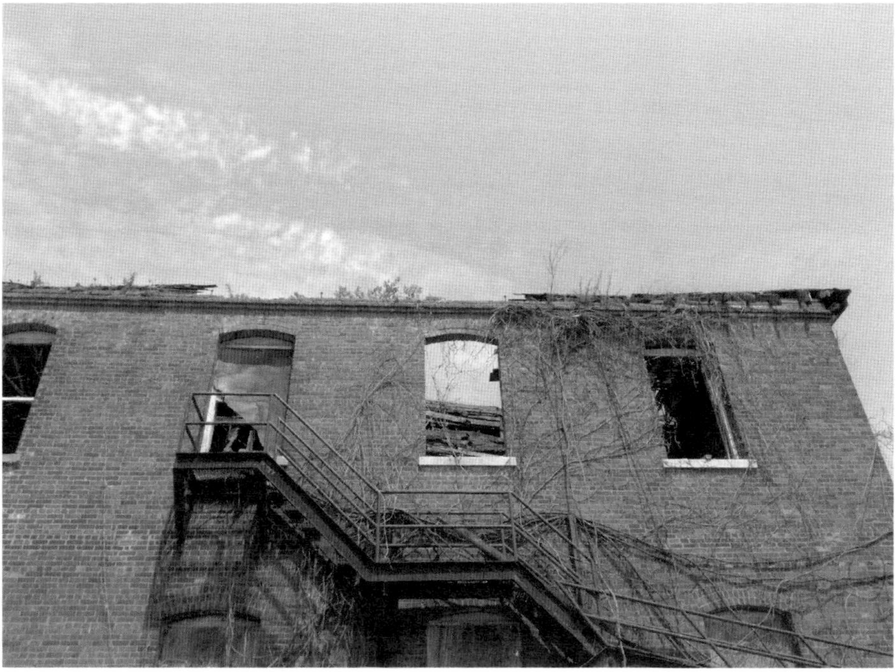

Several buildings at Fort Totten are abandoned and falling victim to the elements. Others await potential restoration. *Author's collection.*

Many of the old buildings have been repurposed and are now used by the New York City Fire and Police Departments as well as the U.S. Army and Coast Guard. The most architecturally stunning building is the nineteenth-century Officers' Club, which is now used by the Bayside Historical Society. Much of the peninsula is now under the jurisdiction of the parks department as Fort Totten Park; there is even a public swimming pool! But there are plenty of buildings that are abandoned, and the condition of these varies from mostly intact to crumbling. A peek inside one building revealed ornate vintage woodwork. The old, circa 1829 Willet homestead still stands, too, and there are plans to stabilize and restore it. The juxtaposition of living with decaying is stunning. A vine-covered, crumbling, early twentieth-century building with a buckled roof stands just across the street from the swimming pool. Fort Totten is very much both a living place and an eerie time capsule, with many nooks and hidden corners to explore. And even if you're not so much of a military history buff, go for the waterfront views alone!

Fort Tilden

Samuel J. Tilden was the governor of New York in the 1870s, but he was belter known for being the 1876 Democratic presidential candidate who won the popular vote but lost the electoral college to Rutherford B. Hayes. Though he died in 1886, Tilden was remembered in 1917 when the U.S. Army built Fort Tilden at the western end of the Rockaway Peninsula (on the site of earlier defenses dating back to the War of 1812). The World War I version of the installation was minimalistic, with barebones structures and equipment but no permanent buildings. The fort became more impressive starting in the 1920s, as new defenses were constructed. Still, it was not until the 1930s that buildings were constructed. By the time of America's entry into World War II, Fort Tilden had become a full-fledged military installation, with more than ninety buildings on the site.

After the war, some of the barracks were converted into housing for veterans. With the start of the Korean Conflict, the apartments were turned back into barracks as troops were once again stationed there. The base was abandoned in 1974 and turned over to the National Park Service as part of the Gateway National Recreation Area.

I knew that I had to see Fort Tilden for myself. From everything I'd read, it sounded like a real hidden treasure.

I ventured to the Rockaways on a pleasant, sunny, summer day and parked at neighboring Jacob Riis Park in a lot that is reminiscent of the huge lots at Jones Beach. This popular park with its amazing beach was opened in the 1930s and has some stunning Art Deco architecture to show for it. As much as I was fascinated by the sand and the surf and the architecture, I had to focus on the task at hand. I crossed over from Riis Park to Fort Tilden Park and was greeted by three friendly penned horses and several old buildings. These were the ones that have been repurposed by some nonprofit arts groups. As I walked farther on, I saw a large, warehouse-like building that was, like several of the park's structures, fenced in and off limits. But, as I soon discovered as I walked along a gravel path, there were plenty of other ruins waiting to be explored. I climbed into one circa 1940 concrete building that was filled with colorful, well-executed graffiti. I stepped over dozens of beer bottles and cans as sunlight streamed in through the holes where the roof had once been. The discarded drink containers were not the only evidence of recent human presence. There was a solitary sneaker, a red sweatshirt and other remnants of a sleepover (or hangover, perhaps). It's always fascinating to see how nature reclaims unused buildings, and Fort Tilden is a great place to witness that and take some dramatic photos.

The highlight of a visit to Fort Tilden has to be Battery Harris East and Battery Harris West. These were the locations of two massively powerful sixteen-inch guns. Each gun could fire 2,100-pound projectiles for a maximum distance of 44,680 yards, or twenty-five miles. When the batteries were built in the early 1920s, the guns were originally exposed in the open air, but a large concrete roof or hood was built over them in 1941–43 to protect them from aerial bombardment. The concrete encasement, along with the bunkers behind them, are still in place. I was eager to see them, but I was not even sure I was going in the right direction. I kept walking, about to turn around and give up, when suddenly I came upon the massive concrete structure that is Battery Harris East.

Battery Harris East has the added bonus of wooden steps that lead to the top of the bunker, for a stunning view in all directions. There are other paths that lead deeper into the park, and the remains of other structures are to be found as well. The full Fort Tilden experience could easily take up an afternoon.

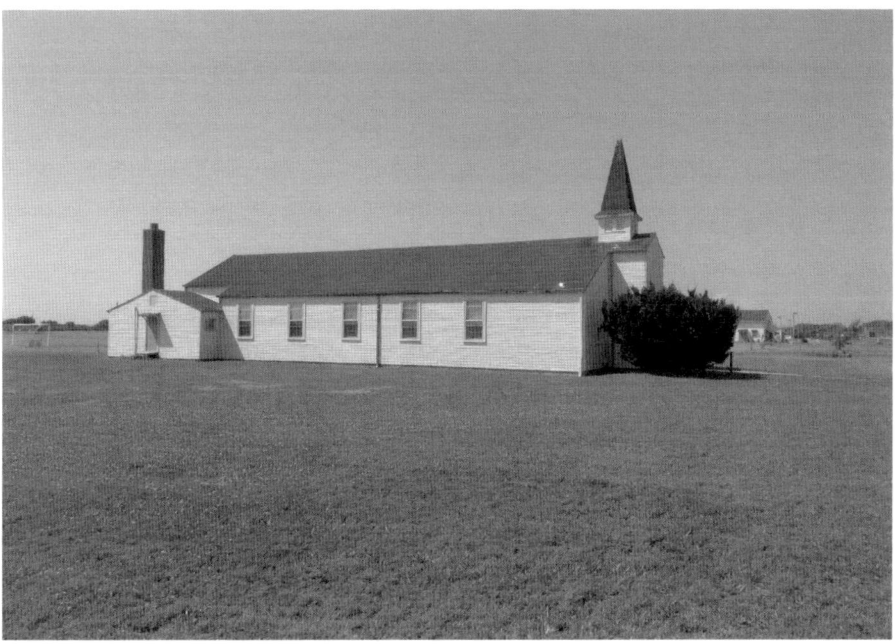

Some of the buildings at Fort Tilden are in current use, while others are abandoned. *Author's collection.*

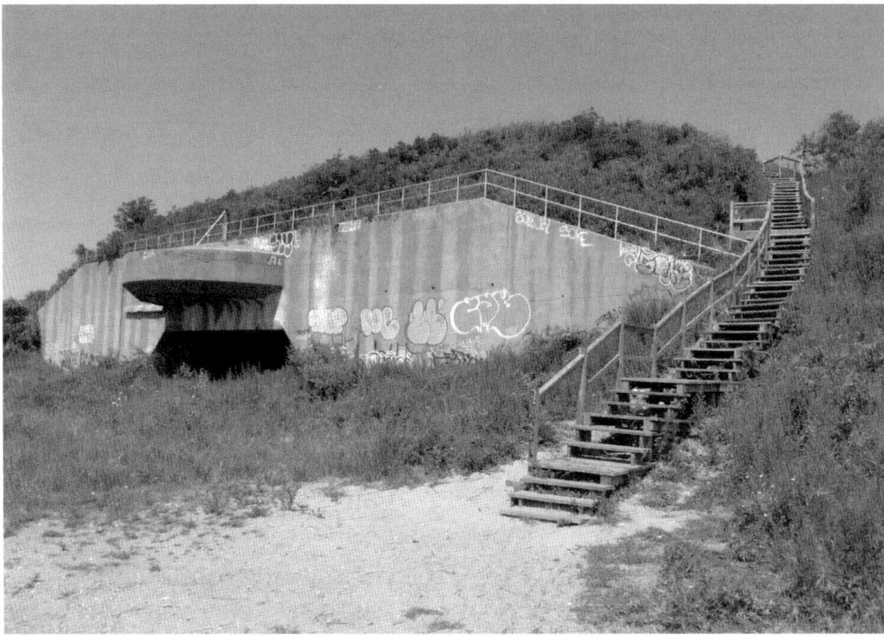

The remains of Battery Harris East at Fort Tilden. *Author's collection.*

After World War II, Fort Tilden became home to the Sixty-Ninth Anti-Aircraft Artillery Battalion, and one thousand men were stationed there, with four batteries of 90mm guns. Each battery had four guns for a total of sixteen guns. But this defense was not good enough for changing and improving offensive technology. What if Soviet bombers appeared over our skies? How could we stop them? The Nike missile program was created in 1945 with the purpose of developing a missile that could target a fast-moving, high-altitude plane. The Nike missile (later known as the Ajax missile when a newer version called the Hercules missile was introduced) was the first surface-to-air missile. It was 32 feet long and weighed 32,000 pounds. It had a range of thirty miles, a ceiling of 70,000 feet and a maximum speed of Mach 2.25.

Now that missiles were in production, the government had to figure out where to place them. Dozens of strategic sites around the country were selected, including nineteen missile batteries in the New York metro area, one of which was at Fort Tilden. The Nike Ajax missiles were later replaced with Hercules missiles, which were faster and more powerful than their predecessors. Today, a relic missile stands erect at the entry to Fort Tilden Park and seems almost to be a toy—but it's not. By 1974, this system had been decommissioned.

THE BREEZY POINT LIGHTHOUSE

Just down the road from Fort Tilden, on the northwestern corner of the Rockaway Peninsula, is the small seaside community of Breezy Point (population four thousand). Composed mainly of homes and beaches, there are a smattering of stores and restaurants in this community, much of which is marked as "private" and is off limits to the rest of us mere mortals. On the beach just off of Palmer Drive and Beach 216th Street stands a structure that looks like a large lifeguard station or a small lighthouse. It is, in fact, neither. Known as the Breezy Point Lighthouse, it was actually built in 1943 as part of the war defense effort.

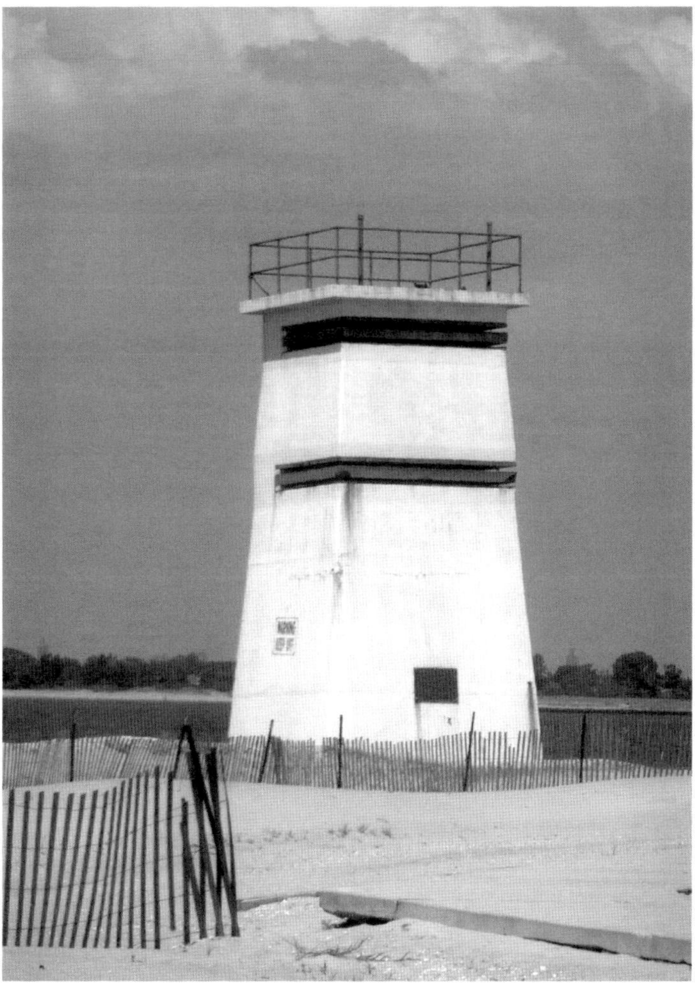

The Breezy Point "Lighthouse." *Author's collection.*

When I first found out about the Breezy Point Fire Control Tower, I erroneously thought it had something to do with spotting fires. In fact, its purpose was to help coordinate targets with the nearby gun batteries at Fort Tilden. The targets for these batteries would be ships, which would be in motion. Having more than one reference point was necessary to help calculate the proper angle of fire. The building was disguised to look like a lighthouse, but it also looks like a rook from a giant chess game.

Since it was just a short hop from Fort Tilden, I went to check out the pseudo-lighthouse. Driving along Rockaway Point Boulevard, you can feel both a physical and mental distance from the rest of New York City. Breezy Point has a very interesting, small East End village feel to it. As I drove, I spotted the tower (which is not really very high), and the next challenge was finding a place to park that was not private or illegal. Unsuccessful in that regard, I quickly ran out of the car and snapped some photos of this World War II remnant, which is still in decent condition and is perhaps the most physically remote piece of hidden history in all of Queens.

THE SOLEMN DOUGHBOY

The 1.7-acre, steeply sloped triangular Doughboy Park at Woodside Avenue, Fifty-Second Street and Thirty-Ninth Road in Woodside, is named after the $5,000 statue that has stood there since 1923. (It was dedicated on Memorial Day of that year.) A memorial to the casualties of World War I, the statue was originally called *Returning Soldier*. The site is appropriate, for it was a mustering ground for Woodside residents who were leaving for the war. The sculptor was a rising star in the art world, a Flushing resident named Burt Johnson (his sister had married the brother of the famed sculptor Augustus St. Gaudens), and his design was one of fourteen submitted to the Woodside Community Council. Ten Woodside men died in World War I.

This doughboy is nothing like most other sculptures of soldiers. It is not an action pose, and this soldier has a bandaged head and looks quite pensive and somber. The granite pedestal is inscribed with the words "Lest we forget." In 1928, the American Federation of Arts selected the Woodside Doughboy as the best war memorial of its kind. Plaques were later added to commemorate local World War II dead and 9/11 victims.

An article about the sculptor in the *Long Island Daily Press* in September 1922 proclaimed:

> *Perhaps the Woodside citizens, who gave him the commission, expected he would choose some ambitious design, something which looked as if it ought to cost a lot of money. Perhaps there was even a little disappointment among them when he submitted just a simple figure of a returned soldier, with gun and helmet, standing at ease. The design was felt on second thought to be beautiful in its simplicity and to make an irresistible appeal. The title is "The Returned Soldier" and the idea is most effectively expressed.*

The statue was originally part of a play area for the kids at adjacent PS 11, but in 1956, the city decided the land was too steep for a play area, and ownership was transferred to the parks department, which converted it into the park that exists today. The move to create a park was also designed to protect the sculpture from neglect and abuse. That year, the sculpture had been removed from its base twice—once by vandals and another time by police, who were afraid that it would topple.

Johnson was ill at the time he was working on the sculpture and died of a heart attack a few years later at the age of thirty-six. The sculpture was restored and conserved in 1990 and received a grant for further restoration again in 2017.

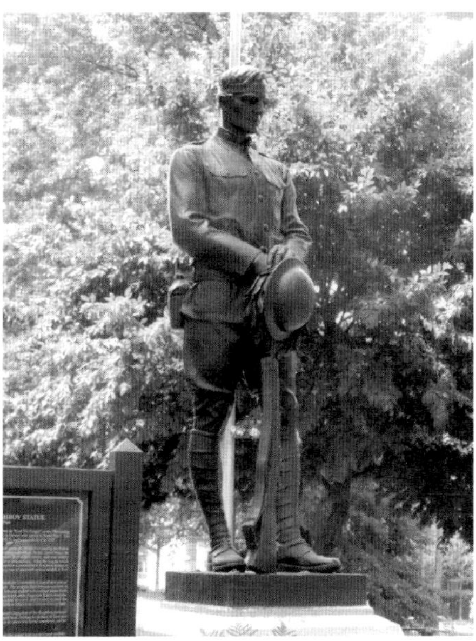

The statue in Doughboy Park, Woodside, is a somber reminder of the horrors of war. *Author's collection.*

Chapter 3

Cars and Trains, Trolleys and Planes

When the first settlers arrived in Queens in the seventeenth century, it was country, far removed from the quickly growing city of New York. For a long time, the only way to get to and from Manhattan was by ferry. In the meantime, transportation within Queens was changing and improving as trolleys and railroads began to appear to speed travel within Queens and across Long Island. Things really started to change around the turn of the twentieth century, with bridges and tunnels across the East River allowing Queens to truly become part of New York City. The extension of the country's first modern highway into Queens was another transportation milestone. Meanwhile, Queens was at the forefront of the city's aviation, with several important airfields appearing between World Wars I and II. In fact, the first transatlantic flight took off from Queens eight years before Charles Lindbergh's solo flight. In this chapter, we'll explore the hidden history of a variety of modes of transportation in Queens.

Clang Clang Went the Trolley

Historic preservationists love the words "adaptive reuse," because that phrase means that some important old building is going to be saved rather than demolished. In New York City, if a building is not a City Landmark, or a museum or private residence, then adaptive reuse is often its best hope of survival. With land prices what they are these days, profitability is king in Queens, and if a buck is to be made, it will. Once in a while, an old building suits a need and can be repurposed.

And so it is that you may notice an odd structure at the entry to the Tower Square shopping center on Northern Boulevard at Woodside Avenue in Woodside. Your first impression may be of some kind of gatehouse to an ancient castle. Actually, the twin-peaked building was formerly a trolley terminal belonging to the New York and Queens County Railway Company. (The name can still be seen on the building, along with the words "Waiting Room.") It was built in 1885, when trolleys clanged all around the city (actually, in 1885, Queens was not yet part of New York City), and Woodside was a hub of sorts, a meeting point for trolleys coming from Manhattan, Brooklyn, Flushing and Jamaica. By 1937, times were changing, and the bus was now the preferred mode of surface mass transportation. The building's trolley days were over, and it was later used by a trucking company. By the 1970s, it was sitting abandoned and in jeopardy.

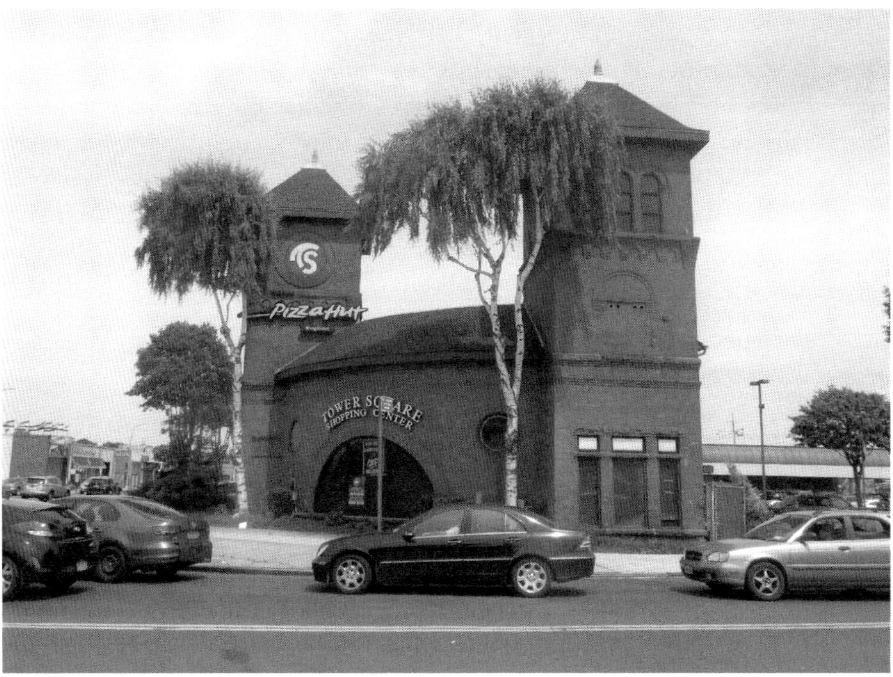

The Tower Square building is a remnant of the trolley days of Queens. *Author's collection.*

Though it stands proudly today, in 1987, the Romanesque Revival building was slated for demolition when a new shopping center was being constructed at the site. Local residents had gathered at the site as a bulldozer and backhoe were rumbling into action and about to smash into the brick towers of the unique structure when, with literally seconds to spare, a New York City Buildings Department inspector issued a stop work order on a technicality—the crew did not have a special permit to operate the backhoe and bulldozer. Also showing up to the site at that moment was the chairman of the Landmarks Preservation Commission. Though it was not (and still is not) a landmark, the hope was that the delay could allow talks to take place with the developer to allow the old building to be reused and become a symbol of the new shopping center. Happily for Queens history buffs, that is exactly what happened.

A NEW SIDE OF SUNNYSIDE

The construction of a tunnel under the East River during the first decade of the twentieth century to allow for train travel between Manhattan and Queens was a huge innovation that forever changed Queens and all of Long Island. No longer was commuting to the "city" an impossible ordeal. In conjunction with the new East River railroad tunnel that was being built, a huge new rail yard was planned for the Sunnyside neighborhood of Long Island City, which drastically altered the area.

The first step was to obtain the real estate that comprised the site of the proposed yard. Advance work on the Sunnyside Yard was already in full swing by 1903, by which time half of the houses purchased thus far had been torn down or moved to another location by their owners. One of the last obstacles to the construction of the yard was overcome late in 1907, when the Pennsylvania Tunnel and Terminal Company acquired 108 lots (with four houses) that belonged to a holdout, a real estate speculator from Manhattan named John McGrane, for $156,962.

To create this massive yard facility, fifty-two streets were obliterated (though many of them at that point existed in name only on maps that had not been translated into reality), and many colonial-era homes were among the more than 246 buildings demolished or removed. The natural features of the area were also eliminated. More than 2 million cubic yards of "Sunnyside Hill" (which was 70 feet high at its apex) were excavated and part of that used to fill in the 40 acres of low-lying marshy areas nearby that was also to become part of Sunnyside Yard. At its peak of construction, there were several hundred men on the Sunnyside site working with several giant steam shovels and supplied by numerous freight railcars. Work on the project also involved the construction of eight roadway bridges and seven railroad bridges, as well as numerous buildings on the site, including a 253-foot-long boiler house and substation and a 160-foot-long Inspection and Machine Shop. There was also a 258-foot-long Stores and Commissary Building that held supplies for Pullman cars and dining cars. This yard was the largest of its kind in the world when built, at 153 acres, with 73 miles of track and the capacity to hold 1,550 train cars. The yard is, of course, still in use today, but it is far removed from its glory days when rail travel was king.

THE LONG ISLAND MOTOR PARKWAY

When you think of Queens highways, perhaps the first thing you picture is bumper-to-bumper traffic for miles. There may be too many cars on the road now, but there was a day when not only were there not many cars, there also were no highways. It was the beginning of the twentieth century, and the automobile was starting to become popular. The problem was, the dusty roads in the New York area were created for horses and carriages, not motor vehicles traveling at much higher speeds.

Enter automobile enthusiast William Kissam Vanderbilt Jr. (1878–1944), who came from old money; his grandfather, the wealthy Commodore Cornelius Vanderbilt (1794–1877), was responsible for the construction of the original Grand Central Terminal. William K. Vanderbilt was a car nut at a time when scant few people owned one. In 1901, Vanderbilt briefly held a speed record when he drove his Mercedes five miles in a time of about seven minutes (a little more than forty miles per hour). His Vanderbilt Cup Races, held on Long Island's ramshackle roads beginning in 1904, were his impetus for creating a smooth, safe, dustless road.

The ambitious project, the planning for which began in 1906, sought to create a seventy-mile-long road through central Long Island, from Queens all the way to Riverhead. One of the biggest challenges was obtaining the property, or right-of-way, to build the parkway. Farmers and estate owners had to be convinced to allow a road to be built through their land. Holdouts would mean an expensive and inconvenient shift in the roadway's course.

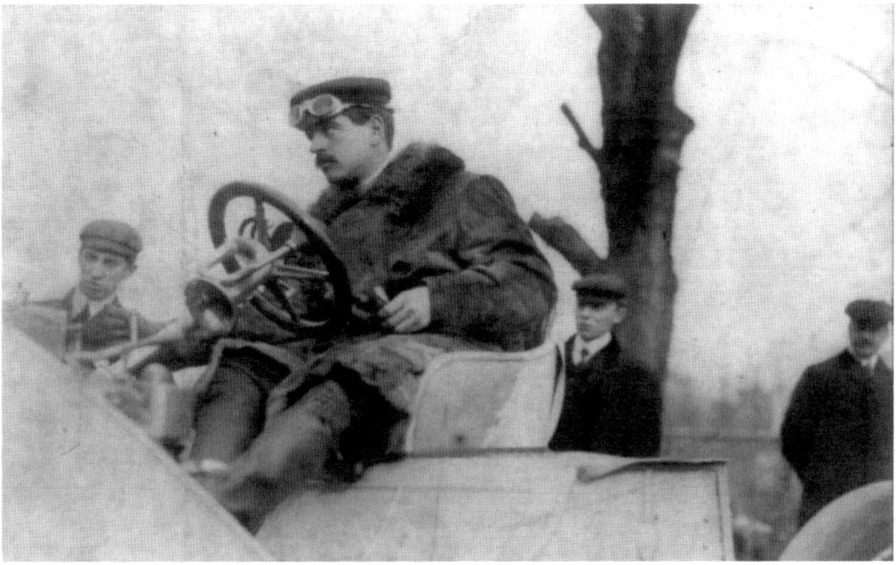

William K. Vanderbilt. *Library of Congress.*

Queens was the western terminus of the world's first limited-access highway. The highway was touted as a great place for automobile designers and manufacturers to test their cars under "true road conditions." From the beginning, the parkway was envisioned as a highway for the wealthy—after all, at that time, before the Ford Model T, automobiles were still affordable only by the privileged. The investment prospectus for the Long Island Motor Parkway explains: "The numerous golf, fishing, yachting, and shooting clubs will be conveniently and speedily reached and can be more fully made use of by their members."

Besides being the country's first concrete highway, one of the other unique features of the parkway was its complete grade separation from other existing roads—all streets and railroad tracks were crossed above or below grade, which meant there were many bridges along the parkway—sixty-five, to be exact.

On June 7, 1908, the first ceremonial shovelful of dirt was turned over with a gold spade in Bethpage in front of several hundred spectators. The president of the Automobile Club of America said on the occasion: "All hail, those pioneers—Mr. Vanderbilt and his associates—who for the motorists of America and the world are thus blazing the trail for the motor roads, the motor streets, and the motor bridges of the future."

Work progressed at a moderate pace. In September 1908, a race-car driver named Joe Tracy tested the completed portions and was able to reach sixty miles per hour on the turns and reached one hundred miles per hour over a straight stretch. "The cement highway makes an excellent racing road, because it is absolutely dustless, and on account of the grayish color it does not blind the driver even in the glaring sun," said Tracy.

About nine miles of roadway were complete by the end of 1908, from Westbury to Bethpage. In 1909, the parkway was extended west from Westbury to Mineola and east from Bethpage to Dix Hills. The section from Bethpage to Lake Ronkonkoma was opened in 1910. By 1912, the parkway extended as far west as Springfield Boulevard in Queens, and by 1926, it had reached its westernmost point, what is now Horace Harding Boulevard in Fresh Meadows.

This expensive new highway was not free for motorists. The toll on the Long Island Motor Parkway was originally set at $2.00, then fell to $1.50, $1.00 and, finally, $0.40 in the 1930s. There were twelve toll lodges at entry/exit points along the way (connecting to nearby local roads), some of them designed by famous architect John Russell Pope (designer of the Jefferson Memorial).

The years that followed the opening of the parkway saw the rise of Queens and Long Island's population and the construction of the more modern, wider Grand Central Parkway/Northern State Parkway in the early 1930s. With the Motor Parkway seemingly doomed to obsolescence, William K. Vanderbilt met with New York City parks commissioner Robert Moses in 1937 to discuss giving the city the title to the portion of the road in Queens. The Long Island Motor Parkway shut down in April 1938 and was sold to New York State for $80,000 (a fraction of the $6 million it had cost to build). Parks commissioner Moses quickly obtained several Queens portions of the parkway's right-of-way for use as the "Queens Bicycle Path"—today this section survives within Alley Pond Park and Cunningham Park in Queens. The opening day was a big event, with hundreds of riders partaking in the festivities.

From a July 1938 article about the opening of the bike path:

> *"The way to progress, sometimes, is to go backward," Moses said on that memorable day. And since that time many a cyclist has gone backward on the impossible hills of the two-and a-half-mile track. "Fifty miles of additional paths exclusively for bicyclists are planned," Moses continues, "which would turn the calendar back 40 years." The winding parkway*

extended westward to Springfield Boulevard Queens, in 1911 and as late as 1921–1925 a yearly patronage of 120,000 warranted construction to Horace Harding Boulevard.

Bicyclists could rent a bike at Alley Pond Park, and in the weeks after the bike path opened, an average of three hundred bikes a week were rented, this in addition to the four hundred to five hundred riders per week who brought their own bikes to the former highway.

The Queens section of the parkway features five of the original sixty-five bridges, most of which no longer exist. The bridges and the road reflect a snapshot of what was then state-of-the-art roadway technology. Some of the original roadway material was a patented form of reinforced concrete. The parks department later repaved the roadway with additional asphalt, but some original concrete and asphalt surfaces, markers and fence posts are visible along the route.

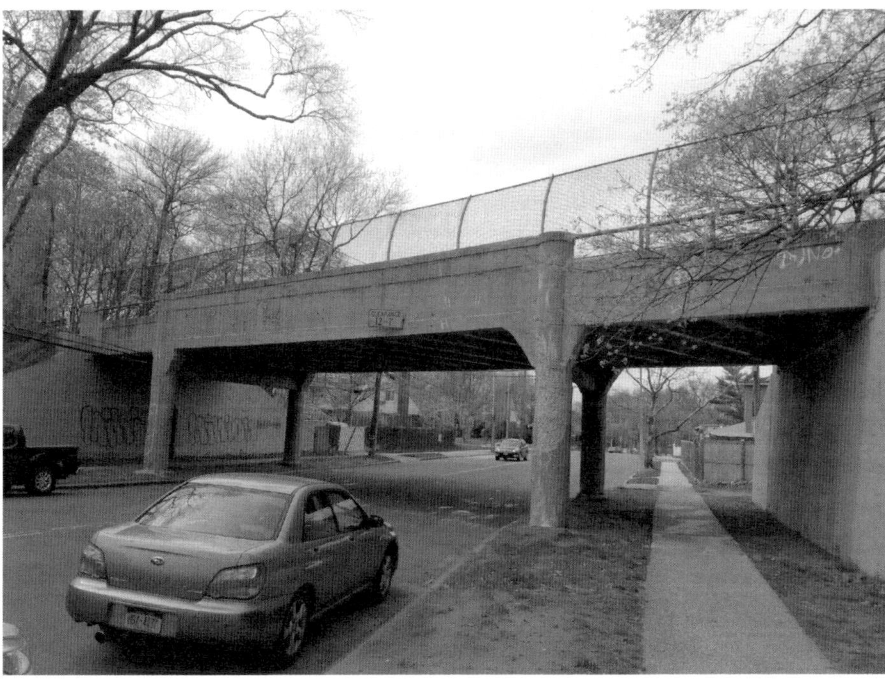

The Long Island Motor Parkway Bridge over Francis Lewis Boulevard is still intact. *Author's collection.*

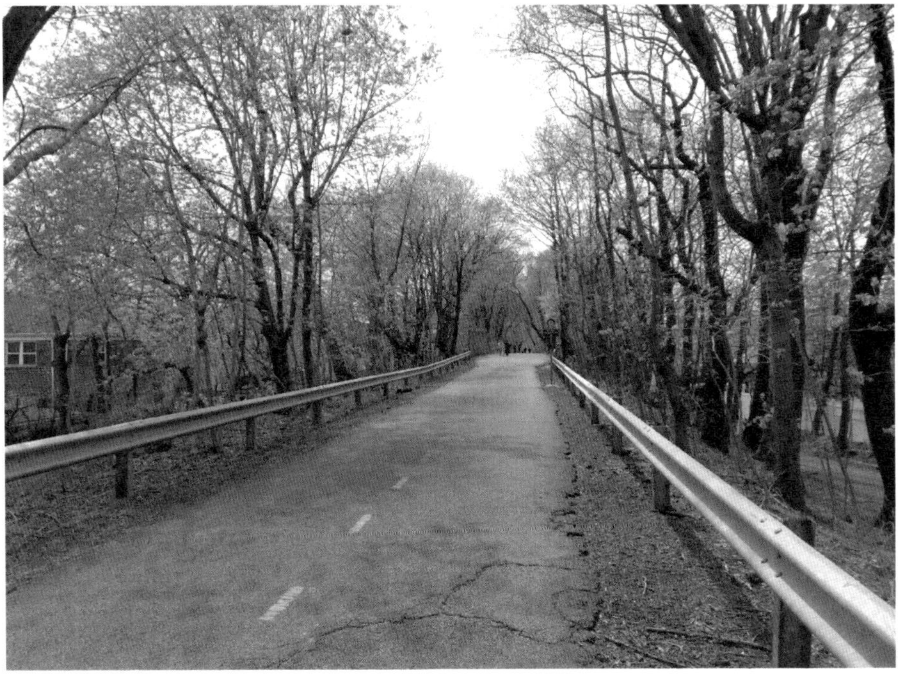

A stretch of the original Long Island Motor Parkway is preserved in Alley Pond Park. *Author's collection.*

Queens residents should be thankful for Moses's affection for bicycling, because almost all of what remained of the historic highway in Nassau and Suffolk Counties was completely demolished over the years, as new infrastructure, homes and commercial development was built.

In 1986, the parks department rehabilitated the section of the parkway through Alley Pond and Cunningham Park. It was incorporated into the New York City Greenway program in 1993 as part of the Brooklyn-Queens Greenway. In 2002, the parts of the Long Island Motor Parkway located in Cunningham and Alley Pond Parks were placed on the New York State and National Registers of Historic Places.

FIRST TRANSATLANTIC FLIGHT

While Charles Lindbergh became the first person to fly solo across the Atlantic, his 1927 flight was just the culmination of a long aviation journey that began in the spring of 1919 in Rockaway, Queens.

After the Wright brothers' first flight in 1903, the field of aviation advanced quickly. By 1910, flight pioneer Glenn Curtiss began to develop the flat land in central Nassau County as airfields, and others followed suit. World War I sped up advances in aeronautical technology, and airfields were built all over the New York City area, including the Naval Air Station Rockaway at Fort Tilden on Rockaway Beach, which opened in 1917.

In 1918, the Curtiss Aeroplane and Motor Company began building a seaplane (aka flying boat, which could float on built-in pontoons) designed by company founder Glenn Curtiss. The NC-1 (Navy Curtiss-1), the largest seaplane in the world, found a home at Naval Air Station Rockaway, where it would be tested and prepared for a potential long-distance flight. With a range of 1,200 miles, the possibilities were exciting. The three-motored NC-1 could carry a ten-thousand-pound load and could reach speeds of between 80 and 100 miles per hour.

In November 1918, the NC-1 seaplane set a new record at Rockaway Beach by carrying a total of fifty-one people on a flight. This was exciting, but the navy had even bigger plans for the plane and for the next three versions that the Curtiss Company was building. By the end of February 1919, the NC-2 had been finished and delivered to Rockaway Beach, and the NC-3 and NC-4 were under construction.

The navy's plans for a transatlantic seaplane flight were first made public in February 1919. A seaplane was ideal for two main reasons. It could land on the water and be refueled by a naval vessel; and it could theoretically survive for a while at sea if the engines failed and it was forced down.

Once the plans became public, newspaper reporters eagerly followed the progress of the plane preparations. It soon became clear that the navy wanted to send more than one of these planes across the Atlantic. Glenn Curtiss himself visited Rockaway Beach in April 1919 to inspect the NC-2, which had made a successful twenty-minute test flight, laden with a 28,500-pound load, a record for a seaplane.

Soon after that, the NC-2 was deemed unfit to make the flight across the Atlantic when it could not lift off from the water due to a pontoon problem. That did not deter the plans for the other three planes. Thirty-two airplane mechanics departed for ships located at the Azores Islands and Lisbon, Portugal, where the navy planes were expected to make stops along their way across the Atlantic. As the weeks passed, there was much secrecy over the testing of the planes and their state of readiness for the voyage. A one-hundred-yard buffer zone was established around the perimeter of the hangars, and only those with proper credentials could get past.

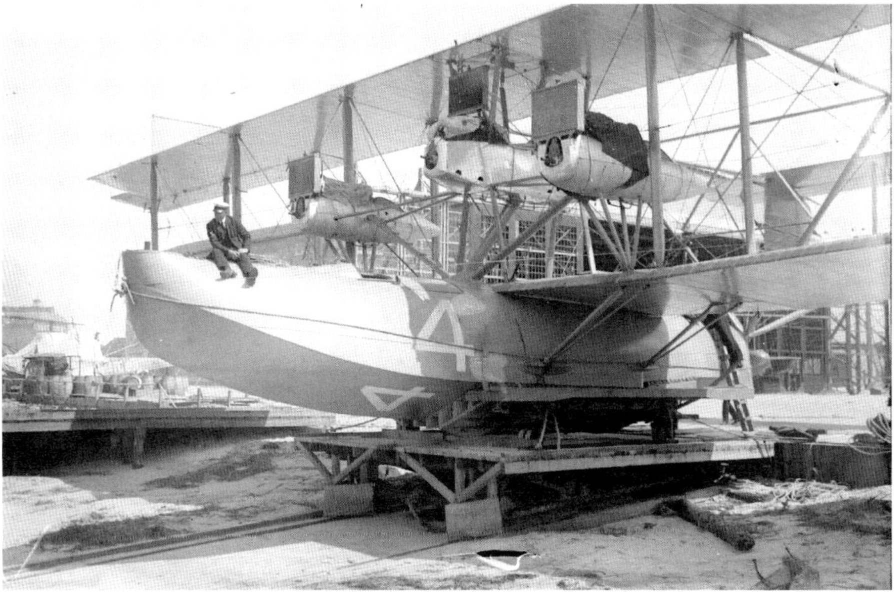

The NC-4 seaplane being built at the Rockaway Naval Air Station, 1919. *Library of Congress.*

The U.S. Navy decided to fly the NC-1, NC-3 and NC-4, but on April 25, the NC-3 failed to take off from the water. Instead, the NC-3, carrying a load of 29,500 pounds, zoomed around the water like a boat. On April 28, the NC-3 was finally successful in lifting off and made a one-hour, fifteen-minute flight. Lieutenant Commander Richard Byrd (who would later be in the running against Charles Lindbergh for the first nonstop transatlantic flight) was to make the first leg of the trip to Newfoundland.

The planes cost about $250,000 each and were made specifically for transatlantic flight. They were officially commissioned as U.S. Navy ships on May 3. Once again, the NC-3 failed that day, but the NC-4 took off fine. Dates for departure were set and reset several times, and delays and setbacks occurred. On May 5, tragedy struck when a different seaplane, an HS-1 model, crashed at the Rockaway base and killed two navy men. On the very same day, the NC-1 was damaged by fire.

The three planes finally took off on May 8, each with a crew of six men: a commanding officer, two pilots, a radio operator, an engineer and a reserve pilot/engineer. What a sight it must have been to the gathered onlookers who saw the three planes flying together over Jamaica Bay on their way to Halifax, with NC-3 as the flagship. The crews were provided with coffee and sandwiches and condensed food rations.

Before liftoff, J.H. Towers, the commander in chief of the flights, said of their chances of making it across the ocean: "It is up to us now, and we are going to try. Guesses aren't worth much, but if you want mine, here it is: We'll get there."

A contingent of navy destroyers was ever-present along the planes' route. NC-1 and NC-3 arrived in Halifax, Nova Scotia, a 540-mile journey, in nine hours, but NC-4 lost contact with the other planes and was forced to land at Chatham, Massachusetts, due to engine trouble. In making this trip, NC-1 and NC-3 had set another aviation record—the longest flight across water, 220 miles. The two planes took off for the next destination, Trepassey Bay, Newfoundland, on May 10, while NC-4 was being repaired in Massachusetts, its crew still hopeful to continue on and catch up to the other planes. Fifty miles after takeoff from Halifax, one of NC-3's propellers malfunctioned, forcing it to return to Halifax for repairs. It took off again a few hours later.

There was talk of NC-1 and NC-3 leaving Newfoundland without NC-4, but on May 16, all three planes were together again and ready to take off

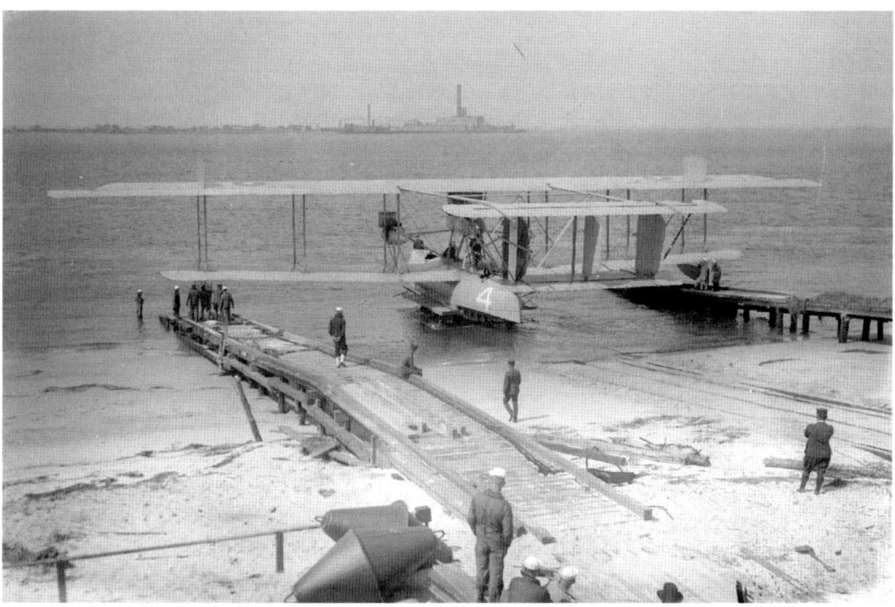

The NC-4 seaplane ready for a test flight. *Library of Congress.*

from Newfoundland to head out on the longest stretch of the journey. The newly reunited planes took off within three minutes of each other.

Just before the trio arrived at the Azores, NC-1 went down in the fog eighty miles from the islands (and eventually sank after the crew was rescued and an unsuccessful attempt was made to salvage the plane in heavy seas). NC-3 went eighty miles off course in the fog and was also forced to make a water landing, spending fifty-two hours in the water. Its wings, tail and hull were severely damaged, and it had to be towed to the harbor by a destroyer. Only NC-4 landed safely at the port of Horta in the Azores. A short hop on May 20 from Horta to Ponta Delgada, Azores Islands (150 miles), took one hour and forty-four minutes.

From Ponta Delgada it was over open water again, the last stretch of the Atlantic and on to Lisbon, Portugal (eight hundred miles), on May 27, which took nine hours and forty-four minutes. At this point, it was official! The NC-4 had become the first aircraft to go all the way across the Atlantic! It was greeted with a twenty-one-gun salute and ringing church bells as a waiting crowd cheered.

The NC-4 took off from Rockaway Beach at 6:07 p.m. on May 8, 1919, for the first leg of the trip, which was from Rockaway Beach to its unexpected stop at Chatham, Massachusetts (300 nautical miles). The flight took five hours and forty-five minutes. Once the plane landed, it was a few days before it embarked upon the next leg. On May 14, the plane left Chatham headed for Halifax, Nova Scotia (320 miles), which took three hours and fifty-one minutes, experiencing engine trouble but surviving without incident. On May 15, NC-4 departed Halifax for Trepassey, Newfoundland (460 miles), which took six hours and twenty minutes. On May 16, it left Trepassey with the other planes for Horta, Azores Islands (1,200 miles), taking fifteen hours and eighteen minutes to arrive.

From Lisbon, there were a few more hops to get to Plymouth, England (where it arrived on May 31), which was 775 miles away from Lisbon and took a total of eleven hours and thirty-five minutes. The total 4,005-mile trip took two days, six hours and forty-three minutes of flight time (twenty-three days overall!). It was a momentous occasion that made headlines all across the country.

The secretary of the navy sent his congratulations to the crew: "All the people of America are happy over your successful flight, which has been an epoch-making event in the history of the world. My congratulations and greeting and good wishes."

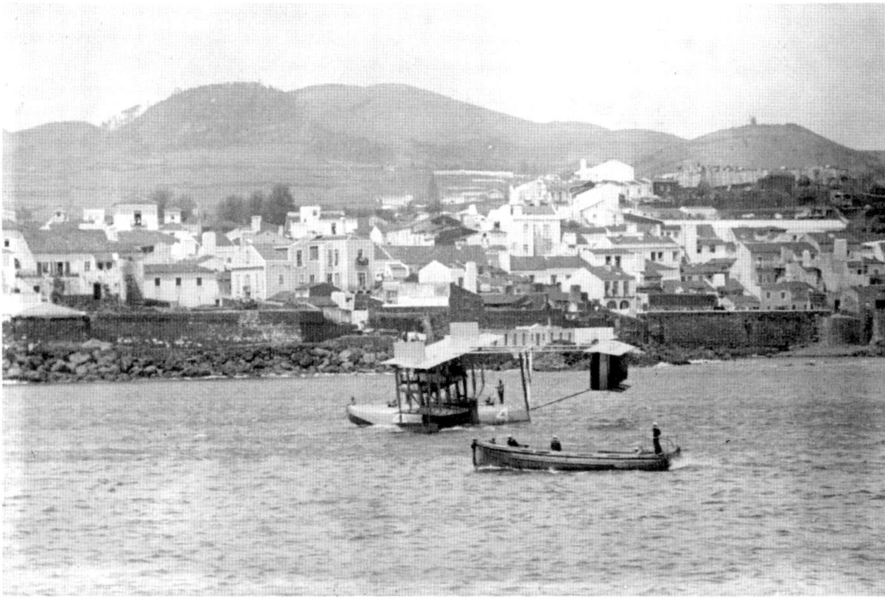

NC-4 lands at the Azores. *Library of Congress.*

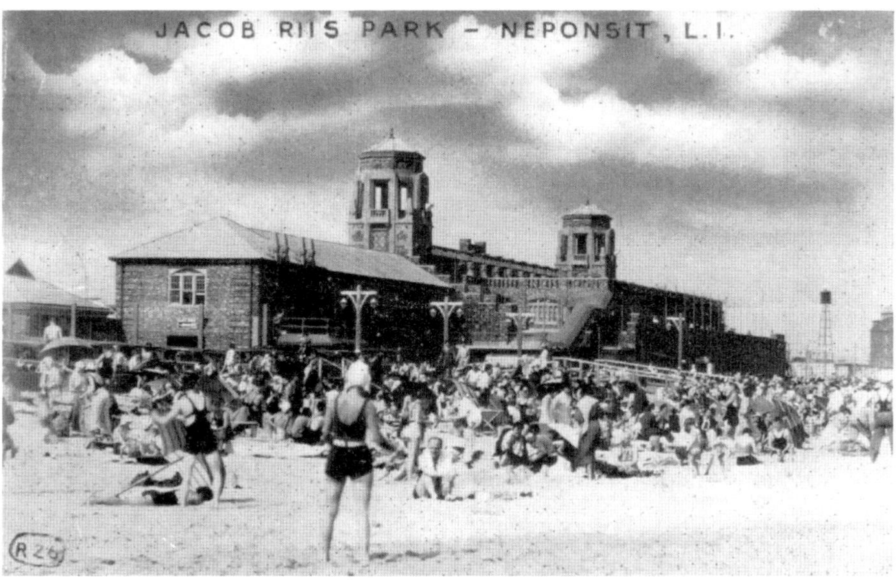

The Art Deco–style Jacob Riis Park Bathhouse Building as seen in a 1930s image. *Author's collection.*

The NC-4, NC-3 and NC-1 crews returned to the United States on a steamship (ironically named the *Zeppelin*) after receiving ovations in Portugal, Spain and England. They were greeted by an honor escort of five seaplanes, two blimps and numerous naval and private boats. The aerial greeting was to have been much larger, but heavy rain prevented that.

Naval Air Station Rockaway was in operation until 1930; its functions were transferred to Floyd Bennett Field in Brooklyn. The historic Rockaway site was demolished to make way for Jacob Riis Park, and Queens' important role in aviation history was soon forgotten. These days, you can walk along the beach where the famous naval seaplanes were tested and repaired and frolic in the water where the planes took off. The centerpiece of the park (part of the Gateway National Recreation Area) is a sprawling Art Deco masterpiece, the Jacob Riis bathhouse (1932), with its two octagonal towers. The bathhouse fell into disrepair after enjoying several decades of a glorious heyday. Repairs were finally begun in the 1990s, but they were not finished. For years after that, the Art Deco structure has sat abandoned and waiting for another lifeline, hoping to avoid a fate similar to the historic naval air station that once stood on the very same spot.

GLENN CURTISS AIRPORT

One of the most important early Queens airports began in 1929 as a seaplane base in the North Beach section of Astoria, fronting Flushing Bay. The base was founded by Richard F. Hoyt, chairman of the Curtiss Wright Corporation; flying ace Captain Harry Rogers; and William T. Carey, a Panama Canal engineer. The Curtiss Wright Corporation had been formed the year before by a merger of the Curtiss Aeroplane and Motor Company (founded by air pioneer Glenn Curtiss, who had arrived on Long Island in 1910 and opened up its first airfield in Mineola) and the Wright Aeronautical Corporation (founded by the Wright brothers). Once the seaplane base was up and running, it wasn't long before the site's potential for a land airport was explored. Eleanor Roosevelt and Charles Lindbergh attended the dedication of Glenn Curtiss Airport on September 24, 1930, just two months after Glenn Curtiss's death. The airport was built on the site of what had been an amusement park and resort that had opened in 1886. It attracted up to sixty thousand people a day at its peak but closed when Prohibition set in.

The new airport quickly rose to prominence, receiving many prominent visitors and serving as the setting for several important flying milestones. In 1931, Captain Frank M. Hawks, transcontinental speed flier, set a record when he landed at Glenn Curtiss Airport after a 1,400-mile flight from Fort Worth, Texas, in just over eight hours. Hawks was flying a Curtiss Hell Diver biplane with a special passenger—the humorist Will Rogers—whom he was flying around the country on a speaking tour for a Red Cross Relief Drive.

In August 1932, more than two hundred planes entered a weekend of veterans' air races that were held at the airport. Events included acrobatics, parachute jumping and spot landings. Entrants included James Doolittle and Charles "Casey" Jones. The event was overseen by several big names in flight, including Amelia Earhart.

In August 1932, John O'Meara set a new glider record from Glenn Curtiss Airport. O'Meara, who was only twenty years old at the time, was towed in his glider, the *Chanute*, by a plane that took off from Curtiss Airport. When the plane reached an altitude of 3,000 feet, his glider was released. Air currents took the *Chanute* higher and higher until O'Meara reached an altitude of 7,010 feet, which was an unofficial new record for a glider. O'Meara wound up soaring above Brooklyn and Manhattan for one hour and eleven minutes before his glider touched down safely at Curtiss Airport.

Colonel Charles Lindbergh used Glenn Curtiss Airport extensively in the 1930s. In June 1931, Lindbergh had his plane fitted with pontoons there in preparation for an ambitious trip to the Far East. In July 1931, Lindbergh and his wife were ready for their trip and set off from Washington, D.C., on their way to the family house in Maine to say goodbye to their thirteen-month-old son before embarking on their ten-hop trip to the Far East. From Maine, they would head to Ottawa, Canada, and then northwest through the vast expanse of Canada, across Alaska and then across the North Pacific to Tokyo. It was a sound plan, but they ran into unexpected trouble soon after takeoff when Lindbergh realized that his radio was not working correctly. The Lindberghs made an unannounced landing at Curtiss Airport, surprising the attendants there as his Lockheed Sirius monoplane swooped down from rain-soaked skies. He had the radio tested and repaired, delaying their vacation by a day, and then the Lindberghs set off on their trip.

In April 1932, tragedy struck when thirty-six-year-old Captain Harry Rogers, who served as operations manager for the airport and was one of its founders, was killed in an accident. His plane crashed into Bowery Bay five hundred feet offshore after his engine failed after takeoff from the airport and he was thrown through the windshield when the plane hit the water.

Charles Lindbergh himself had a near miss with tragedy at Glenn Curtiss Airport in 1933. Lindbergh was testing new pontoons on his plane, having just taken off from Flushing Bay, when two other planes carrying photographers swooped in close to try to get pictures of Lindbergh. One of the planes almost hit Lindbergh's, missing it by mere inches. When he landed, Lindbergh warned other pilots to stay away. This didn't stop photographers' planes from following him when he took off for Maine later that day.

The airport made news in 1934, when Mayor Fiorello LaGuardia leased the facility for five years with the option to buy it for $1.5 million. LaGuardia was eager to build a world-class airport in Queens, and he felt this was the perfect location. After the city purchased the site, work on the expanded airport was begun in September 1937—the mayor himself operated the power shovel that dug the first scoop of dirt. The original Curtiss airport was 106 acres. The new airport would add 357 acres of man-made land and 96 additional acres of purchased land for a total of 559 acres.

Construction of the new North Beach Airport (eventually to be known as LaGuardia Airport) was a huge undertaking. A workforce of twenty-three thousand people was on site during the peak of construction. The airport cost a whopping $43 million to build, much more than the $8 million originally projected. Many supported this new airport, but its critics were harsh, and the money being spent was their main complaint. One reporter wrote in the *Long Island Daily Star* in 1938: "While LaGuardia warns the Board of Estimate to trim the budget, to lop off expenditures, he merrily lavishes huge sums on an airport that will bring the city a return of about .006 per cent on the dollar. In other words, virtually nothing."

Tempers flared when the *Long Island Daily Press* criticized the cost of the new airport. Mayor LaGuardia said he would ask the paper's advertisers not to place ads in the *Press*. His attitude was that if New York was not willing to make the investment to become the transatlantic hub of the United States, some other city would.

Built atop seventeen million cubic yards of garbage, the new airport was a Works Progress Administration (WPA) project. It was dedicated on October 15, 1939, before a crowd of 200,000 people. The spectators were allowed to walk around the airfield and wander into its 350- by 165-foot-long hangars. Army, navy and marine planes flew in formation overhead as part of the celebration.

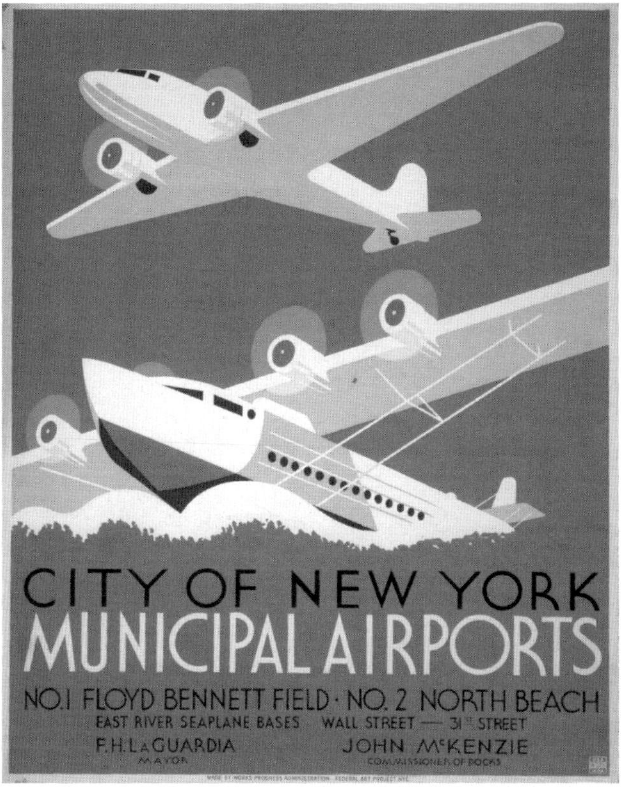

Left: A 1937 WPA poster touts North Beach Airport. *Library of Congress*.

Below: A North Beach Airport postal cover from December 1939 touts it as the world's finest airport. *Author's collection*.

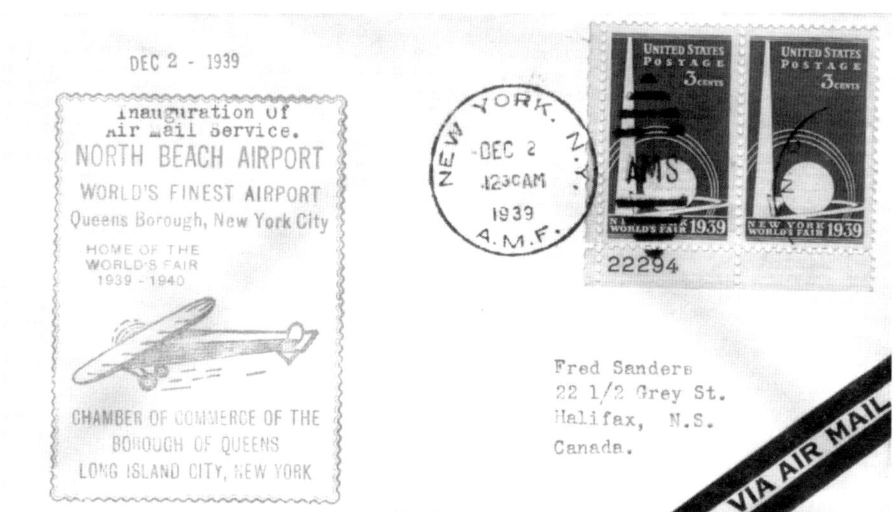

Mayor LaGuardia's dedication speech was a mixture of pride and I-told-you-so: "I can tell you, my friends, if we could transform the disappointment, the opposition and the abuse that Colonel Somervell and I have received into tears, we would have enough to water all of this acreage where we planted grass. But we kept on, and in spite of all we are now completed to the extent that you see the greatest airport in the world."

Eastern Air Lines, Canadian Colonial Airways, Transcontinental and Western Air, American Airlines and United Air Lines were the first carriers to be based at the new airport. By 1941, 90,000 flights took off or landed from the airport. In the years that followed, the airport continued to grow and become more popular; by 2016, there were nearly 370,000 flights entering or leaving LaGuardia. In 2016, a $5 billion improvement program was launched to create a more modern and efficient airport.

Holmes Airport

Just a stone's throw southwest of Glenn Curtiss Airport was another airport that opened the very same year in a meadow just east of St. Michael's Cemetery in Jackson Heights. Its opening was attended by the famous flier Clarence Chamberlin, who was the second pilot to cross the Atlantic, just two weeks after Lindbergh did in 1927. When it opened, just 55 acres of the 220-acre airport were flight-ready. During the opening day festivities, visitors were able to fly in a plane as passengers for five dollars. Chamberlin's presence was not just a friendly gesture; his flying service operated out of Holmes Airport (he even used it as his business address), and he was for some time an officer of the corporation that ran the airport.

Early airport stunts included a five-thousand-foot bullet parachute jump by "Daredevil Krasto" and a "deadstick" landing, in which a pilot stopped his motor at an altitude of five thousand feet and then glided to earth with a dead stick. Another strange flying activity happened in 1929, when the Maspeth Lions Club rented a plane to scatter twenty-five thousand flyers over Queens—flyers that asked residents to participate in a fall cleanup drive! To encourage the flyers to be picked up, they were numbered, with three numbers winning a cash prize upon their return to the club. Sometimes stunts even happened completely unintentionally, as a newspaper headline from 1930 attested: "Aviator 'Knocks Out' Drunk Who Demands That He Take Controls; Man Hurls Stones after Landing."

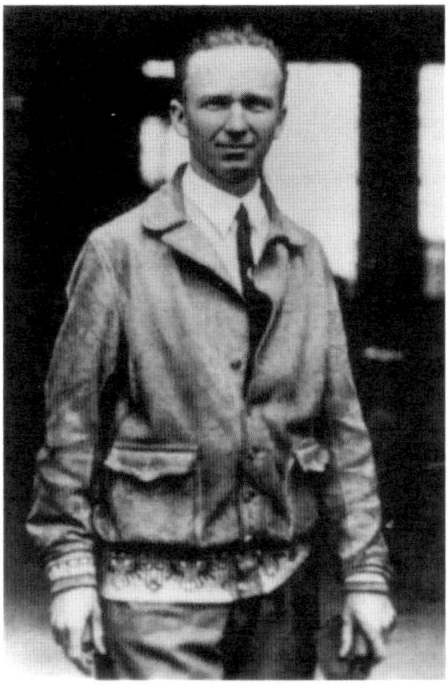

The pioneering aviator Clarence Chamberlin was a major presence at Holmes Airport. *Author's collection.*

The young airport's name briefly changed to Grand Central Airport in 1930, but the name didn't stick, and it reverted to Holmes Airport in 1931. Aside from normal flights, the airport continued to be the scene of some fun and wacky events over the years, such as a combination air treasure hunt and pie-eating contest in 1934. When it was clear that flights alone would not pay for the airport's existence, the owners opened an automobile racetrack on part of the property.

From the start, however, civic leaders in the neighboring communities were not pleased with this airport. They complained of both the noise and the danger of low-flying planes so close to homes. One resident complained in a letter to the *Queens Daily Star* that the local residents were promised a first-class airport and instead got only a "Coney Island affair," a stunt airport where planes flew just twenty or thirty feet above the rooftops of local homes. The airport developed a reputation for being a "playground for daredevils," according to one 1930s newspaper article.

Aside from the stunt flights, Holmes Airport was perhaps best known for the fact that between 1931 and 1938, the Goodyear Zeppelin Company had a hangar there. One of its blimps was involved in a spectacle in October 1931, when strong winds prevented it from being berthed for an entire day and it had to be kept aloft the whole time until the winds died down. That same blimp was involved in a fatal crash at Myrtle Avenue in Flushing the following year in which one of the crew members died. A crowd of five thousand people turned out to gawk at the wreckage.

In July 1935, Colonel Harold Fowler, the first deputy police commissioner in charge of traffic, made headlines when he took off in a blimp and surveyed traffic conditions on highways in the Bronx, Manhattan, Brooklyn and then back to Queens. He made no comment about his flight other than a very vague "I saw a number of things I wanted to see" and said that he would be giving his report directly to the police commissioner. But Fowler was back in the air again several more times, flying over all five boroughs. When he flew in August 1935, he actually broadcast his traffic-related comments through shortwave radio live on the WINS station. This was not exactly your average traffic report, though. As the headline in the *Brooklyn Daily Eagle* read: "Police in Blimp Scold Autoists." Fowler identified specific cars on specific highways and gave them instructions such as "Don't be so hasty there" and "Don't crowd."

As soon as Mayor LaGuardia announced his intent to lease Glenn Curtiss Airport for potential purchase and development, the operators of Holmes Airport could see the writing on the hangar walls. A much larger, better airport so close would mean the end for Holmes. By 1935, Holmes Airport was already up in arms, complaining that Holmes had paid $300,000 in taxes over the six previous years and now the city would take Glenn Curtiss over and it would pay no taxes while Holmes continued to pay, giving it an unfair advantage. Holmes Airport attempted to file an injunction to stop the mayor from buying Glenn Curtiss Airport, but the Queens Supreme Court rejected that and said the city had the right to do as it pleased with Curtiss Airport.

The fears were realized in 1937, when construction on North Beach Airport began. Anthony "Speed" Hanzlik, the pilot-manager of Holmes, expressed concern that private fliers were being pushed out of the New York City area and recounted how the prominent families such as the Whitneys, Vanderbilts and duPonts were using the field. "Private flying has contributed more to aviation than all the rest of the branches put together, yet now they want to shove us out in the cold," said Hanzlik. Among those on the side of the airport was the Queens Flying Club and a state senator named Phelps Phelps, who said that Holmes Airport was important because it was the only emergency landing spot for planes taking off from North Beach. But the new airport was not the only threat. Proposed real estate developments also threatened the airport's existence; any buildings of more than a few stories in height would have made it impossible for planes to take off or land at the tightly hemmed-in airport.

In July 1939, all seemed lost for Holmes, as a housing development was slated to be built on city property in the middle of the airport. "Holmes Airport Closes July 12," read the headline in the *Long Island Star Journal*. But that didn't happen, and in the months that followed came a last-ditch effort to save the airport, which was still a busy place, with twenty to thirty planes taking off or landing daily.

The beginning of the end came in September 1939, when the city moved to extend Seventy-Seventh Street right through the airport, from Astoria Boulevard to Patterson Avenue (Thirty-First Avenue). The airport sought a temporary injunction to prevent the city from erecting light poles on the street, which would have prevented planes from taking off or landing. The injunction was deemed not necessary when one of the city's lawyers promised that the city would not erect any light poles. Then, WPA workers showed up and started digging holes and planting trees along the newly extended street, which would certainly have prevented planes from taking off or landing.

The airport operators again sought to have their injunction granted, and a judge issued a temporary stay against the planting of more trees until he could make a final decision. But the city continued to plant trees anyway—there were more than sixty large trees in place by the time the airport's attorney went back to the judge, who was not pleased, and he said that someone could go to jail if the court's order was not obeyed. Oddly, in the end, the judge refused to make the temporary order permanent, thus allowing the city to continue planting trees. It was noted in his decision that the airport still owned 128 acres that it could develop.

In February 1940, E.H. Holmes, founder of the airport, filed for bankruptcy with more than $3 million in liabilities. The setbacks were too much, and the airport finally closed for good. Once that happened, the abandoned field became a weed-filled dump. After World War II, this huge lot was seen as an ideal location to provide housing to returned war vets. An 1,874-unit emergency veterans Quonset hut housing complex was built on the site in 1946 to help alleviate the housing crunch for more than fifty thousand homeless Queens families living in cramped quarters with relatives or friends.

When, in 1950, the Bulova watch company announced plans to build a watch assembly plant on the northern twenty-five acres of the old Holmes Airport site, there were complaints from the Northern Queens Home Owners Civil Association of Jackson Heights, fearful that one factory would lead to another and destroy the residential character of the neighborhood. Bulova executives were probably wary by now; their previous attempt to build a factory in Forest Hills had been defeated. The factory was the first to be allowed under a new city regulation that permitted light manufacturing in residential neighborhoods. The factory was approved anyway, and the elegant Art Deco building was erected in 1953. By 1952, more than 400 of the original 688 buildings had been demolished, and plans were well under way for six-story apartment buildings on the site. More were demolished in 1953, and the old housing was cleared by 1954. After only a few years, many of the veterans' homes were already in poor condition and were being vandalized. By 1956, there was an infestation of rats living on part of the old airport site. A look at an aerial view of the site today reveals no traces of the former airport.

FLUSHING AIRPORT

After Holmes Airport closed in 1940, thirty-seven-year-old flying veteran Anthony "Speed" Hanzlik, who had been with Holmes for its entire existence, wound up at Flushing Airport, which was then the last private airfield in Queens. Work on the airport, located on a marshy, triangular, 250-acre plot of land south of Twentieth Avenue between Linden Place and the Whitestone Expressway, was begun in 1927. At that time, a pumping station with a pair of ten-million-gallon-per-day pumps had to be installed on the site to drain the marshland. Things stalled, however, and construction didn't begin until 1929. When it did, things moved fast; at the peak of construction, crews were placing one thousand loads of backfill a day to firm up the marshy site. When the airport finally opened in May 1929, the crowd that showed up got more of a thrill than they bargained for, as one of the planes taking off from the field could not gain enough altitude to clear telephone wires at the end of the runway and had to fly under them, just clearing the roofs of automobiles parked on the field by a few feet.

There were a few mishaps at the new airport. In 1933, a stunt pilot lost control of his biplane and crash-landed in the front yard of a home in Whitestone, but his injuries were not serious. In 1934, a plane fell two thousand feet and crashed into marshland near the airport, but both occupants survived. In 1936, a plane that took off from the airport burst into flames and crashed into Ferry Point picnic grounds in the Bronx, killing a woman on the ground.

When Speed Hanzlik arrived at Flushing Airport in 1940, he was given a very special mission. At that point, war had already broken out in Europe, and Hanzlik was an official test pilot to gauge the skills of American men who wanted to become pilots for the Royal Air Force in Britain and help defeat the Nazis. The men would fly over Flushing Bay between the Bronx-Whitestone Bridge and Fort Totten, with Hanzlik giving them orders from the back seat of the dual-control plane. Of the 500 pilots he tested between 1940 and 1941, he passed 362 of them as qualified to fly in Britain's air force. In 1941, Hanzlik was made air director of Queens. At the time, he was also president of the Metropolitan Queens Aviation Association. Though more recent sources have said that this airport was originally named Speed's Airport, I find no such historical references to that moniker.

Over the years of its existence, many rumors circulated about the airport's future. In 1940, it was to be closed and turned into a racetrack. Other ideas for the site included a major league baseball stadium and a housing development. (In 1953, test soil borings were made on the site so developers could see how far down they'd have to drive piles for foundations, and it was a daunting 150 feet before solid earth was reached.)

There were also many complaints from residents over the years; each time, Speed Hanzlik tried to counter or mitigate them as best he could. In 1948, the Flushing Women's Civic Club led a drive to reduce the noise from Flushing Airport's planes; as a result, Hanzlik enacted new rules at the airport, including a new flight pattern, installing mufflers on all planes and banning high-horsepower planes from using the field. The truth was that the airport really was very close to homes and other buildings. Hollywood film crews tried to use aerial shots of Flushing Airport for the 1957 film *The Spirit of St. Louis*, but they gave up when they could not take their film without capturing nearby apartment buildings. When, in 1960, residents of a new nearby co-op apartment complex complained that planes were coming too close, Hanzlik maintained that they were flying at least two hundred feet above the buildings.

In 1967, a private plane collided with a jet over North Carolina, and a congressman from Elmhurst became concerned that Flushing Airport was simply too close to LaGuardia Airport and wanted to inspect the airfield. Hanzlik was confident and proclaimed that there had been only one fatality at Flushing Airport in thirty-eight years, and that was due to pilot error. In September 1968, tragedy struck when two small planes collided over the airport, killing one pilot and one of his passengers, state supreme court justice James Roe, and injuring two of his young passengers.

As the years passed, the airport somehow persevered. When the city announced plans to spend $11 million in improving Flushing Airport in 1972, Congressman Benjamin Rosenthal of Queens, along with the Greater Whitestone Taxpayers Association, strongly opposed the plan, claiming that not only would it be dangerous to have more planes flying out of Flushing Airport, it would also increase noise and air pollution. Not only did they not want it modernized, the locals also wanted the airport permanently closed

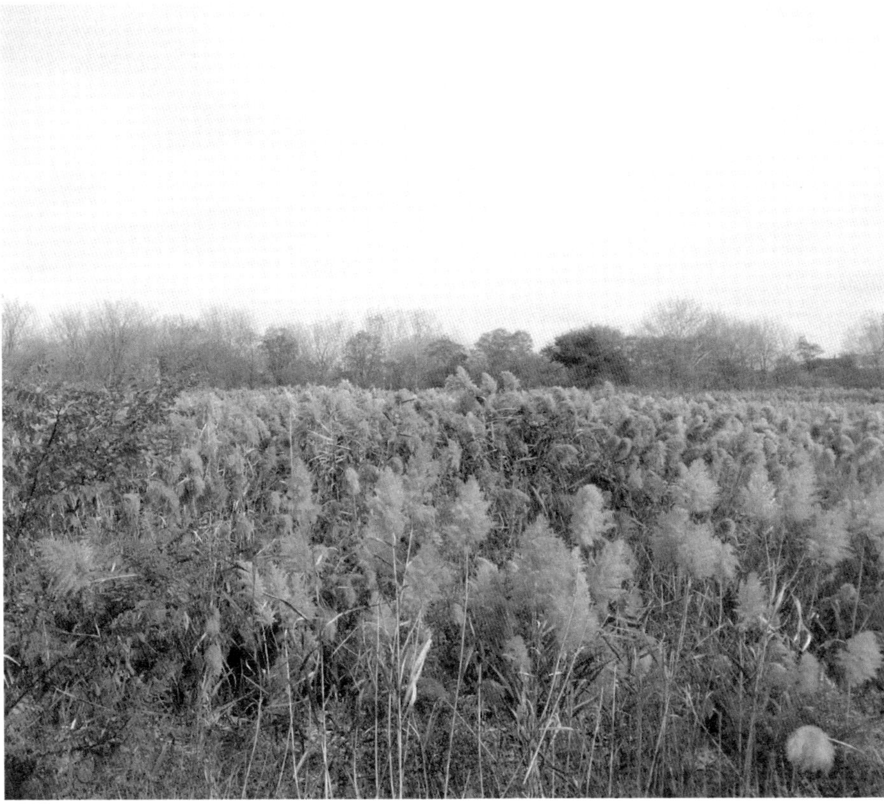

The former site of the Flushing Airport has been reclaimed by nature since it closed in the 1980s. *Author's collection.*

and moved from northern Queens. A 1977 *Flying* magazine article called the airport "a weedy, one-runway slash of asphalt." A 1982 editorial in *Flying* proposed that Flushing Airport be modernized and become an extension of LaGuardia, in essence a "reliever runway" that would allow certain smaller planes to take off and land there instead.

Speed Hanzlik remained at Flushing Airport for many years until his death in 1974, continuing to be the face of the airport and running Speed's Flying Service. The airport itself miraculously remained open until 1984, and there were still traces of it standing as late as 2008, when the old hangars were demolished. The triangle that was occupied by the airport, just east of Linden Place in Flushing, is still quite easily visible in aerial views. In fact, you can still see traces of the old runway in the aerial view.

One of the drawbacks of Flushing Airport was that it was subject to flooding after heavy rains, returning it to its original marshy state. After it closed, it reverted to that state, with much of the area submerged. The property is now an overgrown wetland that looks like a rural wonderland. It is one of the last large pieces of undeveloped land in New York City, patiently waiting for its fate. On the fall day I visited the site, the former airport property, behind a chain-link fence, was filled with colorful "Little Becka" flowers, a pretty red and yellow miniature variety of sunflower.

Ironically, a LaGuardia Airport parking lot is located on the southern edge of the former Flushing Airport. Linden Place, which ran north–south and parallel to the main runway, was closed for years after the airport shut down, deteriorated and flooded. It was redone in 2016 and reopened to traffic.

JAMAICA SEA AIRPORT

Located at Rockaway Boulevard and Springfield Avenue, the 250-acre, $2.5 million Jamaica Sea Airport opened in 1929 and was billed as "the first combination plane port along the Atlantic coast"—it could land both seaplanes and airplanes. Newspaper advertisements in advance of the airport's grand opening touted flying instruction as well as passenger transportation, and a "free bathing beach" that offered refreshments and other recreation. Why just fly when you can swim, too? Like other Queens airports of the era, spectacle was commonplace, because passenger flights alone were not enough to sustain such a venture. The operators of the airport even offered sightseeing trips at "a penny a pound." Soon after it opened in 1929, Queens borough president George Harvey staged a political stunt when he offered twenty-five free sightseeing airplane trips to supporters who wanted to help him retain his position. There were also air races and parachute jumps on "Harvey Day."

The airport's managers and backers had hoped to erect a $30,000 zeppelin mooring mast there for German zeppelins to make temporary stops on their travels and were in discussion with the Zeppelin Company. German officials, however, decided that winds at the ocean-facing site were not favorable for zeppelin stops.

In 1930, Indian motorcycle races were held on the airport's beach and an air circus was held. That same year, a seventeen-year-old Australian

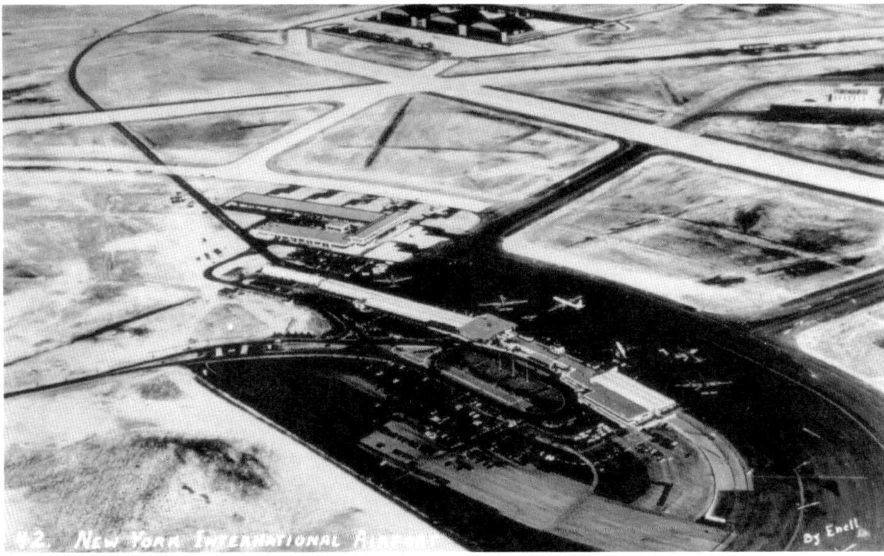

New York International Airport (later known as John F. Kennedy International Airport), circa early 1950s. *Author's collection.*

female aviator named Uva Kimerney walked on the wing of her plane three thousand feet above the airport while a crowd of five thousand watched from below. In 1934, you could fly from the Jamaica Sea Airport to Chicago for thirty dollars—fifty dollars round-trip.

In 1936, tragedy struck when two planes collided one hundred feet over the airport, killing the pilot and passenger of one plane and the passenger of the second plane. Ironically, one of the planes crashed into a billboard for an undertaker.

Interestingly, little Jamaica Sea Airport's fate was tied to that of LaGuardia Airport, and of New York City aviation in general. By 1940, within six months of opening, LaGuardia Airport reached its capacity. The city needed another airport, and fast! The site the city chose in southwestern Queens encompassed the Idlewild Beach Golf Course and the Jamaica Sea Airport.

Construction on Idlewild Airport began in 1942. Originally planned to be twice the size of LaGuardia, by 1945, plans called for Idlewild to be eight times larger than its counterpart ten miles north. Forty-one million cubic yards of sand were used during the first phase of construction to level and fill in the land so it would be stable enough for use as runways. As work progressed, 4,500 people living on or near Jamaica Creek were forced to move to make room for airport construction.

The new airport opened in 1948 and became known as New York International Airport. Jet planes began landing there in the 1950s. Expansions and improvements continued over the years. After the assassination of President Kennedy in 1963, it was renamed John F. Kennedy International Airport. There is no trace of the Jamaica Sea Airport left today, but appropriately enough, it is resting in peace on what is now one of JFK's main runways.

PLANEVIEW PARK AND LAGUARDIA LANDING LIGHTS PARK

There are so many parks in Queens, and each one has its own unique history and amenities. Some are truly enormous, offering all kinds of recreational possibilities (Flushing Meadows–Corona Park, Alley Pond Park and Forest Park). Others, however, are tiny and offer the simplest amenities. There is one such park that might be the city's most rudimentary, scruffy, unpleasant park—were it not for one thing. The park in question is a narrow triangle

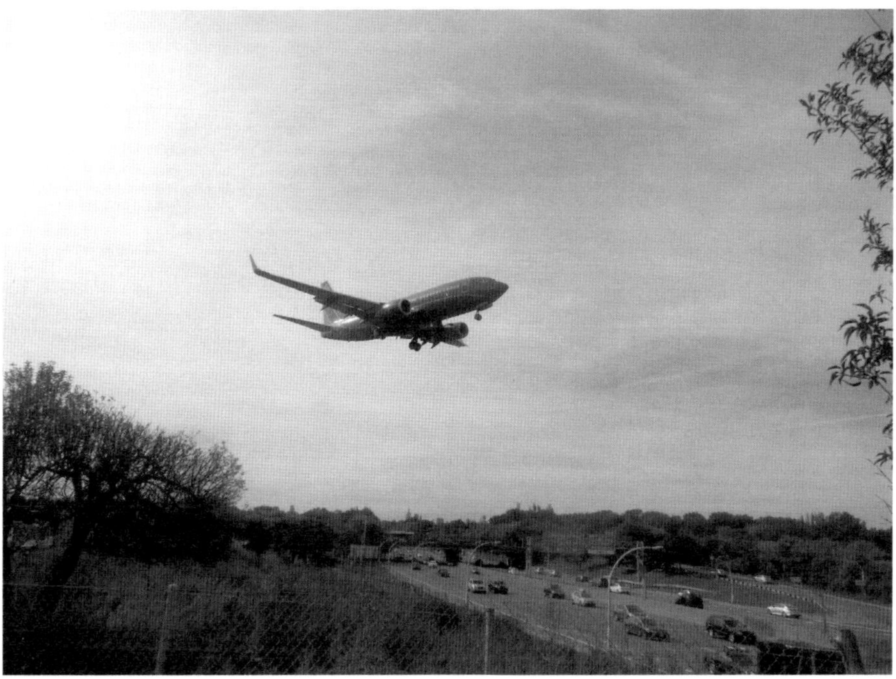

Planeview Park is a highly appropriate name for this tiny patch of greenery. The planes come in so close that you almost want to duck. *Author's collection.*

that is wedged between the Grand Central Parkway and Twenty-Third Avenue, bounded to the west by Eighty-Second Street and to the east by Eighty-Sixth Street.

A clue to the park's saving grace is in its truth-in-advertising name: Planeview Park. The ramshackle, one-acre plot of land in East Elmhurst happens to lie directly in the flight path of planes landing on Runway 4 at LaGuardia, directly across the Grand Central from the park. A steady parade of jets approach from the south, their twinkling lights seen over the nearby Comfort Inn. The planes roar by less than one hundred feet overhead every couple of minutes, and parkgoers can then watch them touch down at the airport. The park attracts many plane watchers, armed with cameras and binoculars, who take joy in identifying and capturing pictures and video of the landing planes (as well as planes lifting off—the roar of their jet engines coming to life is quite jolting). If you were to camp out at the park for a full year, 300,000 planes will have flown overhead by the time you leave. If you visit, you'll also notice that the park abuts the 1,500-student Vaughn College of Aeronautics and Technology, which originated in New Jersey but moved to New York in 1940. Mayor LaGuardia, who laid the cornerstone for the Casey Jones School of Aeronautics (as it was then known), pushed for such a school to be located near the airport.

Planeview Park is one of several patches of green in a direct line to Runway 4 due to Federal Aviation Administration regulations that stipulate that airports must have a large, clear piece of land leading to runways. In 1958, the Port Authority of New York and New Jersey turned over this land to the City of New York for use as parks. Beginning a block southwest of Planeview Park is a diagonal string of nine parcels of greenery that have collectively been named LaGuardia Landing Lights Park. Appropriately, part of Landing Lights Park also happens to be situated on land that used to be part of Holmes Airport.

Chapter 4

The Saved and the Lost

History is often hidden in plain sight. People walk past historic sites every day without a clue as to what exactly they are seeing. Books like this one can offer a fun roadmap to some of the lesser known places and moments in history. The built environment is very fluid, however. In New York City, old is constantly being replaced with new. Even the buildings we now consider "old" likely replaced something even older, which may in turn have replaced something even more ancient. Unless a Queens building has New York City Landmark status, its owner can alter it or even demolish it. This book, and especially this chapter, recounts the hidden history of several important Queens sites—some of which survived the centuries, and some that didn't. Each one has its own story, and as I learned, what separates the lost from the saved is sometimes merely the whims of fate.

The Bloom House Wilts

As I began research on this book, one of the first places I visited was the endangered Bernardus Bloom farmhouse at 90-11 Fifty-Sixth Avenue in Elmhurst. Nestled on a residential street behind the Macy's shopping center and adjacent to the Newtown High School track, the handsome old Empire-style building sat quietly as the centuries passed and what was

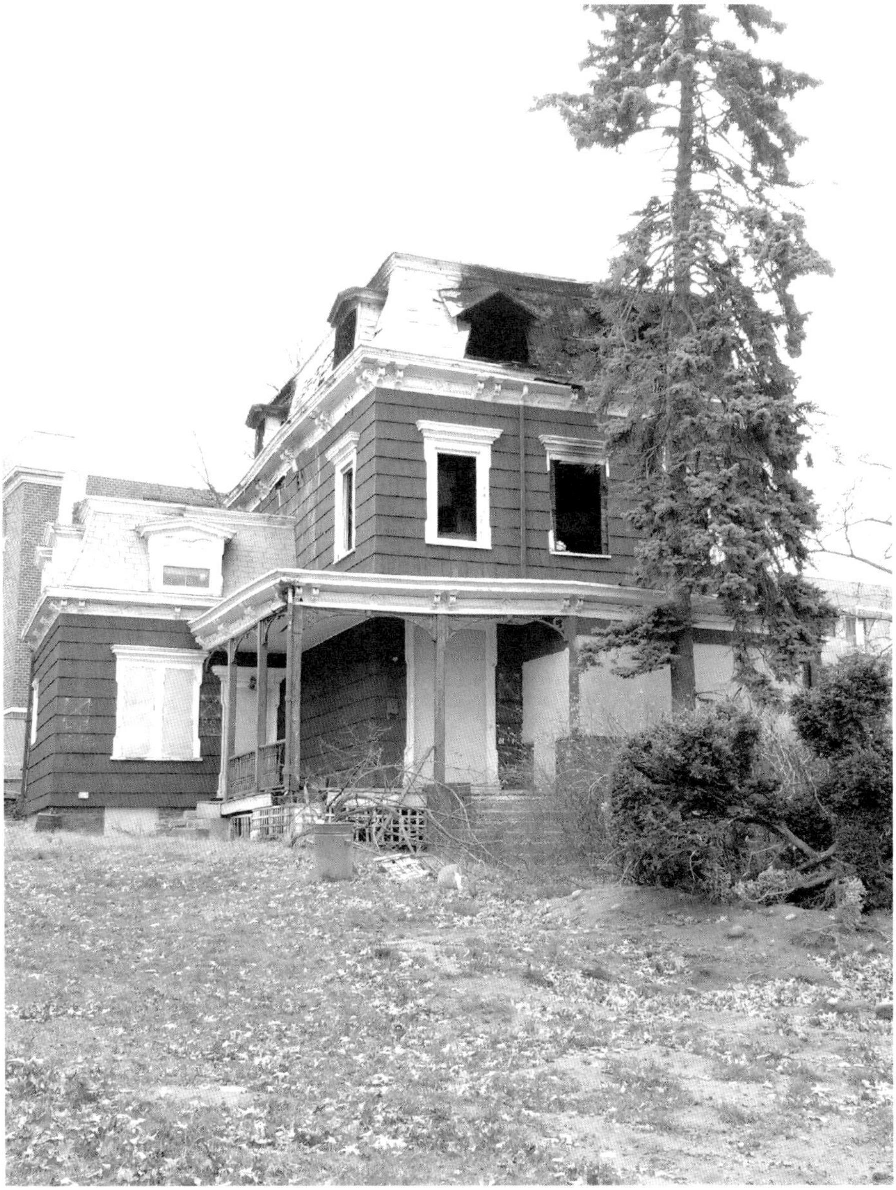

The Bernardus Bloom House in Elmhurst, seen in December 2015, was said to date to the early eighteenth century. It has since been demolished. *Author's collection.*

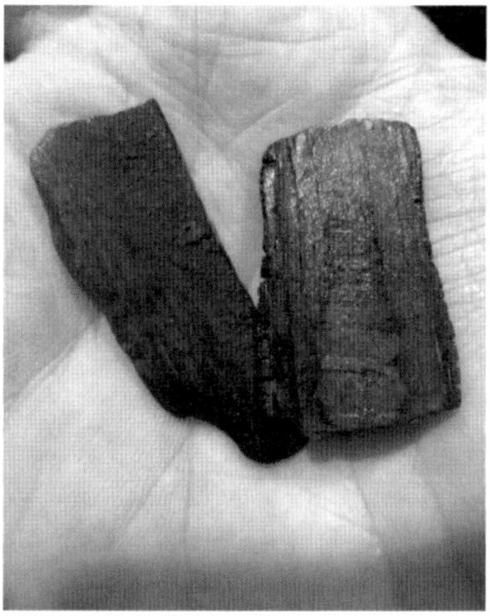

The only remains of the Bloom House are two charred pieces of wood the author found on the grounds while the building was still standing. *Author's collection.*

once the Horse Brook, directly across the street, was filled in, and as houses were built on its street and the streets around it. Though its most recent iteration was a mid-nineteenth-century appearance, at least part of the house dated to about 1700, when John Brinckerhoff bought forty acres of land that included the site of the house. The house was sold to Colonel Bernardus Bloom in 1742; after that, it was owned by the Suydam family for some time.

When I visited in late 2015, the house had just suffered a devastating, suspicious fire. I explored the property and took photographs of this severely injured green beauty. Fire had ripped through much of it, but it still stood, maimed but proud and distinct. I had read several articles about attempts to save the house, including a petition to the New York City Landmarks Commission.

When I went back to the site in 2017, the house was gone. Demolished without a trace left. Nothing more than an empty lot. Attention by the news media and valiant efforts of local citizens, the Newtown Civil Association, a congresswoman, a state senator and a councilwoman were all for naught. One of the oldest buildings in all of New York City was no more. I was glad to have captured the old house for posterity and to share it with my readers here as a reminder to seek out hidden history while you still can, before "here stands" becomes "here stood."

A Church Fit for a King

There are plenty of places in New York City where George Washington and other presidents have visited. But how many buildings in the city can claim a king of England as a visitor? Born in 1765, William, the Duke of Clarence, was the son of King George IV and grandson of George III (the one the colonists hated). William was sent to join the Royal Navy during the Revolutionary War at the tender age of thirteen. He served during the Battle of St. Vincent off the coast of Portugal in 1780 and later was stationed in Queens as a midshipman. The teenaged future monarch is said to have worshipped at the St. James Church on Broadway in Elmhurst, known at the time as "The Church of England in America, mission church at Newtowne."

An alleged wartime plot by George Washington to kidnap young William never came to pass, and the future king eventually returned to sea. When he left the navy in 1790, he had the rank of rear admiral. William, aka "Silly Billy," settled into a relatively quiet life, lived with an Irish actress for twenty years and then married an Englishwoman. He would become king in 1830, at the age of sixty-four, the oldest English monarch to assume the throne to that point. William had no children who survived to adulthood, so upon his death in 1837, his niece Victoria became Queen—for the next seventy-five years. William IV was not the only famous William worshipper—General William Howe, commander of the British forces during the Revolution who was headquartered in Elmhurst, also attended services at St. James.

Built in 1735 and officially chartered in 1761 by King George III, the St. James building became a parish hall when a new church was built across the

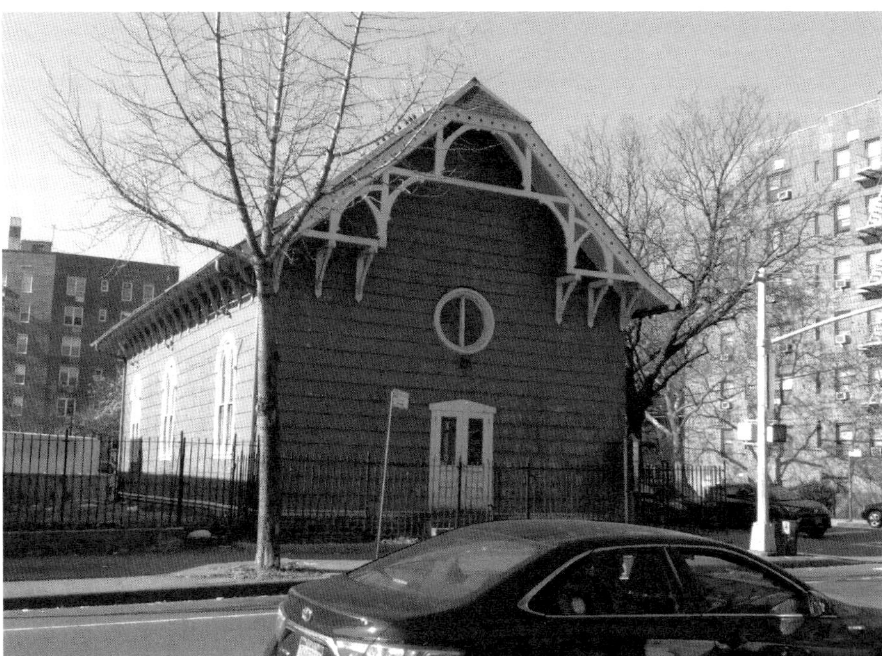

St. James Parish Hall, circa 1735, is now a New York City Landmark. *Author's collection.*

street in 1848. The 1848 church burned down in the 1970s, but the original 1735 building still stands at 86-02 Broadway, its existence in danger for years because it had no landmark status. I had nominated the building as a landmark back in the 1990s but never heard anything from the commission. In 2015, the New York City Landmarks Commission rejected calendaring its nomination, saying not enough of the original was left intact after restorations took place in recent years—giving it the appearance it had during the late nineteenth century after it was remodeled in 1883. The building, for many years a dull gray, was falling apart, and the restoration left it red and restored the Victorian latticework that adorned it following the 1883 renovation. In 2017, the building (New York City's second-oldest religious building after the Friends Meeting House in Flushing) did finally get a hearing date and was officially designated as a New York City Landmark.

A LANDMARK WITH FIVE LIVES

If someone asked you whether you've ever been to King Manor in Jamaica, you might think they were talking about a fancy new Chinese restaurant. But that's not the case (at least until some entrepreneur reads this book and gets an idea). King Manor is actually a Queens historical gem, hidden in plain sight in the heart of Jamaica. I used to see it as I passed by on the Long Island Rail Road years ago (before the view was obscured) and wondered what the handsome old building was. Sitting on a property that is now a city park, the stately colonial King Manor is definitely an enigma. Built in 1750 by Ames Smith, the house led a quiet existence for more than fifty years until it was purchased by U.S. Constitution signer Rufus King in 1805. (King had also been a member of the Continental Congress and the country's first ambassador to Great Britain.)

King Manor has quietly been a museum since 1900, sitting happily in a time capsule in a busy and modern part of Jamaica. Yet this peaceful historic building was saved from destruction or a compromised existence not once, but five times in the course of its history!

Though King found the house to be fairly plain, he made additions and improvements over the years to suit his liking. After Rufus King's death in 1827, the house went to his son, John Alsop King, who would become a U.S. representative and governor of New York. When John King died in 1867, the house went to his widow until her death, and then to his daughter

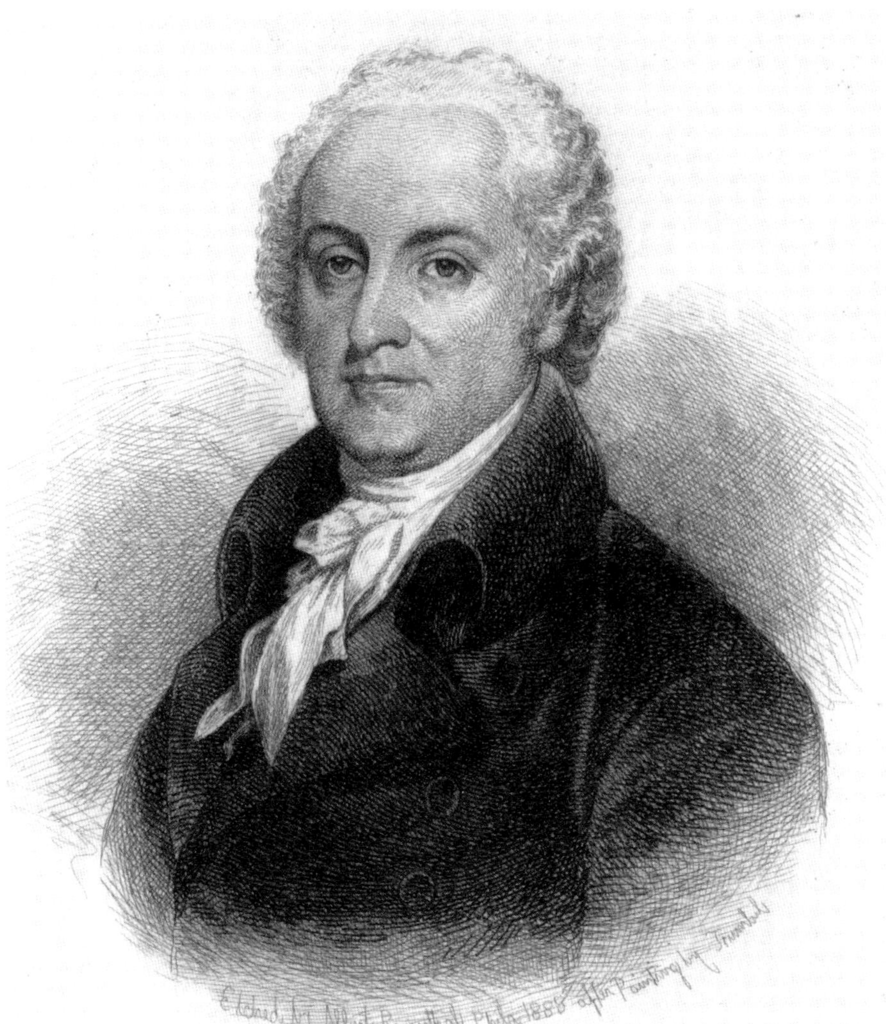

Founding Father Rufus King made his home in Jamaica. *Library of Congress.*

Cornelia, who was the owner until her death in November 1896. Within weeks of her death, there was a stirring of interest among the locals for the town of Jamaica to purchase the mansion for use as a museum and the grounds as a park.

An 1897 article in the *Newtown Register* read, "The dwelling, although unpretentious, is famous and interesting from its historical associations…as there is no one left to take [Cornelia King's] place and maintain it, it must be sold." An editorial in the same newspaper in April 1897 again took up the topic: "We do not see why it should not come into the possession of either the village of Jamaica or Queens County. The Old John Adams house in Quincy, Mass. has become the property of the public, and why should not the public have an equal interest in the historical home of the King family?" An editorial in the *Brooklyn Eagle* in June 1897 put it this way: "If the village of Jamaica should buy the Governor King homestead in Fulton street and set its grounds apart as a public park, their action would commend itself to the public-spirited citizens in that part, of the territory to be included within the Greater New York. We have too few public memorials in this neighborhood, and the preservation of the old King house as an example of early architecture and as a monument to the governor would be an instance of respect for the past which is too rare in these days when everything must give way for modern improvements."

The structure still stands today, thanks to five instances when it was saved from destruction or major alteration.

Save No. 1: The Village of Jamaica did purchase the house (and eleven acres of land) at some point in late 1897 for $50,000, saving it from likely demolition by another buyer. This was a very rare occurrence in those days. The preservation of historic buildings in Queens around the turn of the twentieth century was mostly unheard of, and though local newspapers did decry the potential loss of historic buildings, rarely was anything done to save them. In Elmhurst alone, for example, there were at least three important historic buildings that were lost between 1900 and 1940: the Moore homestead, which belonged to the family of Clement Clarke Moore and was demolished when the subway was being built in the early 1930s; the former Revolutionary War headquarters of British general William Howe, demolished in 1937; and the eighteenth-century Corner House, demolished in 1900. So, it was quite the coup for the citizens of Jamaica to have the common sense to save King Manor.

The village's victory would soon become the City of New York's victory; only a year later, ownership of King Manor was transferred to the New York City Parks Department when Queens became part of New York City in 1898. The newly created King Manor Association was put in charge of the building, while the parks department was in charge of the property behind the house. The house was not fully furnished when it was purchased, and the association had to go about furnishing it in period furniture. By 1900, the work on converting the residence into a museum was in full swing, and the association solicited historic donations. Many came in within weeks, including one of the earliest pianos used on Long Island, a mahogany desk and portraits of George and Martha Washington.

All was well with the museum until 1920, when the Jamaica library's lease was up on its location in a building called Colonial Hall, and the renewal price was too steep for the city to continue to pay. The president of the Board of Trustees of the Queensborough Library suggested that King Manor be converted to use as a library branch as well as administrative offices for the Borough of Queens. Though the parks commissioner and the mayor both approved the idea, it was met with stern local opposition. Converting King Manor to a library and administration building would force the gutting of the furnishings and the loss of the historic context, leaving just a shell of an old building that would be unrecognizable inside. The plan's opponents also argued that the building would not provide adequate space for a library.

According to an article in the *Long Island Daily Star* in 1920, "The suggestion that the King Mansion be used for a Library evoked protest not only from Jamaica and Long Island people but also from societies and individual citizens elsewhere representing patriotic movements and historical study." Save No. 2: Opposition was strong, and by 1921, the King Manor site was firmly rejected as a possibility. The library looked at several other possible sites instead. A year later, $235,000 in funds were approved for building an entirely new library. Once again, King Manor was saved.

Things were okay once again until 1930, when the idea of building a civic center or a general courthouse building for Queens in King Park behind the house was raised. At a meeting of the King Manor Association that year, one of the women attending said: "Our slogan must be 'hands off!'...If we must, we will educate newcomers to the understanding of reverence and loyalty." The president of the Men's Jamaica Village Society, who was one of those who originally helped Jamaica buy the property, said: "It is not wise to oppose the sentiment of Jamaica people in this matter of destroying King Manor and uprooting the park....These buildings and historical spots are dear to us and we will fight, as of old, to protect them."

This civic center idea still had not died several years later. When in May 1935 Mayor Fiorello LaGuardia was anxious to move ahead with selecting a location, the county clerk quickly sent a report to the mayor laying out the reasons why it would be okay to build a civic center in the park, saying the city owned the site free and clear and there was no reason not to use it (so eager was he to get the mayor's consideration that he even included a copy of the deed to the property with his letter). He also included his assertion that not many children use the park, and in the end proclaimed, "There is no better location than this in all of Queens County....It is not a question of taking a park away from Jamaica, but rather putting a beautiful public building in the center of the park." A prominent local attorney also sent a letter to the mayor, telling LaGuardia that he found an "overwhelming" sentiment among local residents he had questioned regarding using King Park for a civic center. Save No. 3: Two days later, Mayor LaGuardia finally ruled out the use of the King site for a civic center, not because he was afraid it would encroach on the historic character of the area, but because he did not want to cut down on Jamaica's already limited park acreage.

Save No. 4: Another thirty years passed before the next scare occurred. A serious fire at King Manor in March 1964 was put out just in time. While the building was saved from being destroyed, the fire did a lot of structural damage, gutting two of the mansion's rooms, with smoke and water damage elsewhere in the mansion. Thousands of dollars' worth of antiques were destroyed. Repairs were first estimated to cost $59,000, $39,000 of which

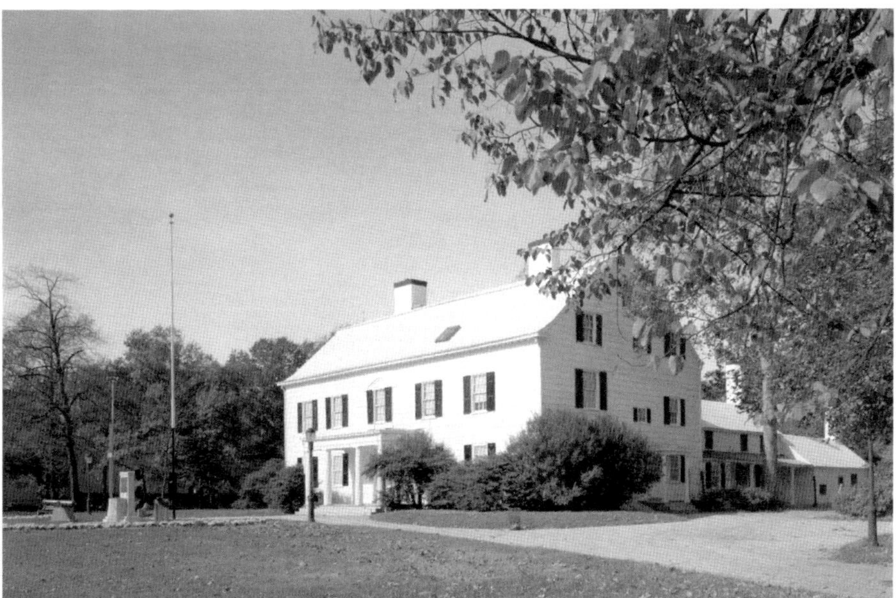

The historic King Manor in Jamaica has survived several close calls that threatened to alter or destroy it over the years. *Library of Congress.*

was to be paid for by the city (for structural repairs to the exterior and grounds) and $20,000 for the interior, to be paid for privately through donations. A call went out for monetary assistance, and funds came in from many different sources, including $50 from the Queens borough president and his staff and $10 raised by a ten-year-old boy from Fresh Meadows who collected nickels and dimes from friends and neighbors. Students from PS 58 in Queens raised $100 after visiting the house and viewing the damage. Though the original goal for the interior was $20,000, one historic house expert put the price at closer to $50,000 after touring the damaged home. By the end of 1965, more money was still needed to complete the restoration. The building was closed for two years while repairs were made; King Manor finally reopened in 1966.

Save No. 5: Another fire happened in 1973 when teenagers were spotted setting fire to the front porch of King Manor. Thanks to an alert woman on a bench nearby, a park laborer with a fire extinguisher and a conveniently passing fire truck, the fire was put out in time and the building saved from destruction.

King Manor was designated a New York City Landmark in 1966 and the interior a landmark in 1976. It still stands strong and proud and is open to the public for tours year-round.

As a footnote to this story—and filed under the category of "lost"—across the street from King Manor stood an eighteenth-century tavern called Pettit's Hotel. In 1790, it was known as the Queen's Head Inn and was run by William Warne. On his way east for a tour of Long Island in 1790, President George Washington slept there, calling it a "pretty good and decent house." The building was demolished around 1907.

IT'S HIP TO BE SQUARE

It is doubtful that Huey Lewis was referring to this building in his song, but he could have been, because the Douglaston Club building has to be one of the coolest squares in the city. Built way back in 1819 by Wynant Van Zandt, one of the oldest buildings in Queens is a cube. It was a fairly large home for its time, probably because Van Zandt and his wife had fifteen children! After Van Zandt died in 1831, George Douglas bought the 120 acres for $25,000 in 1835. George's son William Douglas, a sportsman who raced a yacht in the America's Cup, was the next owner. The manor house originally stood on 175 acres of property, which was sold off in 1906 and

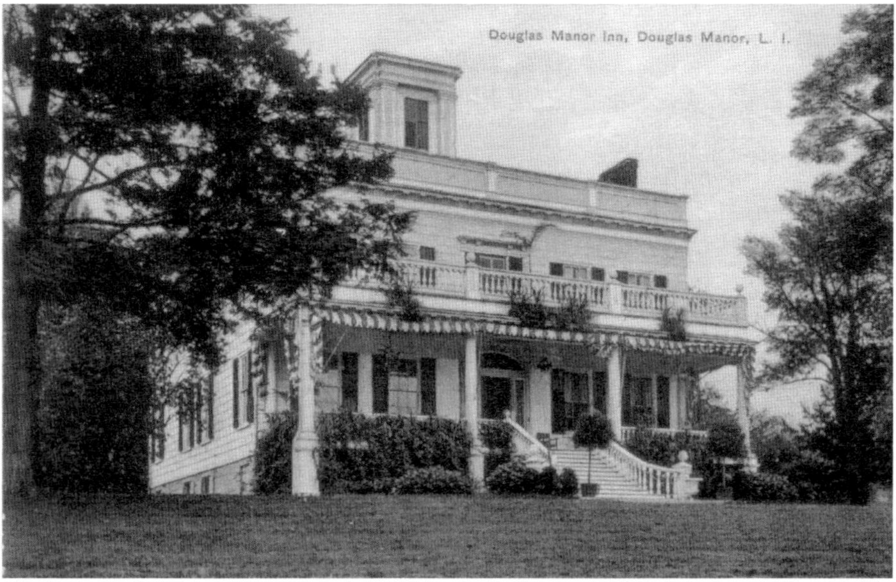

Douglas Manor, circa 1905. *Author's collection.*

developed. The homes that now stand on the former Van Zandt property are all part of the Douglas Manor community, which is a New York City historic district. The third story of the Douglaston Club building was added later, when the building became a clubhouse. The Douglaston Club building is a rarity, as it was the genesis of an entire Queens community.

THE LEGEND OF BODINE CASTLE

The Queens of old was filled with a wide variety of residences, ranging from small cottages to farmhouses to manor houses and mansions. Most of these are long gone now, and many passed away undocumented and unremembered. A few, though, lasted long enough to have been photographed and documented, including a very unique structure at 375 Vernon Avenue (later 43-16 Vernon Avenue) near the banks of the East River in Long Island City. The eighteen-room Bodine Castle, as this Gothic Revival stone building was known, looked eerily elegant.

As I started to research, I began to see some variations in the history of the mansion. One book said that Bodine Castle was built in 1853 by a merchant named John Bodine. Another said it was built in 1851. Small discrepancies are to be expected. I continued to research and encountered another recent source that said the building dated to the eighteenth century and was built by a French nobleman who had secret tunnels and dungeons constructed in it.

Whoa! This was intriguing. Now I had some work to do. I had to uncover the true story of Bodine Castle. Uncovering hidden history means going deeper than common knowledge, debunking old myths and uncovering new ones. It means not accepting only what the most recently published books say. I rarely rely on recent books alone. Where did those authors get their information? In my many years of research, I have found that much history is just borrowed and transferred from one recent source to another, because one author takes as fact what another author writes. But to get to the truth, inasmuch as it is possible, you have to dig deeper.

Before we go back in time, I should tell you that one thing that all sources agree on is that at some point after 1850, the building was owned by and named after a man named John Bodine, who was a member of the Board of Trustees of the Long Island City Savings Bank at its founding in 1876 and in the same year was defeated in his bid for the mayoralty of Long Island City. Bodine sold the place around 1885, after Standard Oil built a refinery nearby and Bodine began to see the transformation of his beautiful neighborhood into an industrial center. The building next was owned by a lumber company, which used it as the lumber yard office. In the 1920s, the building was modernized and updated to handle the task. Stacks of lumber sat on the grounds. Still later, Bodine Castle was owned by Consolidated Edison.

In 1965, Bodine Castle was nominated as a New York City Landmark. A hearing was held in 1966. Con Ed wanted to demolish the building as part of its expansion of services to build a $137 million power plant. In the hearing, a Con Ed representative claimed there was no point in saving the "ugly" building that was erected between 1853 and 1857 by a carpenter named Thomas Anders. A member of the Bodine family spoke and said the castle was built in 1815 by a French baron. More contradictory information! (Sadly, as it happened, the commission denied that it was a landmark, and it was soon after demolished.)

The best way to dig is the actual way you'd dig a hole, starting with the most recent layer and going deeper as you dig. I got back into the time machine and went from 1966 to a 1940 article in the *Brooklyn Eagle* titled "Legendary Ghosts Fill Halls of Bodine Castle." The article described three-inch-thick pine doors and explained that the Frenchman allegedly

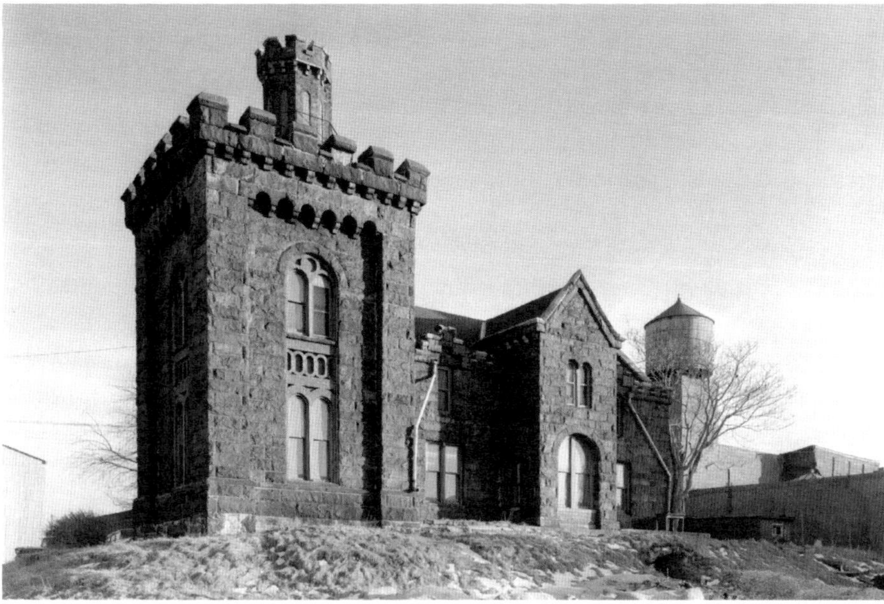

Bodine Castle. *Library of Congress.*

locked his daughter and her lover, a footman on the estate, in the cellar dungeon. When the locals found out, they were outraged. Neighbors armed with pitchforks forced their way inside the castle but found the dungeon cells empty. It mentioned another legend—a later owner's wife was locked in the tower because she fell in love with another man. I went back one year to 1939 and a Works Progress Administration guide to New York City. There I found a brief mention of Bodine Castle and a reference to the cellar dungeon once again.

I had to find more—there had to be more. I went a few years further back, to a 1936 article in the *Long Island Sunday Press* that said Bodine Castle was also supposedly visited by James Fenimore Cooper, who was inspired by the scenery as he wrote plots for some of his novels. If that were true, then the building would have to date to before 1851, when Cooper died. Well before then, if he was planning and plotting novels while there.

In this article's version of events, the nobleman caught his daughter in a love affair with a worker on the estate and chained her in one iron-doored cellar dungeon and her lover in a second cellar dungeon. In this version of the story, the local authorities found out and forced him to set the captives free, after which he sold his estate, disgusted that he could not do as he pleased. An article in the *Long Island Daily Press*, also from 1936, clarifies that papa wanted to hide his daughter away until she could return to France and marry one of her own rank. In this version, her lover was a gardener's assistant. The article also mentions a "ghostly sobbing" that could be heard at night, supposedly the girl crying for her lover.

This was getting complicated. I sent my time machine to 1926 and found a dramatic syndicated article in the *Greenpoint Weekly Star* and other local papers referring to the French nobleman's reasons for coming to America: "after the maddening hysteria of the revolution, he found a place where he could drive away the nightmares of blood and headless men" and that he had further worries, his "willful, high-spirited daughter." He purchased three hundred or four hundred acres of land and built a castle that reminded him of home. According to this version of the story, the Frenchman had a tunnel built leading from the castle that led to the waterfront, from whence he could row his daughter to Blackwell's Island when authorities came looking for her.

"Oftentimes the high-handed methods used by the original owner of the castle to deal with his fiery daughter brought down upon his head the ire of the authorities," the article said. "Several visits were paid by irate Long Island folk in company with local representatives of the law, but each time they appeared at the castle the daughter was not in evidence." It is unclear why it was better for the daughter not to be there at all when the authorities came, as opposed to sitting calmly on a loveseat in the parlor with a deck of cards pretending everything was fine. The possessive Frenchman was also said to have used the tower to keep watch against invaders to his domain.

So far, I had some pretty interesting details, but it still seemed that I was missing more precise information. Nobody recorded the name of this Frenchman? I found that hard to believe, so back into the time machine I went, this time to 1894 and a story in the *New York Times*—pay dirt! By this time, the place was already described as crumbling to pieces, leading me to believe that it could not possibly have dated only to the 1850s, just forty years before. According to this story, Mademoiselle Montcalm de St. Varian, widow of Marquis Charles Edward B. Montcalm, who had been secretary to former president Thiers of France, "some years ago" demanded that the castle be searched. I paused right there to swing on by Google, which revealed that the article was referring to Adolphe Thiers, who was an ex-president from 1873 until his death in 1877. So, her husband must have died sometime between the 1870s and 1880s for this to have taken place "some years ago." This story had nothing to do with the crazy

Frenchman referenced in later articles, but a more recent Frenchman. It seems that Bodine Castle had been used as the meeting place for members of a secret French society called the Cosmopolitan Republican (of which her dead husband was a member); according to Mademoiselle Montcalm de St. Varian, members of the society hid jewelry and other valuables that had belonged to her husband (valued at three million francs) in Bodine Castle after a dispute over the disposition of his estate. The Long Island City police actually performed the search based on a warrant issued by a local justice of the peace, assisted by some workmen, and every inch of the place was searched, but nothing was found. Mademoiselle de St. Varian figured that the members of the society had been spying on her and beat her to the treasures and removed them.

I read on, hoping for more, but the article ended without so much as a mention of the crazy Frenchman and his dungeon-bound daughter! It was also strange that none of the later articles made any mention of this secret treasure allegation.

Based on everything I read, I determined that, first, the building definitely dated to before the 1850s; second, while it's not clear that there ever was a secret treasure, it's likely that the place really was searched, probably after Bodine moved out; third, the crazy Frenchman stories likely have some truth to them—why would a French secret society meet in a random building except that it had a past association with a Frenchman?; and fourth, doing such extensive research has the potential to make my head spin, but it's rewarding, so I don't mind.

A WRECKED CHURCH FINDS NEW LIFE

I've always enjoyed riding the LIRR to Manhattan, because the train goes through cool Queens neighborhoods such as Jamaica, Kew Gardens, Forest Hills, Elmhurst and Woodside. If you pay attention, there's plenty of history to see out the train windows. One thing that always caught my eye was the ruins of an old church just east of Jamaica Station. Whenever I saw the handsome but crumbling old church, I wondered about it. The thing was such a wreck, like some kind of ancient ruin. And then, it wasn't. But, I get ahead of myself. Let's start at the beginning.

There were very few Catholics in New York State in the early years of the nineteenth century. Back in the 1830s, Jamaica, like much of

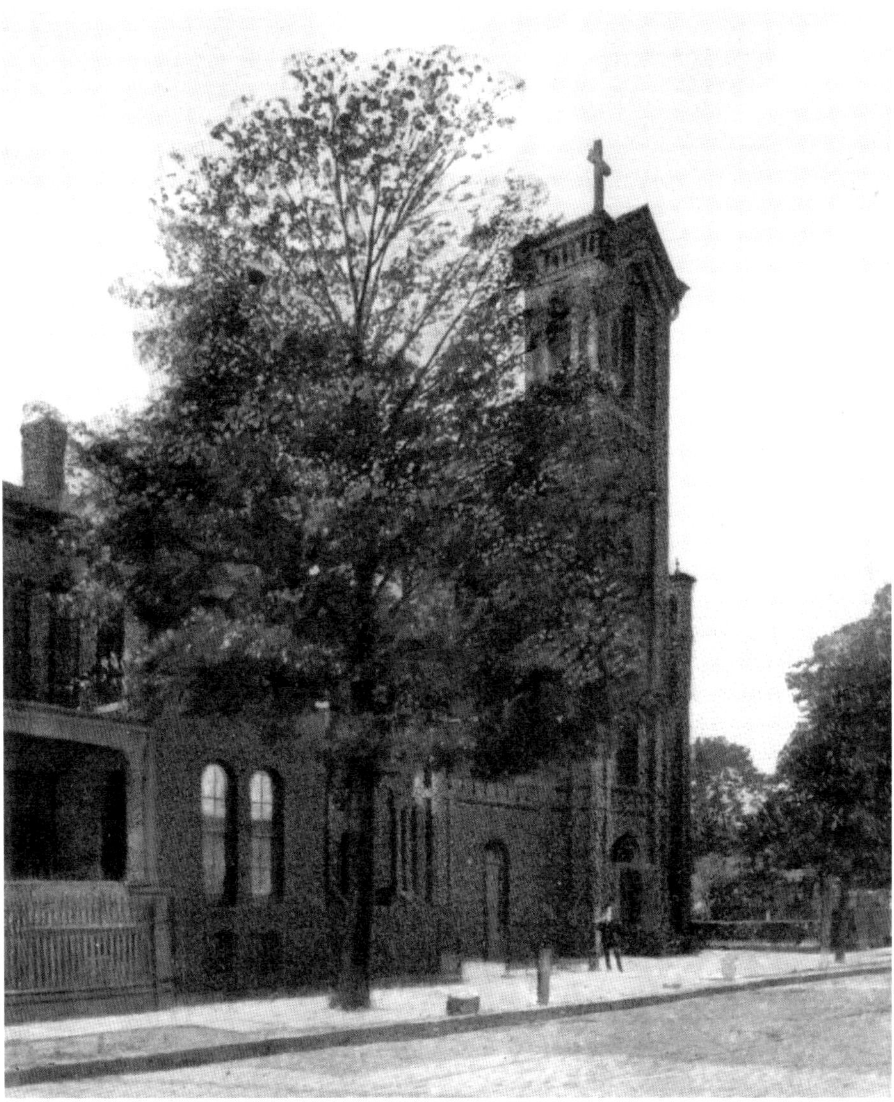

St. Monica's Church, circa 1905. *Author's collection.*

the New York City area, saw an influx of Catholics. The first mass in the area was held in a private home in 1838. Such an increase in the Catholic population warranted the construction of a new church in 1840. The wood-frame St. Monica's was built just south of the Long Island Railroad tracks at what was then Washington Street (now 160th Street). It didn't take long for the parish to outgrow this first building. In

1856, a local mason named Anders Peterson built a new church on the site. This $25,000 red brick building was designed in the Romanesque Revival style.

For decades, the church thrived, as did Jamaica as a shopping and residential area. Future New York governor Mario Cuomo was an altar boy at St. Monica's in the 1940s. By the 1960s, things were looking bleak for the area. Buildings around St. Monica's were condemned to make room for York College as part of the York College Urban Renewal Site. Though St. Monica's was not threatened, the diocese closed the church. The last service was held in June 1973. The city acquired the building, which was vandalized and in disrepair in the 1970s; by the time the state took over the CUNY system in 1978, it was in sad shape. The doors and windows had been boarded up, and the interior was falling apart. Nonetheless, St. Monica's was designated as a New York City Landmark in 1979. What was so important about the church? According to the designation report: "Saint Monica's is one of the only and earliest surviving examples of Early Romanesque Revival architecture in New York, and one of the only Roman Catholic Churches in the city executed in this style."

While a landmark designation can save a building from being intentionally destroyed, it can't prevent a building from crumbling from neglect. State money to fix the building never came through. Most owners of landmark buildings are required to keep them in good repair, but as the state owned it, it was exempt from city laws. Things continued to get worse, and just as the state was ready to spend $700,000 on a study to repair the church, it collapsed during a snowstorm in 1998. Now it was no longer crumbling—it was crumbled.

In 2002, York College was ready to act on a plan to reuse what was left of the old church. It was too late to salvage most of the building, but it was possible to save and reuse the beautiful façade and bell tower. This reuse had to follow strict guidelines, because what was left of the building was still a landmark. The newly reconstructed $7 million building opened in 2009 as the 9,700-square-foot York College Child and Family Center, with room for one hundred children of college students, housed in eight classrooms, with a parent/staff resource room, a food preparation area and offices.

A Tale of Two Town Halls

Before Queens became part of New York City in 1898, the individual towns in Queens County had their own local government, and thus their own town halls. If you have ever driven through Flushing, you may be familiar with the Flushing Town Hall, which is one of Queens' best-known and most architecturally unique structures. Built in 1862, this beloved building became a New York City Landmark in 1968, thus ensuring its continued existence. It is home to the Flushing Council on Culture and the Arts and hosts concerts and other cultural events.

The Victorian-style Jamaica Town Hall, built in 1869 at the corner of Jamaica Avenue and Parsons Boulevard, was not so lucky. The building had a wide array of tenants over the years, including the Jamaica Opera Company, which occupied the third floor in the late nineteenth century. The company performed light opera, plays and minstrel shows. Stars such as Lillian Russell, John Drew and Tom Thumb performed there. In the years that followed, the building's tenants included the Jamaica Traffic Court and Municipal Court, seven veterans' societies, two city marshals, Jamaica's police department and an art society. Foreclosure auctions were held on the steps, and various groups (including the Boy Scouts) used the building to hold meetings. In 1935, a crowd of 1,200 Republicans filled the entire town hall for a rally where President Roosevelt and his New Deal were mocked.

Despite all the use the building got, its time was soon to be up. By 1939, the city decided the building had to come down. The main reason was the widening of Parsons Boulevard between Jamaica Avenue and Hillside Avenue. A 1939 article in the *Long Island Daily Press* said the site was "long considered one of the most valuable pieces of business property in Jamaica." A "For Sale" sign was put on the building; after no takers materialized, it was sold at public auction in December 1940 by the city. The twenty-year lease stipulated that a new building costing at least $50,000 must be erected within seven months. The first buyer, who had offered $393,000 for the twenty-year lease on the property and planned a department store for the site, forfeited his $4,500 deposit when he never followed up with the rest of the first year's rent of $17,650, which was to be paid within ten days. A second auction attempt in February 1941 had six potential bidders in the room, but nobody made an offer. The city vowed to raze the building anyway, even if nobody wound up taking the lease. Other lease restrictions

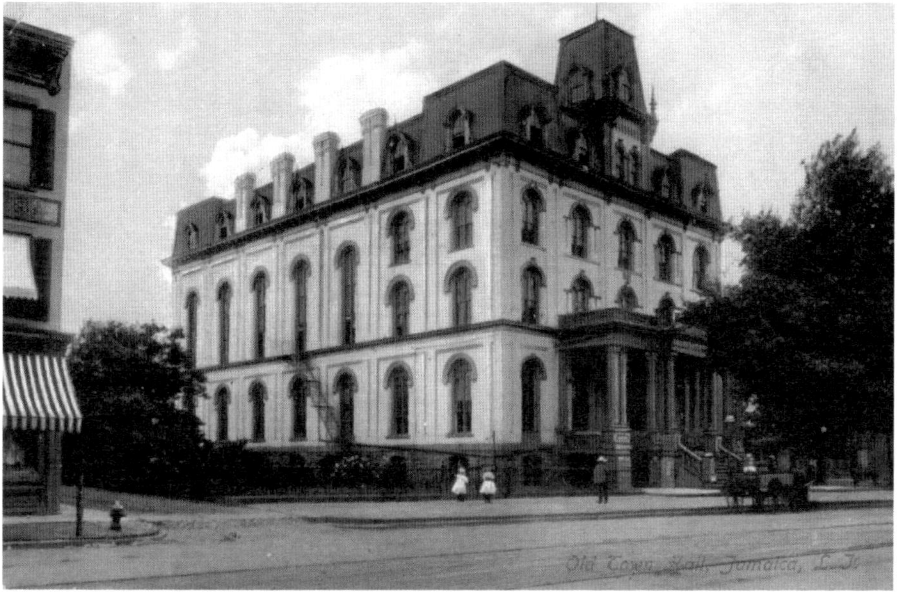

The Jamaica Town Hall and Flushing Town Hall were built in the same era, but the former was demolished, while the latter survives. *Author's collection.*

were removed for the third attempt at selling; now all that was required was that the buyer demolish the town hall and cart the materials away. The third time was not the charm, either. The city gave up and put out bids for demolition, with plans to lease the front part of the site afterward and build a public health center on the back part. By mid-June 1941, demolition had begun. Locals were excited when workers reached the cornerstone (which, oddly, was not at the base of the building but above the second-floor level). What historic keepsakes would be found inside? None. The cornerstone was empty. It took forty men two months to demolish the building. The former site of the building is now occupied by a McDonald's.

THE TENEMENT MASTERPIECES

One of the most aesthetically impressive historic districts in Queens started out as basically a bunch of tenement buildings. Back in the late nineteenth and early twentieth centuries, German immigrants were seeking a new place to call home other than overcrowded Lower Manhattan, Yorkville or

Brooklyn. A German immigrant named Gustave X. Mathews (1871–1958; born Matheis) began buying up farmland in Queens on the Brooklyn/Queens border just after 1900 and formed a building company with his brothers. He hired fellow German Louis Allmendinger as his architect. Allmendinger's designs were striking—aesthetically pleasing brick row houses (the buildings had to be stone because of new building codes) that featured the use of contrasting light and dark brick colors and stone ornamentation in Romanesque and Renaissance Revival styling.

Between 1908 and 1914, the Mathews Company built more than three hundred row houses in Ridgewood. The attractive buff- and amber-colored façades were not the only positives about these buildings. These "new law" tenements were mandated by New York City to have better ventilation and living quarters, and they accomplished this while creating a pleasant layout and living quarters for middle-income families. The buildings had a standard six apartments each, two per floor. Mathews produced the houses for $8,000 each and sold them for a $3,000 profit. Building en masse saved money and resulted in cheaper sale prices. So industrious was this company that in 1911, it received 25 percent of the tenement house permits issued in the borough of Queens.

In 1915, the Tenement House Department of New York City selected the "Mathews Model Flats" as the "most up-to-date method of housing for the masses at a minimum of cost" and exhibited them at the 1915 Panama-Pacific Exhibition in San Francisco. After the land in Ridgewood was developed, Mathews also built similar houses in Astoria, Long Island City and Woodside.

The last commission of the Mathews Company is a bit of hidden history, one that I walked past every day on my way home from junior high school, along Grand Avenue in Elmhurst. The distinctive, Art Deco light and dark tan attached brick buildings located on the west side of Grand Avenue just south of the bridge over the LIRR tracks were a sign to me that I was getting close to home on my walk from Maspeth. I did not realize it at the time, but I was walking past the last hurrah of Allmendinger and the Mathews Company. In the 1930s, the company designed 150 houses on Seventy-Ninth Street, Calamus Avenue, Grand Avenue, Elks Road and Ankener Avenue in Elmhurst. Styles and tastes had changed a lot since the earliest of the Mathews houses had been built in Ridgewood, and these last Mathews homes were rather modern and angular but still had that distinct use of two-toned bricks to create visual appeal.

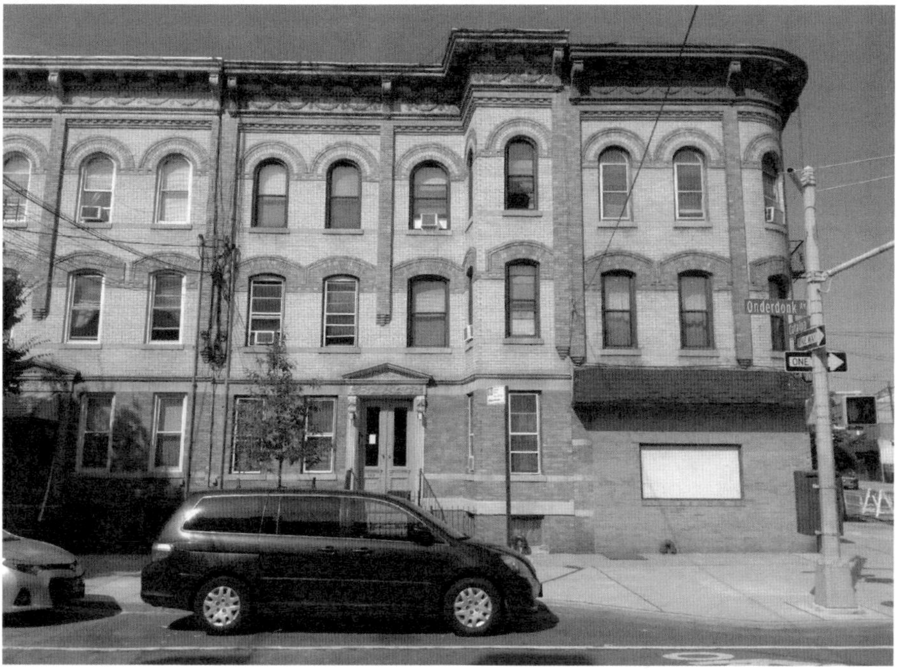

Tenement masterpieces in Ridgewood. *Author's collection.*

Many of the Ridgewood buildings were placed in the National Register of Historic Places in 1983, and two historic districts (Ridgewood North and Ridgewood South) were approved by the New York City Landmarks Commission in the years that followed.

Chapter 5

Famous Folks

Queens has been home to some pretty famous folks. As we've seen in chapter 3, none other than the commander in chief of British forces in America during the Revolutionary War was headquartered in Queens, and future king of England William IV was stationed there when he was but a young prince and midshipman. But wait, there's more! In fact, there's much more. It would take an entire book to cover all the illustrious folks who've made Queens their temporary or permanent home over the years, but all I've got is a chapter to spare, so I've picked a select variety of famous Queens-related folks. Step into the time machine with me as we look at some of the more notable and interesting people who've been associated with Queens, from governor/inventor and Maspeth resident DeWitt Clinton to the alleged logs of our most famous log-cabin dweller, Abraham Lincoln.

Clinton's Summer Hideaway

For centuries, Queens was a bucolic countryside. Even the "towns" like Flushing, Newtown and Jamaica were basically tiny villages surrounded by farms. Back in the day, wealthy Manhattan residents built their country homes at choice locations in Queens, which they would reach by ferry across the East River and then by horse and carriage. It was fascinating to know, as I walked through one of the most industrial parts of Queens in the southern reaches of Maspeth, that this was once one of those prime "country" home spots.

A grand two-story, four-chimneyed house was built in 1724 on a scenic piece of land near the Maspeth town dock by a judge named Henry Sacket, who died in the 1750s. It was then bought by Walter Franklin, an importing merchant who also had a house on Cherry Street and Franklin Square in Manhattan. (It would become the presidential residence of George Washington in 1789.) During Franklin's ownership, the Maspeth house was the Revolutionary War headquarters of British general Joseph Warren. Warren directed the departure of the troops that left Newtown Creek from the nearby dock on September 15, 1776, heading for the invasion of Manhattan.

Franklin died in 1780, while the war was still raging, and the house went to Franklin's sister and her husband, Colonel Isaac Corsa, a New York City merchant and veteran of the French and Indian War. But before occupying the house, Corsa had run into trouble in August 1776, when General George Washington ordered him arrested and thrown in jail for supporting the British. After Corsa, who was described as "small in stature and juvenile in appearance" died in 1807, the house passed to a politician named DeWitt Clinton, whose wife was Maria Franklin, Walter Franklin's daughter. Clinton was quite famous by this time. He was, at the time he moved in (for eight months of the year), mayor of New York City after having resigned his office as U.S. senator to take that job. Then in 1811, he became lieutenant governor of New York. In 1812, he ran for president but lost to James Madison.

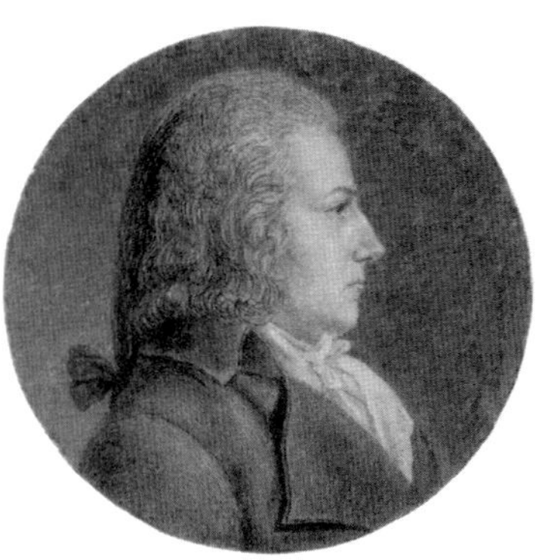

Governor DeWitt Clinton had a summer home in Maspeth. *Library of Congress.*

Clinton had visitors brought from the city to his house by his own private barge up the East River and then along Newtown Creek and a stream called English Kills. While living in this house in 1815, Clinton developed the plans for the Erie Canal underneath the big old buttonwood tree on the property, as the story goes. It is not unreasonable to think that Clinton was inspired by the waterways he took to get to his home from the city, in creating the plans for the Erie Canal. The canal plans helped Clinton get elected governor, during which time

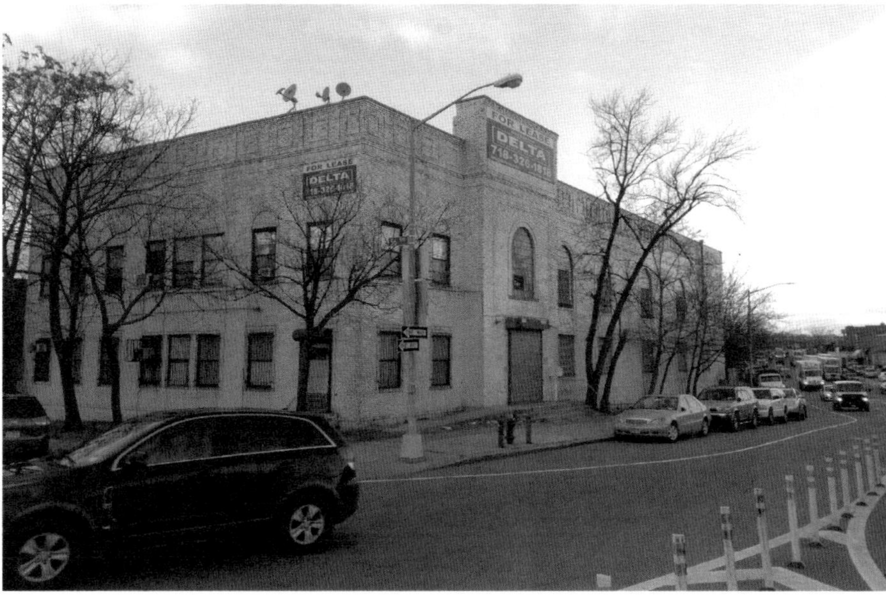

Clinton Hall in Maspeth briefly coexisted with Governor DeWitt Clinton's summer home. *Author's collection.*

he implemented his plans. But the Erie was not the only canal he wanted to accomplish; he also pushed the idea of a canal from Flushing Bay to the Wallabout in Brooklyn that cut north–south and could avoid navigating the treacherous Hell Gate in Upper Manhattan.

After Clinton's 1828 death, the property was eventually sold to his son-in-law, Judge David Jones, in 1842. The memory of the area's famous resident was still fresh. In an 1845 book on Long Island, the first fact mentioned in Maspeth's entry was that Clinton used to live there. By 1850, the creek that Clinton had so loved was still lively with fish, but pollution took its toll soon after. After Jones died in 1848, his widow sold it to an E. Godfrey, and then a dairyman from Elmhurst named Philip Grussy bought it in 1870. He turned it into a beer garden and amusement hall called Grussy's Clinton Park. This was, sadly, the property's last gasp at glory. In the 1880s, one of DeWitt Clinton's sons visited the mansion to see the place where he was born but was denied entry until he revealed just who he was.

By the late 1890s, still in the Grussy family's ownership, the place was a tenement split into four apartments and used to house modest Polish families. In 1901, the house was described as "greatly dilapidated." In 1902, an article in the *Brooklyn Daily Star* reported, "Very little thought is given nowadays to the country home of DeWitt Clinton….[It] is being permitted practically to go into ruin." By then there were already smokestacks of big factories nearby. The area was changing fast. In 1919, again there was a cry to save the old place, but nothing was done. The beautiful gardens that surrounded the house were now gone.

Around this time, a large amusement hall opened near the Clinton house. Called Clinton Hall, it was built at Fifty-Sixth Road and Fifty-Eighth Street. The place underwent expansion, and a 1927 newspaper article proclaimed the opening of the rebuilt Clinton Hall. Said to be the largest dance hall on Long Island, it also had ballrooms and bowling alleys, basketball courts and a pool room. The chandelier in the ballroom weighed in at two tons and had two thousand lights.

Meanwhile, things were looking bleak for the old Clinton house. The building was vandalized and finally was destroyed by fire in 1933. As for Clinton Hall, the amusement days eventually ended, and the building was later used as a laboratory. When I visited while writing this book, the place was for rent—another legacy of DeWitt Clinton's time in Maspeth that could potentially be lost.

The creeks and fish are long gone now, and as I stood in front of Clinton Hall, it was hard to imagine the peaceful waterfront scenery that DeWitt Clinton had enjoyed in the 1810s.

When All Through *Which* House Not a Creature was Stirring?

The modern concept of Christmas was born in 1822, when Dr. Clement Clarke Moore, professor of Oriental and Greek literature at the General Theological Seminary in Manhattan, wrote a fun holiday poem that was meant strictly as momentary entertainment for the family gathered at his estate, Chelsea, at Twenty-Ninth Street in what is now known as Chelsea. He recited the poem "A Visit from St. Nicholas" for his niece, who lived in Troy. She jotted it down, and the next year, her father sent it to the *Troy Sentinel*, which published it anonymously. It took twenty-two years for Moore, who felt it too trivial to be affiliated with, to acknowledge that he was the author.

Though he himself was born in Manhattan, Moore's ancestors were early colonists in seventeenth-century Queens. In about 1662, his great-

great-grandfather Samuel Moore built a home in the recently settled village of Newtown (now Elmhurst) after receiving a grant of eighty acres of land. This Moore homestead stood for almost 270 years and by the 1920s was revered as one of the very oldest structures still standing in Queens and one of the most storied places in the city. But its existence was precarious by this time. As with most relics of the distant past, change was inevitable, especially as the twentieth century arrived. What was once a sleepy but important village was developed as a suburb of Manhattan. This process only sped up with the incorporation of Queens into New York City in 1898. As more people moved to Elmhurst, transportation improvements were necessary, one of which was the extension of the IND subway line into Queens.

By the late 1920s, plans were advancing for the subway, and unfortunately for the Moore homestead, it was sitting right atop the planned location for the subway tunnel. Its existence was doomed; it was announced that the Moore house was to be demolished so the city could excavate and build the tunnel.

With this announcement in 1929 came many newspaper articles and much public mourning of the loss of the historic place. Borough president Harvey wrote to the board of transportation, which was due to acquire the property, asking that the house be preserved because it was where Moore was inspired to write the poem. Meanwhile, Harvey himself received letters from various "experts" who weighed in on the Moore house's impending destruction. A member of the real estate firm that had represented the Moore family for one hundred years expressed doubt that Moore ever set foot in Elmhurst. The Girl Scouts of Queens County visited the doomed house determined to defend the honor of the legendary homestead and solve the mystery of whether Moore was inspired by his childhood there. The commissioner of the Queens Scouts said, "We will not let go unchallenged the statement that he did not receive his inspiration in Elmhurst." The Girl Scouts were given a tour by Major J. Moore Perry, one of the Moore descendants, who owned the house at the time.

That same year, a schoolboy wrote a letter to the editor of the *Daily Star* newspaper:

> *I recently read an article published in your paper concerning the Moore homestead. I was surprised and much grieved to learn that the railroad company was going to tear it down. Now, we have stood enough of letting people tear down historical homesteads, but when it comes to the Moore*

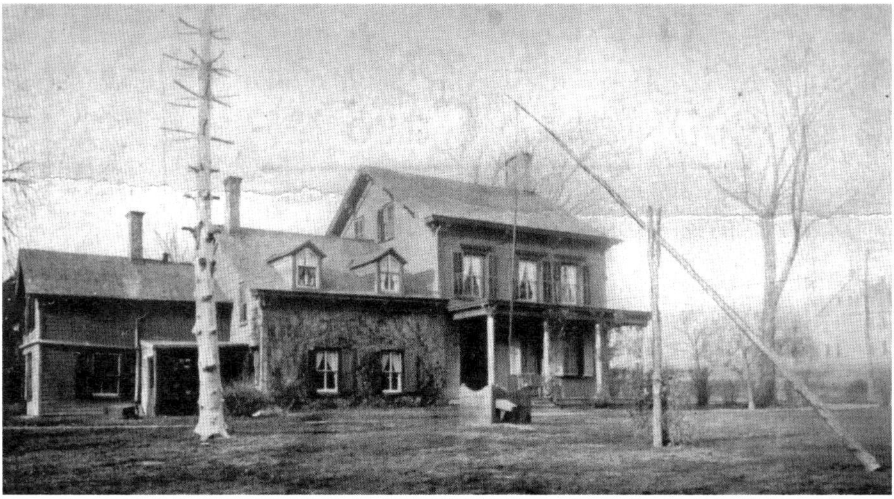

The Moore homestead, which stood in Elmhurst from about 1662 to 1932. *Author's collection.*

> *homestead, things are going a bit too far. I am sure it would not harm to let the subway go around the house instead of directly beneath it. Now, are we, the men of tomorrow, going to stand for this?*

That was the beginning of decades of misinformation being spread about the house and Moore's and his famous poem's connection to it and to Newtown. Some articles proclaimed that Moore was born in the house (he wasn't). Others said that he wrote the poem in Queens (he didn't). But the one thing most sources seemed to agree upon was that Moore drew inspiration for the poem from his childhood visits to the Moore homestead.

Despite public outcry to save the building, the Moore house was demolished in 1932. "Moore Homestead Sacrificed for 5-Cent Fare" one newspaper headline read. As of 1935, barns, sheds and a gardener's cottage were still standing on the property. A granite marker was in place by 1944 to denote the "birthplace of Santa Claus." In December 1944, the *Long Island Daily Press* printed the poem and said, "Dr. Moore's poem is a fusing of his childhood Christmas Eves in the old Moore Homestead." The controversy or uncertainty fifteen years earlier seemed to have been settled by popular demand. The future of what was left of the historic site was uncertain. Many locals wanted it to be turned into a park. A 1950 article in the *Long Island Star* had the headline "Santa's Birthplace to Be Sold." As of 1951, an old barn and a well still stood on the property. In 1953, the last tenants

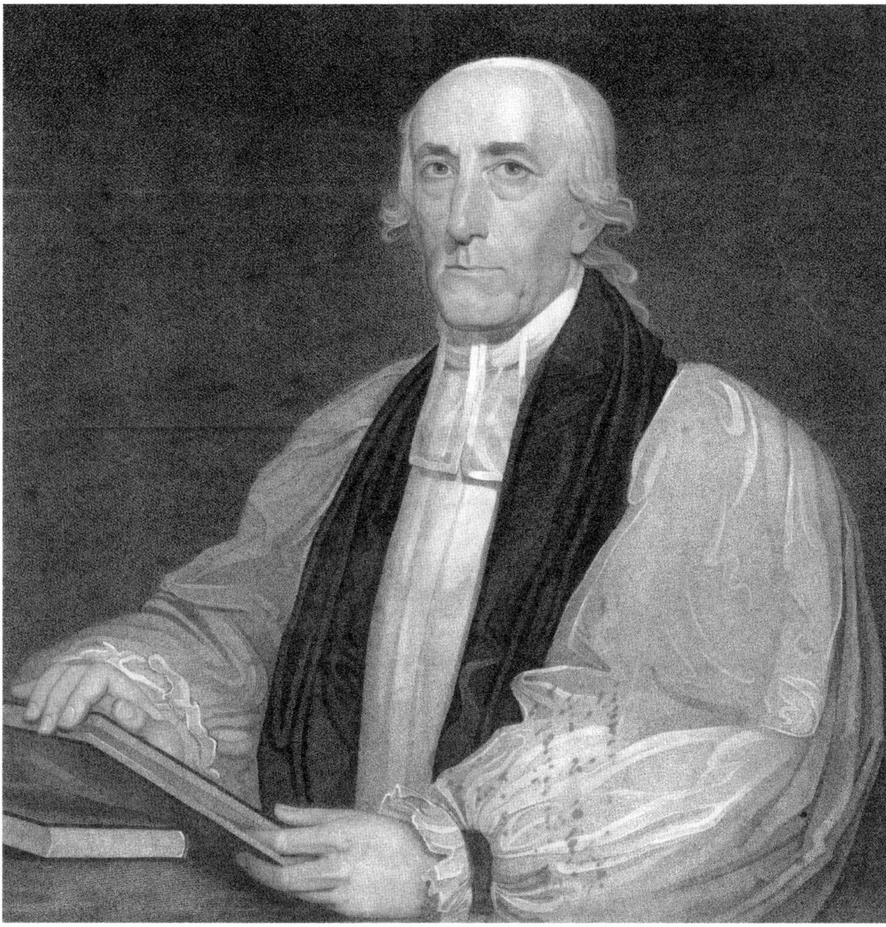

Bishop Benjamin Moore, father of Clement Clarke Moore, was born in Newtown (Elmhurst). *Library of Congress.*

on the property, the Ebbetts, moved out. They had lived in the old carriage house that still stood. Mrs. Ebbett was the daughter of the former longtime caretaker of the Moore estate.

The last of the old outbuildings were torn down and in 1954, efforts began to turn the property into Elmhurst Playground. As a young kid, I spent many a sunny day in this playground, which was just a block away from my childhood apartment building (which was part of the eighty-acre Moore estate). In 1987, the city renamed the park Moore Homestead Playground. On the New York City Parks Department website page for this park, it says, "Clement Clarke Moore Homestead." Having researched Elmhurst history for many years, I thought it was cool that toddler me romped around on the site where Clement Clarke Moore got his inspiration for "A Visit from St. Nicholas."

So cool! Except for one small detail. It's wrong.

It's all wrong.

Problem is, the Moore house that is celebrated as being "the" Moore house was not in fact "the" Moore house, rather "a" Moore house. It seems that there were several Moore houses built by the family over the years. In doing my research for this book, I found a series of newspaper articles written by a man named Arthur White in the 1920s and 1930s, in which he explained in great detail the true story of the various Moores and their various homes. I was intrigued and excited. Could almost one hundred years of common knowledge really be wrong? Who was this Arthur White, anyway, and could I trust him against the vast tide of knowledge that proclaimed otherwise? Turns out, White, who died in 1952 at the age of ninety-three, was known as "probably the best versed man on the history of old homes in Queens," as one article referred to him. He lived in or near Elmhurst for eighty years and was the son of the founder of the *Newtown Register* newspaper. Seems pretty trustworthy to me.

I uncovered some excellent information using White's articles as a starting point, but digging deeper, I found much more detail to back up what White wrote.

The original Moore house was not the one I wrote about above. The first Moore home in Queens was the one built by the English immigrant John Moore, who arrived in 1652 and was the second pastor of Newtown. That house, which was located in the heart of the village just off Broadway at St. James Avenue, served multiple functions as church, school, meeting hall and the minister's home until his death in 1657. This building has been gone for hundreds of years (though a part of it allegedly still existed, repurposed as part of a different house in another part of town, as late as about 1900). The Moore homestead that fell victim to subway excavation in 1932 was the second of the Moore houses to be built, by the son of John Moore. The third Moore house dates to when Samuel, the builder of the Forty-Fifth Avenue and Broadway homestead, moved out in 1684 (leaving the home to his brother Benjamin) and settled in Astoria in a house that stood until around the turn of the twentieth century. The fourth Moore house was built a little after 1700 and was located in Woodside, adjacent to where the Moore-Jackson Cemetery still stands. It lasted until the 1920s.

The fifth Moore house was built about 1734 at the northwest corner of the intersection of what is now Broadway and Woodside Avenue by a branch of the Moore family. This house was later known as the Witte House and was still standing as of 1903 (where Elmhurst Hospital stands now). It was actually the sixth Moore house that had the Clement Clarke Moore connection. In 1734, Benjamin Moore, owner of the old house at Forty-Fifth Avenue, gave his son Samuel (born 1711) a parcel of land west and north of the Moore Homestead (including an orchard). It was on this land, on the southern side of Woodside Avenue, near the intersection with Broadway, that Samuel Moore built a home. It was described in a 1921 article in the *Newtown Register* as a "low, shingle sided house, which with its ancient barn, far surpassing it in size and with its mill for pounding corn or samp, stood…under the shade of two or three great trees." This house was where Clement's father, Benjamin Moore, was born in 1748. Benjamin later moved to Manhattan, where Clement was born, but the Christmas holidays would have included time at his grandparents' house.

Grandpa Moore died in 1788, when Clement was nine years old, and Grandma Moore died in 1796, when Clement was seventeen. By this time, Samuel Moore had amassed an estate of about eighty acres, and it extended west all the way to Sixty-Ninth Avenue in Woodside. The house and estate then passed to Samuel Moore's son Jacob Moore. An Englishman named John Davis wrote of his time in Newtown circa 1800–01: "Farmer Jacob Moore, brother to Bishop Moore, of New York always entertained me with a hearty welcome. Everyone acknowledged his daughter [Hannah] was charming: A maiden never bold; Of spirit so still and quiet, that her motion Blush'd at ltself. Indeed, the manners of the whole family were worthy of the Golden Age."

In 1834, nine years after Jacob's death in 1825, the Moore house was sold, and the property was divided among several owners. It stood for much of the nineteenth century and was widely known as the house where Bishop Moore was born. By the late 1880s or so, the house where Clement Clarke Moore's father was born had been demolished and replaced with a new little house. It was, according to an 1898 *Newtown Register* article, guarded by "two or three chained creatures—whether wolves or dogs—[that] tend to discourage antiquarian researches in case any one should desire to make them."

The modest little house was in turn demolished soon after, and in its place was erected a large apartment building in the early 1920s. As soon as I uncovered all this hidden history, I was compelled to visit the site for myself to see firsthand where the old house had stood, to see where Moore was situated when he visited his grandparents as a child. This new information I had gathered also proved that my childhood apartment building at 80-20 Broadway, just a block east of the Moore home site, stands on the former Benjamin Moore estate, on the very grounds that likely inspired the famous Yuletide poem. As I walked along Woodside Avenue on a cold winter's day just after Christmas, I marveled at the huge transformation the site has undergone over the years. Where a carwash is today was likely where the Moores' horse-drawn carriages once approached.

The whole thing was fascinating for another reason. Clement Clarke Moore's father, Benjamin, was quite famous in his own right. Not only was he the second Episcopal bishop of the United States, he also happened to be the one who gave a mortally wounded Alexander Hamilton his last communion as Hamilton lay dying of a gunshot wound in the Manhattan home of a friend after the infamous duel with Aaron Burr in 1804.

So why was nobody in more recent years aware that this was the actual house where Clement Clarke Moore likely had his childhood Christmas inspiration? Probably because the house fell some years before Clement

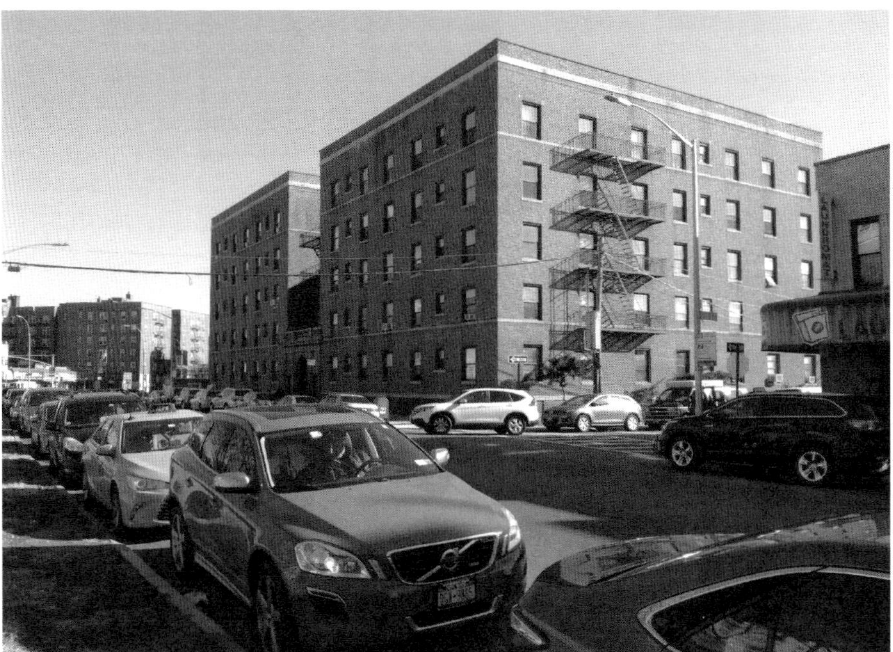

The site of Bishop Moore's home is occupied by a large apartment building. *Author's collection.*

Clarke Moore became the kind of icon that the twentieth century and the growing cult of Christmas in this country brought him.

With all this said, Moore's home in Chelsea was on a hill and offered a picturesque scene itself. Plus, it is likely that Moore visited the 1662 homestead at least a couple of times when he was a boy. It was the home of his uncle, after all, and the family's ancestral homestead.

Though we still have nothing in Clement Clarke Moore's own words to prove he was inspired by his time in Queens, we do have the words that a British Revolutionary War officer wrote to a friend: "The heightened joys that filled up every day even in the severity of winter months, in the sweet village of Newtown on Long Island, where we frequently had our quarters and cantonments. I hope I may be indulged this small tribute of grateful remembrance and affection for many agreeable families of that place; to the Moores, of that neighborhood, I am particularly indebted, a family ancient and respectable; to the charms of their company, to the hospitable attentions of their numerous connections, I owe many hours of festivity and innocent mirth." Reading this testimony, I am convinced. I can well imagine how Moore could have been inspired as a child in Newtown by the cozy comfort of his grandparents' home.

THE MAURICE HOUSE

Even the most industrial or commercial areas of Queens harbor hidden remnants of the past that are completely unassuming at first glance. These buildings have history that is just waiting to be discovered. I found one great example on Rust Street in Maspeth, which runs between Flushing Avenue and Maspeth Avenue and is pretty hardcore industrial. There are train tracks on the west side and plenty of industrial buildings on the east side. It's pretty much the last place you'd expect to find any traces of Maspeth's nineteenth-century history, but there at the corner of Fifty-Seventh Road stands an old house with stories to tell. At a quick glance, the house clearly has some age to it, but the surprise is just how old it actually is and who lived there.

The Maurice House was home to a lawyer named James Maurice (1814–81), who built it way back in 1841, making it one of the oldest surviving buildings in this part of Queens. James Maurice was a state assemblyman in 1850 and again in 1866 and served one term as a U.S.

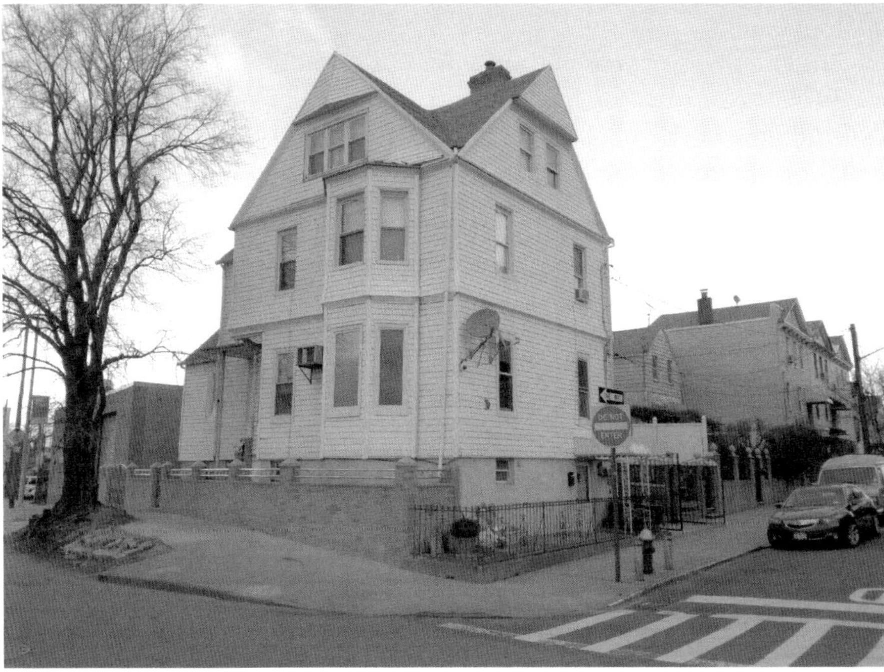

The James Maurice House is one of the oldest buildings in Queens. *Author's collection.*

congressman from 1853 to 1855 in the Thirty-Third Congress representing the First District (Hempstead, Jamaica and Newtown). Maurice Avenue is named after him.

The house was the scene of a locally important moment when the first meeting to discuss the formation of Mount Olivet Cemetery was held there in 1850. After his death, his library of nine thousand fine books of English literature was auctioned, including one hundred Shakespeare volumes and the first English translation of *Don Quixote* and an 1838 book on the Bayeux Tapestries. The Maurice property was seventy-two acres in size and for a long time remained undeveloped (known as Maurice's Woods and used by many for picnics and playing), until it began to be sold off in 1920 (1,100 lots) and houses were built. The house remained in the family until 1909, when Maurice's sister died, leaving no more heirs. Today, it stands clad in white siding, its original form still visible, the former home to one of Maspeth's most illustrious citizens.

LORD'S MANOR HOUSES

After Samuel Lord emigrated from England in 1824, he had hardly any money. He borrowed $1,000 and began a dry-goods store in Lower Manhattan. When his wife's cousin George Taylor joined the business, the name of the firm became Lord & Taylor, and a New York City retail legend was born. The store moved and expanded, and Lord became wealthy. Queens soon became a second home to Lord. Around 1850, he began to spend time in Newtown (Elmhurst). He even built a "country" version of his famous store at the corner of Grand Avenue and Broadway in 1860 and lived in a fine home across the street (which burned down in 1873). For several years, this was his only residence, and he would drive by carriage to Williamsburg, Brooklyn, every morning, whence he took the ferry to Manhattan and then returned every evening the same way. Before long, he owned one hundred acres in and around Newtown. Among his real estate projects was building four identical large homes on what he called Clermont Terrace, right in the heart of the village.

According to the *Newtown Register* newspaper: "He conceived the idea of making Newtown a sort of manor town, after English ideas. He built that expensive row of houses on Clermont Terrace to further carry out that pet scheme. But he was doomed to disappointment. Such a scheme was repugnant to the American idea." This was Lord's idea of the suburb, and it was far more lavish than what would eventually take hold throughout Queens and the rest of Long Island.

An 1859 advertisement in the *New York Herald* proclaimed that there was available on Clermont Terrace "within one minute's walk of the railroad depot a two-story house, with kitchen and attic, containing nine rooms, with garden sufficient to grow all the vegetables for a large family, and privilege of a beautiful playground containing two acres." An 1862 ad in the *New York Times* was for "Two of those Beautiful houses, situated on Clermont Terrace, Newtown, L.I.; each house contains thirteen rooms, has all the modern improvements, with large garden and shaded lawn in front of two acres, with circular carriage road, completely protected from the main road; only two minutes from railroad depot, and thirty-five minutes from New-York."

Evidence of the failure of Lord's plan mounted over the years as the land was divided. In 1885, at least two of the houses were altered to accommodate two families. The failure of his development to achieve his goals was one of the reasons he went back to England, where he died in 1889. As seen in the postcard shown here, the homes on Clermont Terrace circa 1906 still had

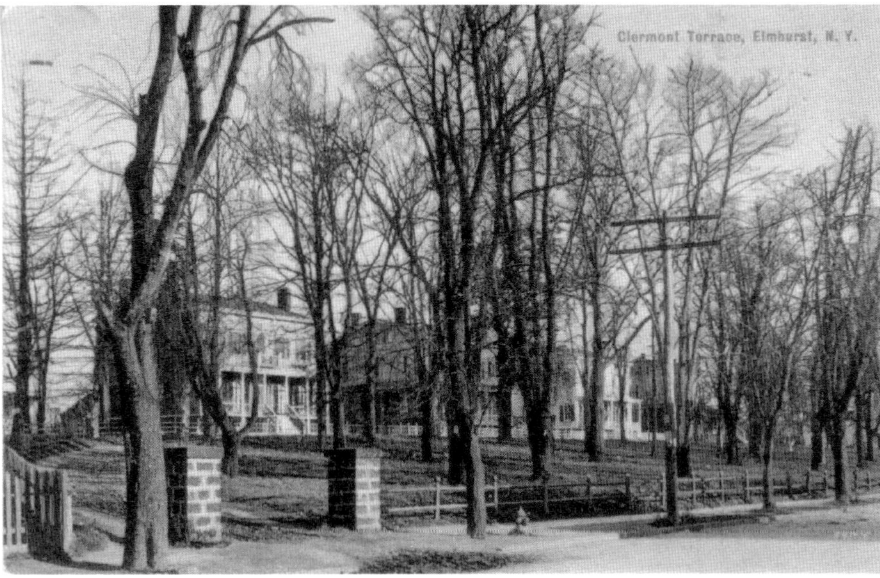

Above: Clermont Terrace was an experiment in middle-class housing created by Samuel Lord. *Author's collection.*

Opposite: The last remains of the groundbreaking Clermont Terrace development, as seen in 2017. *Author's collection.*

large front yards, but that was not to last much longer. In 1915, a Clermont Terrace "plot consisting of fifty-two lots right in the heart of Elmhurst, with frontage of 475 feet on Broadway" was offered for sale at $125,000.

Two of the mansions were demolished in the 1930s, at least one of them a victim of roadway construction; today's Dongan Street cuts directly through where one of the mansions stood. The last of these houses, which by the 1970s had been turned in to five apartments, somehow stood intact until 2006, when it was mostly demolished to make way for a multistory apartment building.

What used to be elegant Clermont Terrace, a semicircular road (or access driveway) to the four houses that started and ended on Broadway, is now just a sad, unpaved, hilly trash dump of an alley off of Dongan Street known as Claremont Terrace. (It ends just south of the railroad tracks and runs parallel to Broadway.) But Claremont Terrace holds a sliver of hidden history. When I wrote above that the last of the houses was "mostly" demolished, it's because as of this writing, at the end of 2017, the front steps to the northernmost and last of the Lord houses were still

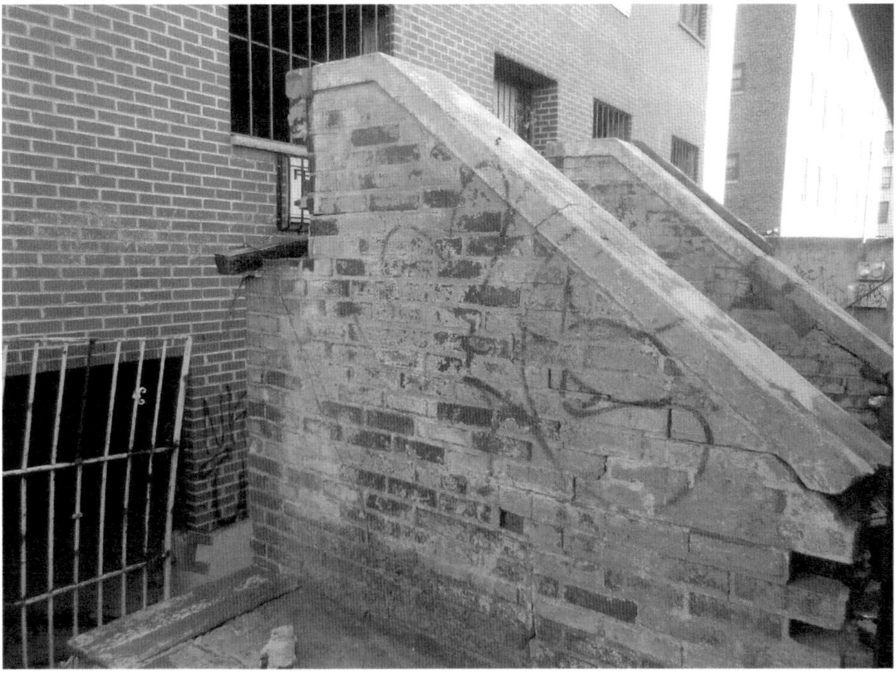

standing. It was a thrill to peek through a cutout in the wood construction fence and see (and touch!) the steps to a house that the founder of Lord & Taylor had built. It is only through a quirk of fate that this last remnant still survives. Because construction of the new apartment building was abandoned, the staircase also remains (but who knows for how long), a vestige of a pioneering experiment in suburban housing.

Lincoln's Logs

Everyone knows that Abraham Lincoln was born in a log cabin, but how many people know that the cabin that is on display at the Abraham Lincoln Birthplace National Historic Park spent several years in storage in a basement in northern Queens?

Born in Hodgenville, Kentucky, on February 12, 1809, Lincoln was not famous for several decades, so there was nothing special about his birthplace, and thus no reason to expect that the little cabin would survive long. And it didn't. The original one-story log home was torn down in 1838 (and supposedly used for firewood) to make way for a road.

By 1865, all that visitors to the birthplace found were some rocks denoting the site of the former chimney. In the 1890s, an ambitious New York restaurant operator named Alfred Dennett, in partnership with a Kentucky speculator named James Bigham, purchased the Lincoln birth site farm, determined to create a shrine that would attract lots of visitors (and earn lots of money). But the site alone was not enough—it was empty. What would attract visitors?

Dennett decided to re-erect the Lincoln cabin on the exact spot where it had stood. To do so, he purchased a different and bigger cabin, a mile north, from a man named Davenport. He had Bigham disassemble, move and reassemble the two-story cabin as a one-story cabin on the Lincoln birthplace site. In 1895, Bigham invented a story that said the Davenport cabin was actually the birthplace cabin that an admiring local physician had purchased and moved a mile north. In reality, the cabin likely dated to after 1840. When the cabin attracted few visitors, Bigham and Dennett decided to take their show on the road.

Bigham took the cabin apart and had it exhibited at the 1897 Nashville Centennial celebration, along with a cabin that was purported to be the birthplace of Jefferson Davis. In 1899, Dennett brought the logs to New York City with him. In 1901, they were shipped to Buffalo and reassembled for the exposition there. Somewhere along the way, there was confusion, and the Lincoln and Davis logs were mixed up. The Lincoln cabin logs were next stored at Coney Island before making their way to College Point, Queens. Dennett was broke and eventually was declared insane and committed to a mental hospital in California.

A man named David Crear, a friend but also one of Dennett's creditors, had by now come into possession of the cabins. Crear was not sure what to do with them. By 1904, the logs were being stored in a vacant annex (owned by Crear) to the Poppenhausen Institute in College Point. The logs were stored there until 1905, when the building was torn down and they were moved to the basement of the nearby Warren Collins residence. In 1906, the Lincoln Farm Association purchased the cabins from Crear for $1,000, but as he would say, he received only $975 because, as part of the deal, the Lincoln Farm Association sold him a subscription for $25. They intended to create a Lincoln birthplace site worthy of visitors and managed to eventually raise $350,000 in contributions from more than 100,000 American donors giving between $0.25 and $25.

In 1906, the logs were removed from the Collins basement and set off for a slow journey back to Kentucky that was designed to attract much attention

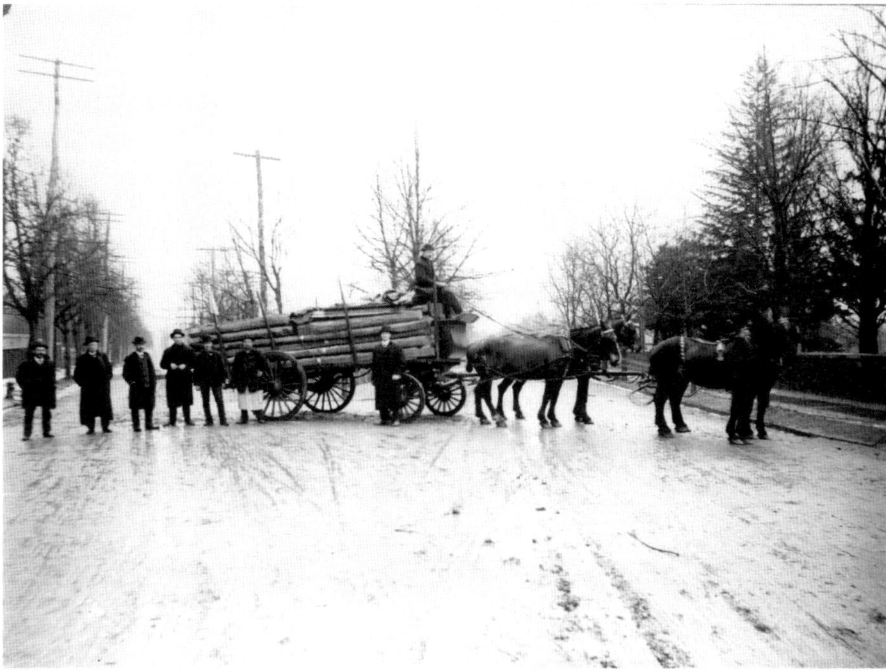

Purported Lincoln birthplace cabin logs being removed from storage in College Point in February 1906. *Library of Congress.*

and interest. The logs' removal from their Queens storage place received some media coverage, enough for several articles and a news photographer to capture the moment on film. As the procession passed the College Point Public School, the schoolchildren serenaded the wooden remains with "The Star-Spangled Banner" and "My Old Kentucky Home." The logs were stored in Long Island City until June 1906, whence they were loaded onto a railroad flatcar for their journey to Louisville, Kentucky. Stops along the way attracted large crowds. After arrival in Kentucky, the logs remained in a warehouse in Louisville until 1911, when they were taken to the Lincoln birthplace site and reassembled inside the new temple-like memorial building designed by John Russell Pope—at a smaller size to allow visitors to walk around the cabin. President William Taft presided at the official dedication ceremony for the memorial building.

Originally 142 pieces when it left Queens, the enshrined log cabin was now made of 63 logs as reconstructed by the Lincoln Farm Association. There it stands to this day, and even now the webpage of the U.S. National Parks (which now runs the site) for the Lincoln birthplace site is careful not to discuss the actual provenance of the log cabin that is standing there, calling it neither fake nor real but "symbolic."

Conflicting testimonies by those who lived in the area in the nineteenth century were given in the early twentieth century as to the authenticity of the preserved cabin, but Robert Todd Lincoln, the president's son, stated unequivocally that, in his opinion, the Kentucky cabin was a fraud. So, while it is unlikely that the actual "Lincoln" logs spent time in Queens, the logs that are on display at the symbolic log cabin at the Lincoln Birthplace National Park most certainly did.

The Crocheron House's Infamous Guest

First known as the Bayside Hotel, the Crocheron House was built around 1854. Perched on a hill overlooking Little Neck Bay (just off what is now the Cross Island Parkway), this large hotel boasted great views and fine cuisine and entertainment. There was a two-hundred- by three-hundred-foot platform, with a pavilion jutting out over the bay. The stables could accommodate 150 horses and carriages.

The hotel received many prominent visitors, including General Ulysses Grant. While Grant may have been more famous, no visitor was more infamous than William Marcy Tweed (1823–78). Tweed was just another ambitious New York City politician early in his career. He rose quickly through the ranks of local politics, starting out as a city alderman at age twenty-seven and was elected to Congress in 1852, before he'd even turned thirty. In the late 1860s, he became the leader of Tammany Hall, the New York Democratic powerhouse that gained power and numbers by luring immigrants and the poor. Known as "Boss" Tweed, he was infamous for his schemes and financial shenanigans that left him and his crooked cronies rolling in the dough. When he got his mitts on the beautiful new courthouse at 52 Chambers Street (also known as the Tweed Courthouse, it is still there today), for example, he wound up increasing the cost of the building by $8 million based on inflated invoices and unnecessary repairs. He was also involved in a shady land-buying scheme based on insider knowledge of the widening of Broadway.

During the peak of his power, Tweed was king of New York City and lived large with the stolen fortune at his disposal. One of his pleasures was heading to the Crocheron House, which was owned by his pal Joseph Crocheron.

Tweed and his associates used to go to the hotel for a day and a night and wind up dropping $1,000 in the process.

Tweed's bold pilfering from the people of the city eventually caught up with him. Critical cartoons drawn by Thomas Nast and published in *Harper's Weekly* magazine helped stir public opinion against him. The *New York Times* got a scoop on some of Tweed's misdeeds and published the details. In October 1871, Tweed was arrested, freed on bail and reelected to the state senate in November, but in December, he was indicted for fraud and felony. He was convicted and sentenced to twelve years in prison. He served nineteen months and was then released on a legal technicality. The city filed millions of dollars in civil lawsuits to recover the money Tweed stole. He was arrested again and thrown in jail but managed to escape. And where did he go? To the Crocheron House!

As the story goes, Tweed was brought to the hotel by horse-drawn carriage from Manhattan. Hotel proprietor George Hill recalled to a visiting newspaper reporter years later:

> *Do you see that cupola up yonder? Well, after Tweed's escape from Ludlow Street jail in 'seventy-five, looking for a refuge from his enemies, where did he go? Why, right down here, of course. They hustled him up to the cupola, reached by a ladder, and so he pulled up the ladder after him. For two days and nights the refugee was hidden in that tiny room, where he could see everything, but where he was himself unseen, now and then letting down a pail by a rope and hauling up his terrapin and champagne, banqueting in silence and security till at last his friends sent him word that all was ready, and at dead of night they took Tweed from the Crocheron House across the bay in a small boat, and from Throgg's Neck hurried him to the railroad by fast horses. There an engine and tender awaited him, and without stopping Tweed was hustled over the Canadian frontier.*

From there, Tweed fled to Spain, but he was captured and, in 1876, brought back to New York and thrown in jail, where he died in 1878.

The hotel, purchased by Joseph Crocheron in 1867, was completely destroyed by fire (along with all its outbuildings, at a total loss of $35,000) in 1878 when a kerosene lamp in a bedroom exploded. The hotel was rebuilt and did well for several more decades, retaining its reputation as a fine spot for dining and recreation. An 1884 article in the *New York Sun* described the scene on a Sunday at the hotel:

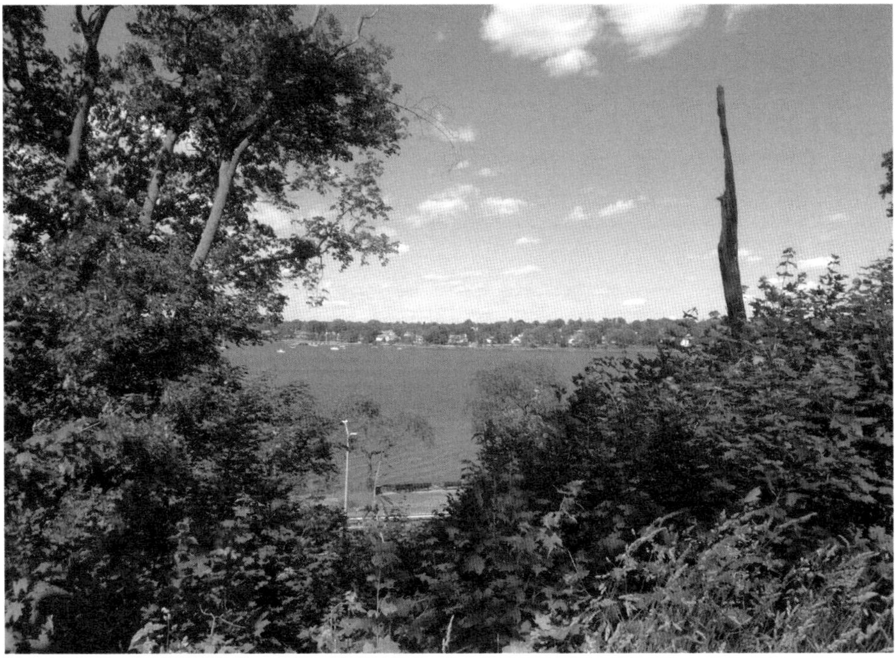

Crocheron Park was the site of the Crocheron House, which was frequented by the infamous Boss Tweed. *Author's collection.*

> *A pavilion fronting the hotel sheltered tables spread with linen whiter than snow and glittering with casters and cruets. The waves washed the foot of the pavilion and a score of white sails were visible on the bay. Scarlet lobsters, cooling cucumbers, delicate heads of lettuce, ripe tomatoes, silvery blue and king fish, succulent steaks, and platoons of wine routes were temptingly displayed. A score of colored waiters in white jackets were within call. The first buggy arrived at 9 o'clock. Two young bloods alighted, patronized the bar and took breakfast in the cooling breeze. By noon drags loaded with ladies, phaetons, carriages, and top buggies were pouring in unceasingly, while stages brought in loads of persons who had come down on the North Shore road.... The tables were fringed with guests, and knots of well-dressed men and women sat beneath the leafy maples, enjoying the breeze and reading the morning newspapers.*

In its heyday, up to eight hundred people came to the hotel to spend the day. A Crocheron House menu in 1905 included the following: mock and green turtle soup; steamed, baked hard and soft clams; hard- and soft-shell crabs and lobsters; bass; eels; sheepshead, frogs' legs à la Newburg; terrapin à la Maryland; chicken, southern style; spring lamb with mint sauce; and roast beef Pommard.

By 1907, the hotel's future was uncertain. There was talk of developing the land it stood on. A puzzling newspaper article that year said that "up to the present time a room in the hotel which Tweed occupied has been kept just the way it was at the time he last occupied it." This would have been quite a feat if the room, along with the entire hotel, burned to the ground in 1878. Memories back then were apparently very short, because even an article about the devastating fire that occurred later in 1907, destroying the hotel for good, said that it was built nearly seventy years prior and had been where Boss Tweed was hidden for a week. And note in the reminiscences stated earlier how the old hotel proprietor points to the cupola, which would not have been the same one Tweed was hidden in, since the hotel was rebuilt.

The city purchased the hotel land in 1925 and, by 1936, had turned it into Crocheron Park. A visit to the park makes a lovely outing, much as it did back in the day, minus the turtle soup. When you walk along the eastern edge of the park, you can see the views and know why this place was such an attractive destination for city folk. And if you glance down at the ground near the roots of some of the older trees, you may find, as I did, a few ceramic remnants of the old Crocheron House complex—bits and pieces of history. Who knows, maybe one of them could be a fragment of a plate that old Boss Tweed himself ate from!

A Company Town Grows in Queens

When you hear the words "company town," perhaps you think of some coal-mining village or a faraway locale out west. But oddly enough, there was a company town in Queens, and it was founded by one of the most illustrious businesses in the borough's history.

The Steinway Piano Company was founded in Manhattan in 1853 by Henry Steinway and his four sons, all German immigrants. The company soon developed an international reputation for building excellent pianos. By 1870, Steinway & Sons was looking to expand. According to William Steinway (one of the sons) in an 1896 interview in the *New York Times*:

> *For several years previous to 1870 we had been looking for a plot of land away from the city, and yet within easy access of it, for the erection of an additional factory, rendered necessary by the extension of our business. There were two reasons why we sought a place outside the city. In the first place, we wished to escape the machinations of the Anarchists and Socialists, who even at that time—twenty-five years ago—were continually breeding discontent among our workmen and inciting them to strike...we felt that if we could withdraw our workmen from contact with these people and the other temptations of city life in the tenement districts they could be more content and their lot would be a happier one. Then there was a growing demand for more room to extend our facilities. The Fourth Avenue* [Manhattan] *factory was inadequate for our wants and we needed in additional shipping facilities near the water and a basin in which logs could be stored in water to keep them moist and prevent them from cracking.*

In addition to buying four hundred acres of land in Astoria in 1870, the Steinways also purchased a twenty-six-room house on a bluff that once offered pleasant views of the waterfront. Built in 1858 from handsome Maine bluestone, the Italianate mansion had belonged to Benjamin Pike Jr., a wealthy optician, and was used by the Steinways as a summer home, a place where the sons and their families could relax during the warm months in a pleasant setting that was still very close to the city. This summer home was quite impressive; the dining room could seat fifty people.

In 1872, William Steinway began to develop the Queens site by first building a sawmill to transform the trees that were growing on the four hundred acres into lumber. Steinway also built iron and brass foundries and a building for finishing and processing the iron piano frames. Along the four thousand feet of Steinway-owned waterfront, there was more than one thousand feet of bulkhead and docks, as well as a canal to allow ships to unload their cargo of raw materials. The Steinway lumberyard had five million square feet of lumber out in the open, seasoning for two years before being put into kilns for use in the factory. It was not so simple as just erecting one building to make pianos; there are a lot of components to a piano and a lot of manufacturing processes that are required. By 1876, there were about three hundred people employed in the Steinway factory. In 1879, a new factory was built that was four stories high, and by 1892, there were six hundred workers at the factory. In 1902, an even bigger Steinway factory was built that took 2,500,000 bricks to construct. Its grand piano varnishing room could accommodate 530 piano cases.

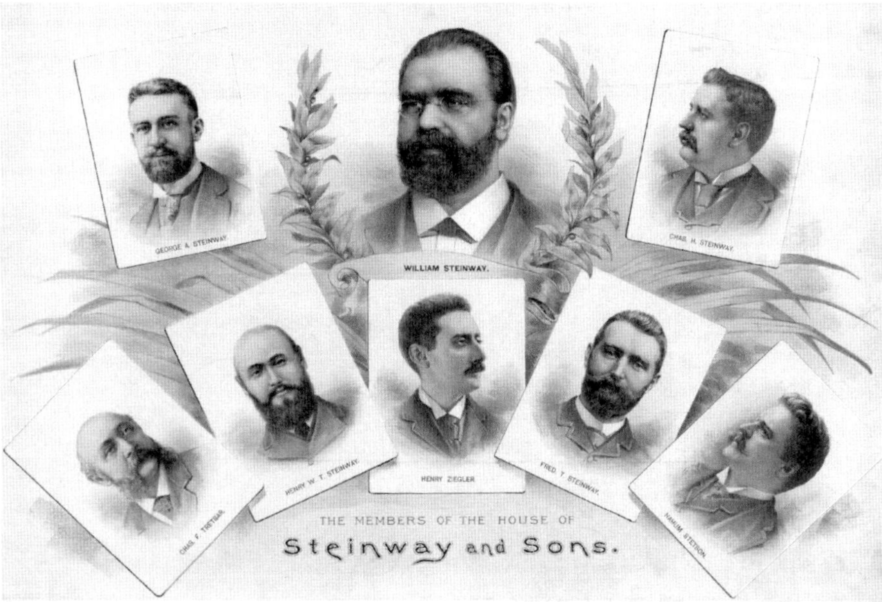

An 1890 print shows the managers of the Steinway company. *Library of Congress.*

But was the elder Steinway satisfied solely with making pianos? As a newspaper article published decades later said of William Steinway, he was "like Alexander the Great, always looking about for more worlds to conquer." Steinway's vision was not for a manufacturing complex, it was for a town. He owned much more land than was needed for simply making pianos. In 1873, he had streets laid out, including 6,500 feet of Steinway Avenue (its official name as of 1905; later, Steinway Street). This main road connected Northern Boulevard (then called Jackson Avenue) with Bowery Bay, the waterfront where their factory was. Sewers were installed and dozens of houses built by his Astoria Homestead Company. This settlement would become known as Steinway Village.

But he wasn't done there. In 1877, the Steinway company paid for the construction of a school for up to five hundred students and paid for a German-language teacher. In 1879, Steinway donations funded construction of the Protestant Union Church. In 1881, the Steinways built a 100- by 50-foot public bath near the waterfront with fifty dressing rooms, as well as a 250- by 200-foot gas-lit park with a fountain of drinking water, for use by employees and their families. They also built the Steinway Free Circulating

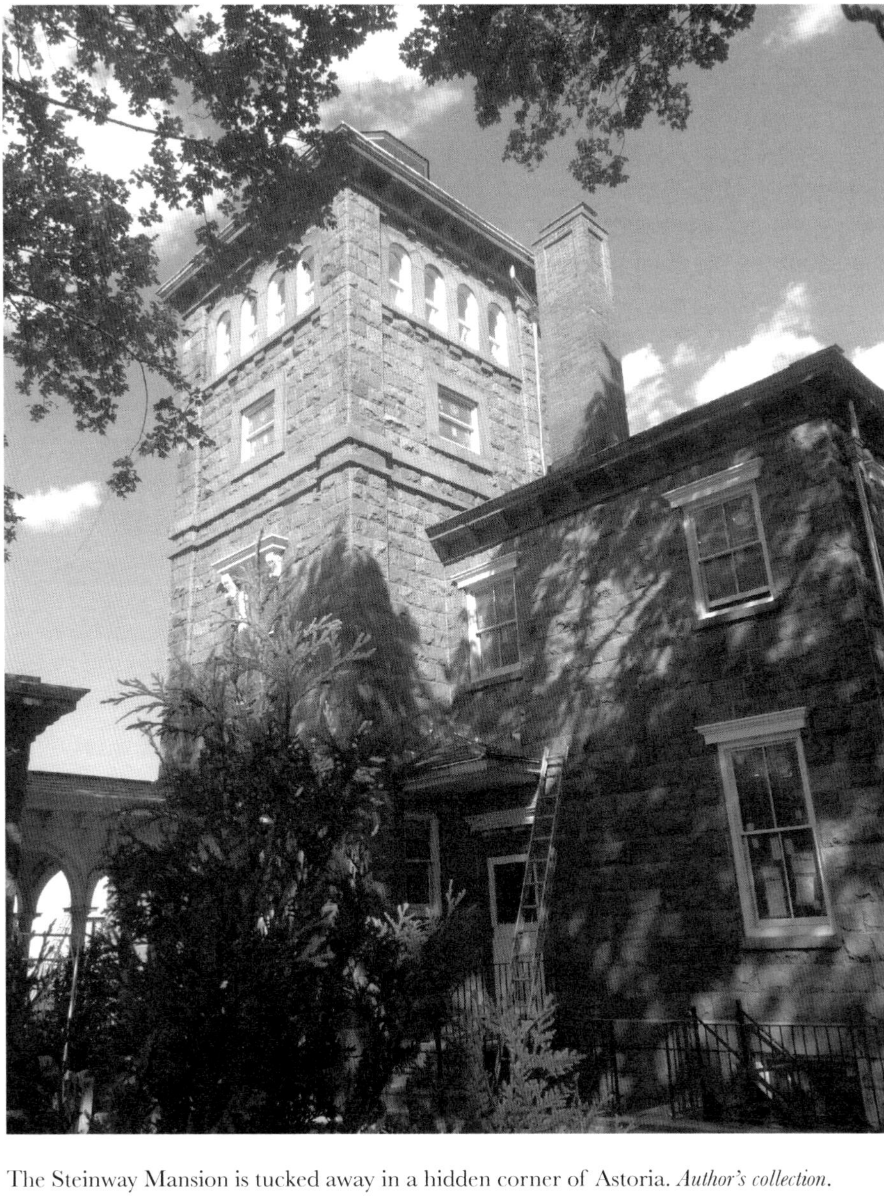

The Steinway Mansion is tucked away in a hidden corner of Astoria. *Author's collection.*

Library and the Steinway Free Kindergarten. By 1881, there were 130 homes in Steinway, built to house piano factory workers. The streets had sidewalks, and numerous trees were planted. Steinway also owned a horse car line that ran from Steinway Village to Hunter's Point.

Steinway actively promoted his settlement, trying to attract both workers and other businesses to this new village. An 1881 newspaper advertisement placed by Steinway & Sons touted the benefits of "Steinway Settlement," requesting the attention of manufacturers, mechanics and workingmen who wanted to live in "comfortable and cheerful homes—in a thoroughly healthy and desirable neighborhood—in the immediate vicinity of, and easy access to, all parts of the City of New York," only two and a half miles from Central Park. It called their attention to the "over one hundred neat and well-constructed Brick and Frame Dwelling Houses and Stores" that were constructed there. A variation of this ad, with more enticements listed as new improvements were built, ran for at least fifteen years in the *Long Island Daily Star*. There were also references to the waterfront becoming a resort, but beyond the bathhouse, this never happened.

Steinway was not a typical company town. Its founder had a charitable streak that went further than just erecting public buildings and parks. In the 1890s, William Steinway granted permission to the Association for Improving the Condition of the Poor to use three hundred acres of Steinway's vacant land for poor families to cooperatively farm on. A total of one hundred farms were allotted on Steinway-owned land, growing potatoes, turnips and cabbage. When, one year, this venture actually made $6,000 in profit, it was offered to Steinway, but he turned it down.

Thankfully, there is much remaining of the Steinway legacy. There is still a Steinway piano factory in Astoria, offering three-hour tours (with no chance of getting stranded on a desert island, thankfully). The Steinway Mansion still stands today but is now oddly in the midst of a highly industrial zone with automotive shops. The Steinway Mansion (at 18-33 Forty-First Street) was purchased from Steinway by the Halberian family in 1926 and was sold again in 2014 for $2.65 million—but as a New York City Landmark (designated in 1967), it is safe from demolition. In 1925, much of the former farmland surrounding the Steinway Mansion was sold off, divided into seven hundred lots.

Many of the original Steinway-built homes still stand, and in 1974, the Steinway Historic District, comprising twenty-nine of the original Steinway Village row houses located along Twentieth Avenue and Forty-First Street, was proposed and then designated as a New York City Landmark. Sadly, the decision was overturned by the board of estimate in 1975 after many of the homeowners complained about the onerous requirements such status would force on them. A visit to what remains of the old Steinway Village is well worth it.

WHITES ONLY, AND ALL THAT JAZZ

Queens has been home to some pretty famous musicians. It's widely known that one of the most popular musical duos in history, Simon and Garfunkel, originated in Queens. In their youth, Paul Simon and Art Garfunkel lived only three blocks apart in Kew Gardens Hills, just east of Flushing Meadows–Corona Park. Paul Simon also has one of the most famous references to Queens ever immortalized in song—"Rosie, the Queen of Corona," in the 1972 song "Me and Julio Down by the Schoolyard."

Beloved jazz musician Louis Armstrong, meanwhile, lived in a modest house at 34-56 107th Street in Corona in the later part of his life, from 1943 until his death in 1971. Upon his widow's death in 1983, she left the house to the City of New York. The building is now a New York City Landmark and a museum, with the rooms preserved as they were when Armstrong was alive.

But that is just the tip of the musical iceberg. Queens was home to numerous popular jazz and soul musicians of the 1940s and 1950s, and they lived in a little-known, beautiful section of St. Albans called Addisleigh Park. But there is a dark and sad side to this story, and the more I researched, the more it shocked me.

Located in a roughly triangular area bordered by Merrick Boulevard, Linden Boulevard and 180th Street, the elegant Addisleigh Park neighborhood was first planned as early as 1892, but the earliest homes date to the 1910s. These older homes are typically in the colonial style. By the 1920s, the dominant style was Tudor Revival, with some architecturally distinct designs. The homes sold fast. In 1931, ninety-one new Addisleigh Park homes were sold in a matter of two months, and twenty homes from a second round of development that same year were sold just from the blueprints, before any of them were built.

By about 1938, the famed jazz composer, singer and pianist Fats Waller had purchased a house at 173-19 Sayres Avenue. (He remained there until his sudden death in 1943.) Waller was known for writing the jazz hit "Ain't Misbehavin'" (among many others) and performing it in the 1943 movie *Stormy Weather*. Not everyone in the neighborhood was pleased with their new renowned neighbor. It was not that they didn't like his music, or that he had loud parties, or that he didn't mow his lawn. It was a simple fact. They were white, and he was black.

Things came to a head in 1939, when a white couple, Mr. and Mrs. George Bouchey, purchased a home in Addisleigh Park. They were not

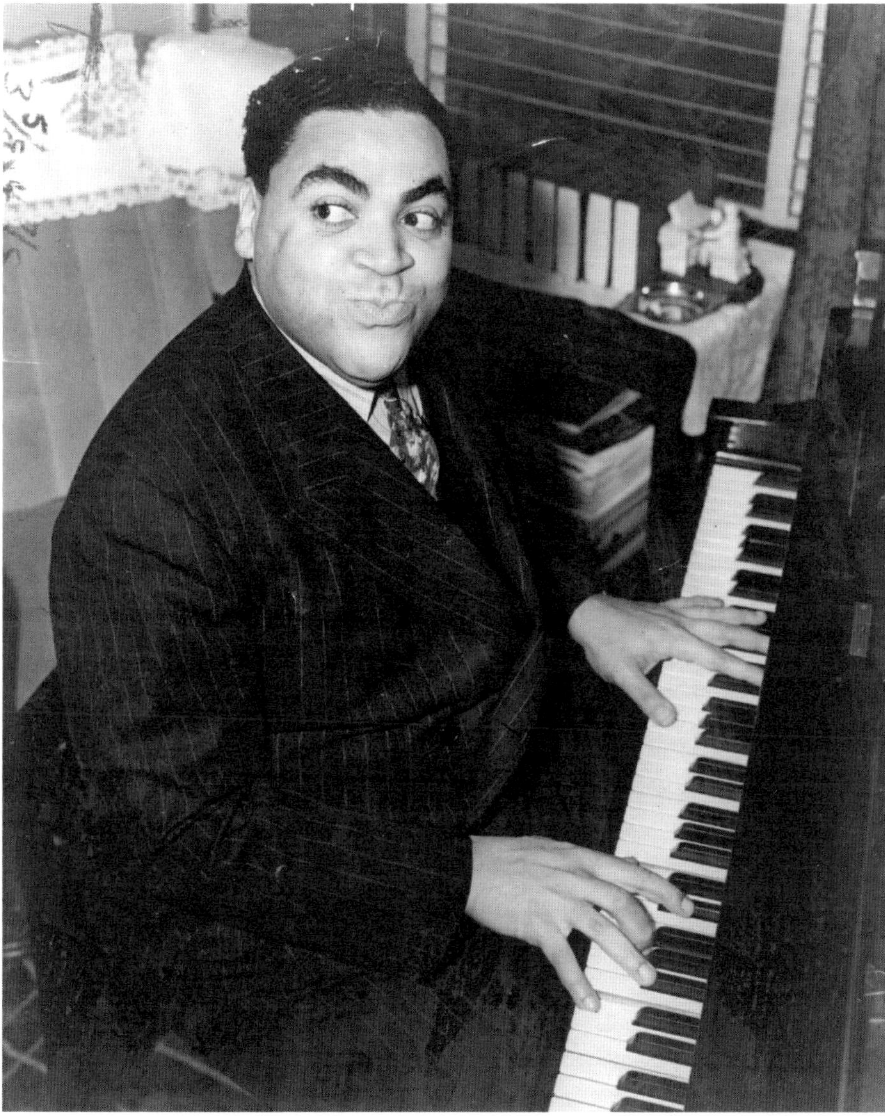

The beloved musician Fats Waller was one of the first African Americans to move to Addisleigh Park. *Library of Congress.*

satisfied with it and asked for their money back, but the real estate company refused. The couple, feeling spiteful, put up a sign on their lawn saying the home was for sale to Negroes. The company, Addisleigh Homes Inc., was horrified and took them to court, asking for monetary damages. The judge ruled that members of the community could sell their homes to anyone they wanted, provided that the homeowners had not entered into any contracts prohibiting such sales.

In 1939, an ugly development happened. A restrictive clause was added into some homeowners' deeds that forbade them from selling their homes to anyone other than Caucasians until the year 1975. By 1942, more than two hundred homeowners had signed the covenant. Still, this clause did not stop folks from selling to whomever they wished. The owners would often "sneak sell" their homes to African Americans to avoid the wrath of their neighbors. These buyers would sometimes come to view the house at midnight, when nobody else would be awake to notice, or even buy the home sight unseen.

When, in 1942, African American bandleader Andy Kirk wanted to buy a home in Addisleigh Park, fifteen white families in the neighborhood demanded that the Queens County Court grant an injunction against the sale. By this time, Fats Waller was not the only famous musician living in the neighborhood—Clyde Barrie, an African American baritone singer, was also a resident. But anti-black sentiment was high. That same year, the neighborhood's white residents received attention when they refused to buy

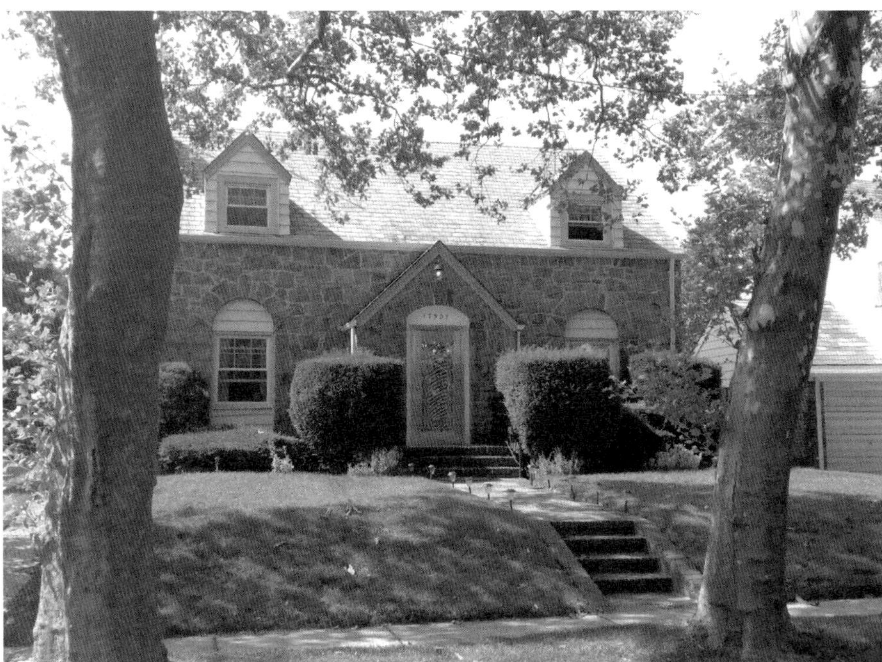

The Ella Fitzgerald House is located at 179-07 Murdock Avenue in Addisleigh Park. *Author's collection.*

a single war bond from an African American "Minute Woman" salesperson going door to door.

Meanwhile, African Americans kept moving in, including several more notable musicians. In 1946, vocalist Lena Horne and bandleader Count Basie bought homes in Addisleigh Park. Other residents included Bill Kenny of the group the Ink Spots and jazz trumpeter Cootie Williams. Racial tensions were escalating. That same year, four black residents had cards placed on their doorsteps that read "Klu Klux Klan, District of St. Albans. Warning. To Negroes Entering St. Albans. Beware." But as one resident pointed out, the cards had to be a hoax, since the correct spelling was "Ku" not "Klu."

Also in 1946, two white Addisleigh Park homeowners, Harold Kemp and John Lutz, obtained a temporary injunction against a neighbor, Sophie Rubin, who had signed the restrictive covenant but was planning to sell her home for $10,500 to an African American merchant named Samuel Richardson. Rubin won a brief victory in the Queens Supreme Court when the judge issued a temporary injunction against the restrictive covenant until a decision could be reached. The most ironic twist to this story was that the would-be buyer already owned a plot of empty land behind the house that was up for sale.

In February 1947, the Jamaica Supreme Court ruled in favor of the injunction preventing the sale of the home. The judge stated that, though "distinctions based on color and ancestry are utterly inconsistent with our traditions and ideals," he said he still had to honor the covenant. According to the judge: "We do not have on our statute books any specific provision which outlaws racial restrictive covenants. This court does not feel that it should judicially legislate by reading into the statute something which the Legislature itself has failed to adopt." There was widespread interest in this case, and many groups rallied around the cause of the defendant. Amicus witnesses who testified for the defendants included lawyers for the American Jewish Congress, the Social Action Committee of the New York City Congregational Association, the Citywide Committee on Harlem, the Greater New York Industrial Union Council and the National Association for the Advancement of Colored People. By this time, there were sixty African American families living in Addisleigh Park.

The defendant appealed, and the Brooklyn Appellate Division upheld the lower court's ruling, but in July 1948, a state court of appeals heard *Kemp v. Rubin* and overturned the two rulings, saying that Sophia Rubin could in fact sell her house to an African American businessman. The ruling found guidance in a recent United States Supreme Court decision, *Shelly v. Kraemer*, that said courts cannot uphold restrictive covenants. African Americans could finally move into the neighborhood without fear of legal repercussions.

Even as more African Americans bought homes in Addisleigh Park, there were still tensions. In 1952, someone set fire to a cross in Addisleigh Park; by this time, the area was described as "expensive private homes owned mostly by Negroes." Other notables who had moved into the neighborhood included the singers Ella Fitzgerald (resident from 1949 to 1956), Rose Murphy, Brook Benton and James Brown; musicians Earl Bostic, Wild Bill Davis, Mercer Ellington (Duke Ellington's son), John Coltrane, Illinois Jacquet (from 1950 to 2004) and Milt Hinton (from 1950 to 2000); baseball players Jackie Robinson (who had already made waves as the first African American major leaguer) and Roy Campanella (from 1949 to 1956); boxer Joe Louis (from 1955 to 1958); and the civil rights activist and professor W.E.B. DuBois (from 1951 to 1952).

Thankfully, perspectives changed with the times. A 1963 newspaper article proclaimed that instead of real estate values dropping in Addisleigh Park, they more than doubled. In 1961, Addisleigh Park resident Mrs. Count Basie (Catherine) was picked as a ceremonial "Locality Mayor" for Queens, and in 1964, she was present at the ribbon cutting for the opening of the new Addisleigh Park East development of eight new high ranch–style houses on Sayres Avenue.

In 2011, the New York City Landmarks Commission designated the neighborhood, encompassing 426 homes, as a historic district. Addisleigh Park is currently about 90 percent African American, and now, because of its landmark status, the elegant, historic homes are protected against demolition or major changes. To walk through the neighborhood is to take in a major site in both civil rights history and jazz history.

THE DUKE OF QUEENS

Aside from the musicians mentioned above, there have been plenty of other famous folks from Queens. The list is long and storied. It seems there was one Queens celebrity or another on practically every corner. And that's no exaggeration. There was even one on my corner, in fact. Well, Mom's corner, to be exact. As kid, I heard an occasional mention from Mom of a celebrity she knew when she was a teenager. Back then, I was a teenager myself and I didn't really think or care to ask her more. As I got older, I revisited the topic once in a while, until recently, as I was writing this book, when I decided it was time for a more thorough discussion. "So you knew Patty Duke?" I said. "Tell me more."

Mom handed me a slightly blurry black-and-white photo dated October 1962. And sure enough, there's Mom standing between two boys, and at the right is Patty Duke, as they stand on the corner of Van Horn and Fifty-Third Avenue in Elmhurst, up the block from where Duke lived and in front of the building where Mom was living at the time. Turns out, not only did Mom hang out with Patty Duke, the actress and her family (mother, sister, and brother) moved into the second-floor apartment of the two-family building at 86-28 Fifty-Third Avenue right after Mom and my grandparents moved out of that very same apartment, around 1960 or so! Of course, Mom kept telling me that she couldn't be sure of the details, and what if she was wrong? Well, a little further research verified that Mom and the Dukes had indeed lived in the same apartment just off Seabury Street and near Queens Boulevard.

Born Anna Marie Duke, Patty had been acting since the age of seven. Before her big break on Broadway, she performed at the Elks Club on Queens Boulevard on Amateur Nights. Though not a native of Elmhurst, she was living there at the time her fame blossomed. Or at least the local newspapers had people believing that was the case. The headline of a March 1962 article in the *Long Island Star-Journal* read "Elmhurst Girl at 15 Zooms Toward Stardom" and described her as a "beguiling creature, with a quick smile" who was living on the top floor of a two-family house near Queens Boulevard with her mother and sister and a parakeet. Though she was in Elmhurst visiting Mom on occasion, the reality was that Patty Duke had moved into the Manhattan home of Ethel and John Ross, her highly overprotective managers. There has always been and still is much misinformation out there about the details of Duke's life. For example, many websites (surprisingly, including imdb.com) claim Patty Duke was born in Elmhurst; in fact, she was born in Bellevue Hospital off First Avenue between Twenty-Sixth and Twenty-Eighth Streets, the same neighborhood she lived in as a young child.

Curious to know more, I wondered what else I could find. I realized there was only one other living person would could shed any more light on this topic, and that was Patty Duke's older brother Ray, an actor whose career had actually kickstarted Patty's. I decided to try to locate Ray Duke and give him a call. He verified some of the timing and details of what Mom had told me. The reason the 1962 article did not mention him as living in Elmhurst was that, by that time, he had joined the army. But as he remembered it, he had lived in Elmhurst for about a year before his military service (just shy of his twentieth birthday). But he was not in Queens much; he only really "bedded there," spending most of his time in the city.

At the time my mom first got to know Patty Duke, she was starring on Broadway in *The Miracle Worker*, which was based on the life of Helen Keller (played by Duke). *The Miracle Worker*, which began its run in 1959 and ended in 1961, made a household name of Patty Duke. That hit was followed with a brief stint in a play called *Isle of Children* (in which she played a child who was dying) in early 1962, as well as the filming of the movie version of *The Miracle Worker*.

But busy though the child star was, sometimes she was in a group of friends who would ring Mom's bell wanting to hang out. Sometimes they hung out in the basement of her boyfriend and his sister, on Fifty-Third Avenue between Van Horn and Haspel Streets. Says Mom, "We hung out there and listened to music and danced. And their mother put out pretzels and soda for us. And once in a while Patty Duke would come." Occasionally, they would walk to the playground and hang out there. "She told us about her life," Mom said. I asked what else Mom remembered about the young star. "She used to wear a cape instead of a coat," she said, a fact that is clear in the photo.

Mom's memories are verified in Duke's 1990 autobiography, *Call Me Anna*, in which she remembered that on those occasional weekends when she would be sent off to her mother's in Queens because the Rosses had other plans, she would hang out with the neighborhood kids and head over to someone's basement to dance. The frightening part she adds to that story is that her managers, the Rosses, were so controlling (she was not even allowed to close her room door when living with the Rosses) that she and her mother lived in constant fear of them finding out she was out hanging with my mom and other Elmhurst kids, and that she would often go out against Mrs. Duke's wishes.

At the time the photo was taken, things were really heating up for Patty Duke. Her film version of *The Miracle Worker* was running in theaters; it had opened that July. Her performance would go on to win her the Academy Award for Best Supporting Actress in April 1963, for which her acceptance speech consisted simply of the words "Thank you" and that was it, making it the shortest speech in Oscar history. When she won, the local papers called her "Patty Duke, of Elmhurst" even though she didn't live in Elmhurst more than on occasionally weekends, according to her autobiography.

She would go on to star in *The Patty Duke Show*, which was filmed in New York City and ran from 1963 to 1966. According to Ray Duke, his mom, by then living alone, moved out of Elmhurst around 1965 or 1966 and then on to Park Avenue in Manhattan. More television appearances and films followed for Patty, as well as a marriage to actor John Astin, all of which kept Duke in the spotlight. It was only years later that Duke's troubled, abuse-filled, tightly orchestrated childhood came to light. Those relaxing times with my mom and the other neighborhood friends from the 'Hurst were not just a way to escape the pressures of acting; they were also the only time and the only way teenaged Patty Duke could ever escape the vise grip of the forces that controlled her every move and finally just be a kid. All in all, it is fitting that the papers called her Patty Duke of Elmhurst, because when she was there was the only time she was allowed to be a real person.

That Crooner from Astoria

The legendary Tony Bennett is not the only famous crooner to hail from Astoria. Born in 1926, Bennett would meet his slightly younger Astoria counterpart on the Billboard charts in the early 1960s. And while both men made girls swoon, only one first gained fame as a television icon who became a recording star.

Born in Astoria to Greek immigrant parents, George Maharis has fond childhood memories of his dad's Astoria restaurant. "I used to love to go into the icebox, it was a big, walk-in icebox. And in the icebox there was always a big keg of sauerkraut, which I used to sit there and eat. And that's where they used to find me." Neither acting nor singing was on young Maharis's mind in those days. The family saw tough times when his father lost the restaurant due to the Great Depression.

He got his start singing on Red Letter Day at Flushing High School, the day the seniors took over the school, pulling kids into the auditorium and having them do funny, embarrassing things. "I was a tough kid. I was really a street tough kid. So, they said 'get up and sing.' So, I got up and sang and they were surprised, and [classmate] Jerry Bock heard it and he asked me if I'd be in this play called *My Dream*." This was not just any Jerry Bock, it was THE Jerry Bock, who would go on to major fame as the award-winning writer of such Broadway hits as *Fiddler on the Roof* and *Fiorello!*

Maharis started off singing in small Long Island clubs in the 1950s. At the time, he was working in Radio City Music Hall as an elevator operator and living in a walk-up, cold-water apartment on Fifty-Fourth Street. He got a part singing in the chorus in a musical and was noticed by famous German movie actor Hans Heinrich von Twardowski, who declared, "You are an actor!"

He studied acting and started getting parts in 1950s television series. After he appeared in four episodes of the police drama *Naked City* and was offered a part in the 1960 film *Exodus*, Maharis's career took off. He was cast as the scrappy Buz Murdock in a dramatic series called *Route 66* about a pair of buddies traveling across the country in a Corvette. The show was (and still is) unique, in that it was filmed entirely on location in a different place across the country each week, highlighting some conflict and new cast of characters the pair get entangled with. Maharis hired one of his brothers to come along and work on the show. The series became one of the top-rated shows on television, and Maharis was one of the best-known actors of the day.

But singing was never far from Maharis's mind, and during the peak of *Route 66*'s popularity, he saw a chance to parlay that fame into a recording contract. Maharis recorded a demo and was signed to Epic Records. He released an album of standards titled *George Maharis Sings*, which spent twenty-nine weeks on the *Billboard* Album Chart in 1962, peaking at no. 10 and ending up as the no. 41 album of 1962. He first found out about his success as he lay in a hospital recovering from hepatitis, when he saw Dick Clark mention him on *American Bandstand*. Toward the end of 1962, Epic had him release another album, *Portrait in Music*, and for a couple of months, both albums were on the charts simultaneously. He also won the *Cash Box* magazine award for Most Promising New Male Singer in 1962.

I asked him how he managed to record an entire album when his filming schedule for the television show was a full-time, seven-day affair. "[Executive producer] Burt [Leonard] promised me that he would cut away a week. As it was I got a day recording and one day for traveling. I got to the studio to record the album and in those days the orchestra was there live and you only had them for three hours. You went into the studio and there was the orchestra. They ran it through once and the next one was your take. That was it. I had x number of hours in the studio and that was it and then I had to get on a plane and fly back to wherever the hell I was to continue doing *66*."

Five more albums followed over the next three years for the actor turned singer (the Rick Springfield of his time). These were extremely well-orchestrated, professional records, and his immense following yielded him five hit singles among the fourteen Epic released, including the highest charting, "Teach Me Tonight," which spent eleven weeks on the charts, peaking at no. 25 on the Hot 100 and at no. 8 on the Adult Contemporary Chart. Several of his singles were listed by *Billboard* in its "Breakout Singles" feature. He also sang a rendition of, what else, "(Get Your Kicks) on Route 66." In 1963, Epic Records took out a full-page ad in *Billboard* magazine to tout Maharis's records, and he went on a twenty-six-city promotional tour. He had ended his run on *Route 66* by then. He made his television singing debut on the *Judy Garland Show*, performing a duet with the star. Interestingly, his rich, evocative voice at times emulates not only Sinatra, but it also sounds a little like, you guessed it, Tony Bennett.

Epic certainly took full advantage of his popularity, but by 1964, the music scene was changing with the Beatles' arrival. His last recording was a live performance he did at the Plaza Hotel (released in 1966—he included two Beatles songs in his set), but his acting career continued. After *Route 66*, Maharis starred in the short-lived 1970 series (thirteen episodes) *The Most Deadly Game*. He appeared as a guest star in numerous television shows during the 1970s and '80s, including *Fantasy Island*, *Barnaby Jones*, *The Bionic Woman*, *Logan's Run* and *Police Story*. After his retirement from acting, he took up painting, much like fellow Astoria crooner Tony Bennett.

Maharis had homes in both New York and California. Some years ago, his longtime New York housekeeper was ready to retire, so she offered to take Maharis out to dinner to mark the occasion. She picked the place, and though his New York home was in the Village and she lived elsewhere in Queens, "she took me to a restaurant on Broadway [in Astoria], and I'm sitting in the restaurant getting these peculiar feelings. I was across the street from where my dad's restaurant was." A long and storied life that had begun in Astoria had come full circle, more than sixty years later.

Chapter 6
Last Traces of Hidden History

As time and progress march on, they leave behind scattered remnants of the past in their wake. Places and things still stand, despite the obliteration of their surroundings—objects and structures that are stuck in a ghostly time warp. Some are hidden remnants and others are in plain sight, neither demolished nor used. Queens is filled with these pieces of the past, in various forms and in various states of decay. We've visited some of these places in previous chapters—Fort Totten and Fort Tilden, for example. In this chapter, we'll explore more glimpses of Queens' past in bits as small as a handful of ceramic shards and as large as an entire abandoned complex of buildings.

The Destruction of Arverne

The Rockaways became a popular summer destination for New Yorkers in the nineteenth century, and numerous hotels and amusements used to line the beachfront. Though much of the area is still used for recreation today, long gone are the grand hotels and the vacationers.

Though much of the Rockaways has changed drastically, no section has been transformed as much as the easternmost Rockaway community Edgemere (aka Arverne). By the late nineteenth century, it was a summer resort, anchored by the massive Edgemere Club Hotel (capacity 250 guests), which stood on the water's edge at Beach Thirty-Fifth to Thirty-

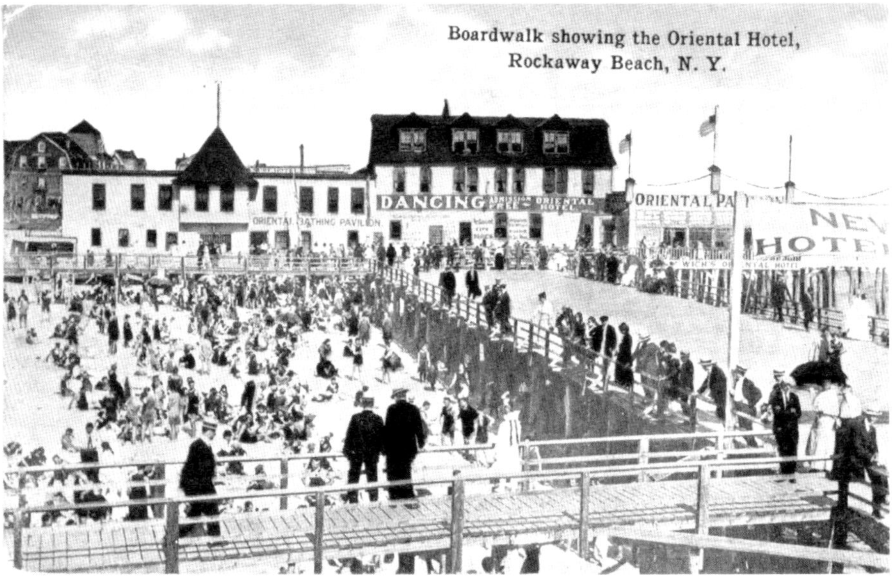

Rockaway Beach, circa 1910. *Author's collection.*

Sixth Streets. At that point, it is said there were only three or four summer cottages in the area, but by 1911, Edgemere had three other major hotels and about one hundred cottages. Other hotels of the era included the two-hundred-room Lorraine (Beach Thirty-First Street), the Frontenac, the Wave Crest, the Coronado (at Beach Thirty-Second Street) and the Lyndeman. The Edgemere offered a private beach, golf, tennis, yachting and rowing, as well as nightly dancing to a ten-piece orchestra in a ballroom overlooking the ocean. According to a 1912 article in the *Brooklyn Daily Eagle*: "At Edgemere are to be found some of the most attractive cottages in or near New York City. Here one sees some of the best examples of modern suburban house architecture."

In January 1914, a major coastal storm destroyed most of the boardwalk at Arverne and swept the Arverne Pier Theater off of the hundreds of piles that kept it fifteen feet above the normal high tide. Arverne suffered a devastating disaster in July 1922 when a fire caused by a lit cigarette tossed by a workman onto the shingle roof of the Hotel Nautilus became a major blaze. More than two hundred buildings, including a railroad station, six hotels and many cottages, were destroyed. The fire caused $2 million in damage and left twenty thousand people homeless. It was a scene of utter devastation that would oddly presage what was to come for the community.

After rebuilding, the area was once again a popular summer destination through the 1940s. By this time, most of the old hotels were gone; times and the community were changing. Arverne was no longer the prime seaside destination it had been, and by the early 1960s, the area was a mere shadow of its former glory.

The beginning of the end came in 1965, when Arverne was designated as an Urban Renewal Area. The process of condemnation of all buildings south of Rockaway Beach Boulevard between Beach Thirty-Fifth and Beach Fifty-Eighth Streets began, and in 1969, the site was cleared as part of the urban renewal plan. And when I say cleared, I mean cleared. A 1969 article explained about work on the section from Beach Forty-Fifth to Beach Forty-Ninth Streets, which included 267 structures: "[The contractor] will level all buildings....A bulldozer will go through and knock everything down and then trucks will come and cart out the rubble." Another contract followed for the removal of 342 buildings between Beach Forty-Ninth and Beach Fifty-Eighth Streets. The clearing was a slow process, and by 1974, there were still "numerous vacant buildings, structurally unsound from repeated fires." The one thing that was left behind was the infrastructure. Street after street was left to crumble as the land between them became completely overgrown.

Construction on new development was to begin as early as 1970, but it didn't happen. A description of the area in 1974 from a local newspaper is not too far from what it looks like today: "Piles of rubble, debris and

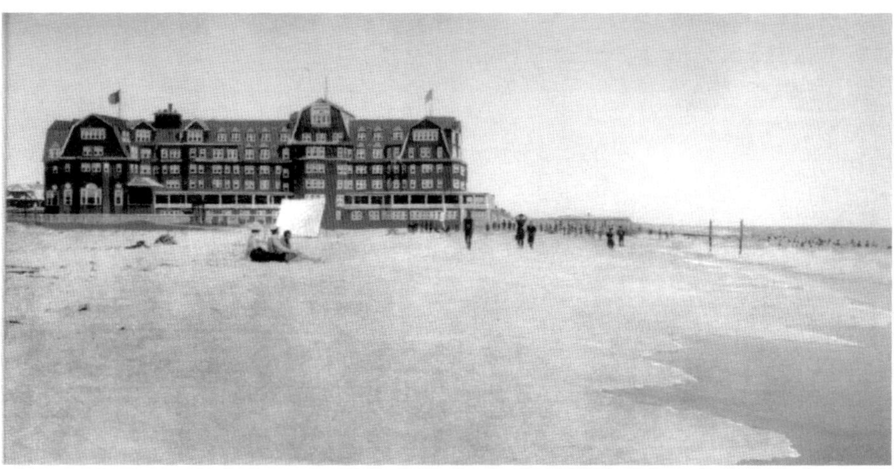

The Edgemere Hotel, circa 1905. *Author's collection.*

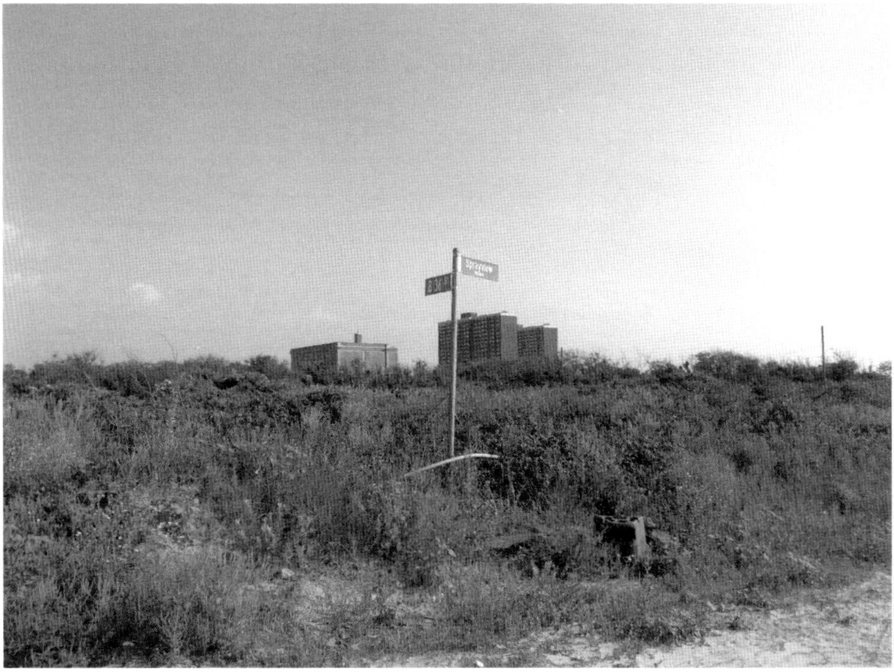

The Edgemere area today. *Author's collection.*

abandoned cars cover the two-mile stretch." In the decades since the demolition occurred, this abandoned twenty-block stretch of beachfront streets has turned into an eerie combination of sand-swept ghost town, wildlife preserve and squatter's paradise. There are rumors of wild dogs in the area.

On my trip there, as I walked along the pothole-dotted road (or what was left of it), I saw a milk crate, items of clothing, broken electronics, brick and stone debris and a sleek-looking somewhat vintage motorboat on a rusting trailer. That's right. A boat. Just sitting there off the side of the "road" in some scrub brush. Who knows how long it had been there. There are also plenty of fire hydrants in this wilderness, and from their frequency you can tell just how populated this area used to be. Perhaps the most eerie thing I saw was the street sign marking the intersection of Beach Thirty-Sixth Street and Sprayview Avenue. Streets that had once been alive were now mere ghosts waiting for the long-promised revival. In the midst of this emptiness stands Public School 106 on Beach Thirty-Fifth Street, a stately old building dating to the early twentieth century. Turn toward the ocean, and there is a boardwalk and people enjoying the beach. Turn back north, and in the distance is Edgemere Avenue and the Rockaway Freeway. The scene is unsettling…and very cool…for its stark contrasts.

Several plans for redevelopment have been touted over the years, but nothing happened. The first sign of life was the new Arverne-by-the-Sea development (with 2,300 residential units, its website proclaims it the "largest revitalization project in the Northeast). It broke ground in 2002 and sits at the western end of the emptiness. The latest plans for the remaining eighty or so acres include a nature preserve, residential units and commercial space. This time, it may actually happen, and the largest ghost town in Queens may finally breathe new life again.

World's Fair Built on Junk

As a kid, I was always looking at the ground as I walked along, picking up all sorts of interesting things (or just plain junk, depending on who you asked). That is one thing about me that has not changed in all these years, and it is a habit that would prove to be very useful when I was at Flushing Meadows–Corona Park recently. As I meandered looking for remnants of the world's fairs, my attention was captured by fragments of ceramic that littered the ground in certain spots near the New York Pavilion. There were an awful lot of them; many were white, but one was jade green, and others had colorful patterns on them. I was excited at the thought that maybe these were bits and pieces potentially dating back to one of the fairs.

Then I thought about it a little more. Why would the fairgoers have been using ceramic dishes and bowls, to such a degree that I was finding this many different sizes and shapes and colors and types of ceramic? It didn't make that much sense, so I "dug" into the topic some more and was surprised at what I found.

Many of us know that Flushing Meadows–Corona Park was created on landfill that was formerly marshy land. But I didn't realize that the park was actually built on a pile of garbage—literally junk. What would become parkland in the 1930s was in the 1920s the Corona Ash Dump, said to be the inspiration for F. Scott Fitzgerald's "Valley of Ashes" as described in *The Great Gatsby* (1925): "a fantastic farm where ashes grow like wheat into ridges and hills and grotesque gardens." For decades, ash and garbage were carted to the site by the Brooklyn Ash Removal Company and dumped. This part

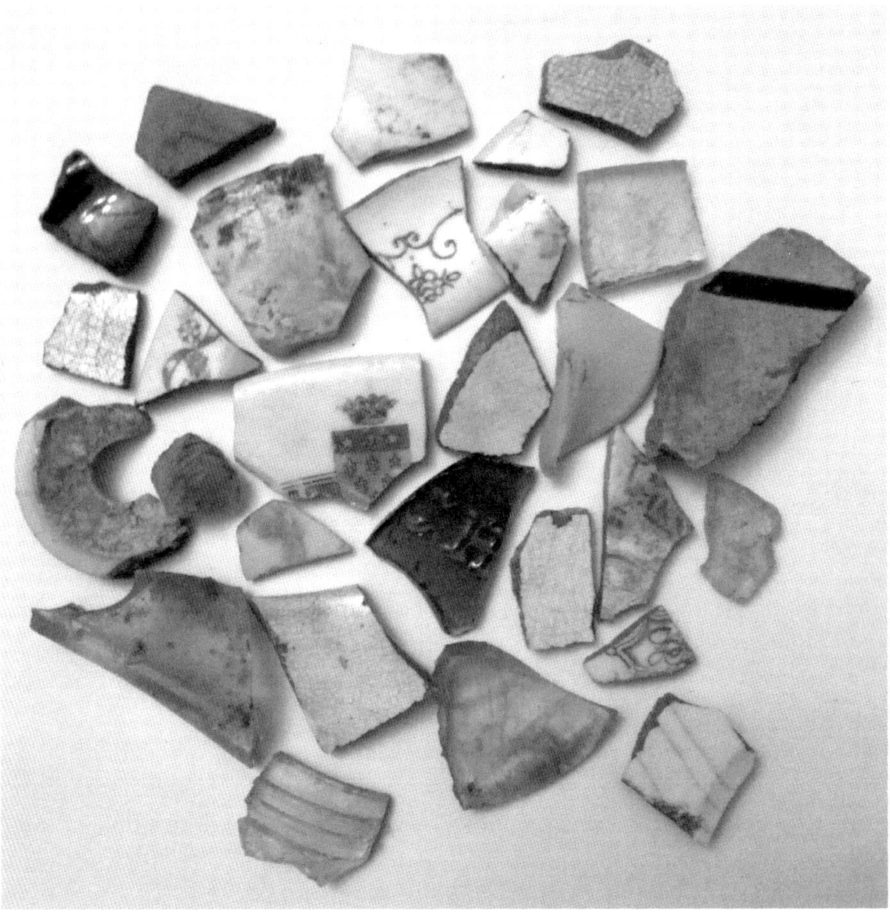

Corona Ash Dump remnants can be found in Flushing Meadows–Corona Park. *Author's collection.*

of Queens was for almost twenty-five years an eyesore and a foul-smelling health hazard. At one point, 110 train cars of garbage arrived each day! The company's contract with the city expired in 1933, and the era of garbage in Flushing was finally over as the site began its transformation into a park.

The remnants of the old dump come to the surface these days especially around the roots of many of the 1,200 old trees planted in 1937–38 in advance of the world's fair, which have forced these bits and pieces to the top—also in bare patches of dirt that may have been bulldozed or disturbed in the years since. So, the pieces I found were deposited there from around 1910 to 1933 (but could be older; the plates discarded in 1910 may have been purchased in 1890, if you think about your own household). The ash dump was ninety feet high at its peak. An official archaeological dig was held at the park in 2001, and it unearthed both fragments as well as whole bottles and other nondegradable items, which were actually put on display in the Queens Museum.

So if you find yourself in the park one day, bending over and picking up a shard of old ceramic, you will be holding both a piece of junk and a piece of history!

FARE (NOT SO) WELL, WORLD'S FAIR

By the 1930s, it had been more than eighty years since the city had hosted a world's fair. The last one was at the Crystal Palace in 1853. A grand iron-and-glass marvel that stood on the site of what is now Bryant Park in Manhattan burned down a few years later. The idea for another world's fair in New York was born in 1935. The success of the 1933 Chicago Exposition was an inspiration, and New York's leaders formed World's Fair 1939 Incorporated with one hundred charter members from all walks of life. The fair (which would cost $155 million when all was said and done) would be paid for by a mix of city, state and federal government as well as private investors.

In 1936, the site of a tidal swamp/garbage dump in Corona, Queens, was selected, and by June, work had begun in earnest to transform it into a fairground. Seven million cubic acres of earth and garbage were moved in creating a fairground out of "primeval bog, spongy marshland, and the accumulated debris and ashes of many years," as the official guidebook explains. The leveling and filling was complete by the end of March 1937, and the site was now ready for construction and landscaping. The plantings were extensive and included 10,000 trees, 500,000 hedges, 400,000 pansies and 1,000,000 tulips and other flowering bulbs from Holland.

The planning of the fair was a huge undertaking. Up to eight thousand people were employed just in the world's fair corporate offices. The federal government agreed that the nations of the world should be invited to participate and build exhibit pavilions. All told, sixty foreign countries were represented; even the Soviet Union agreed to participate. There were one thousand exhibitors, many of which were corporations demonstrating their state-of-the-art products and showing off their visions of what the world of

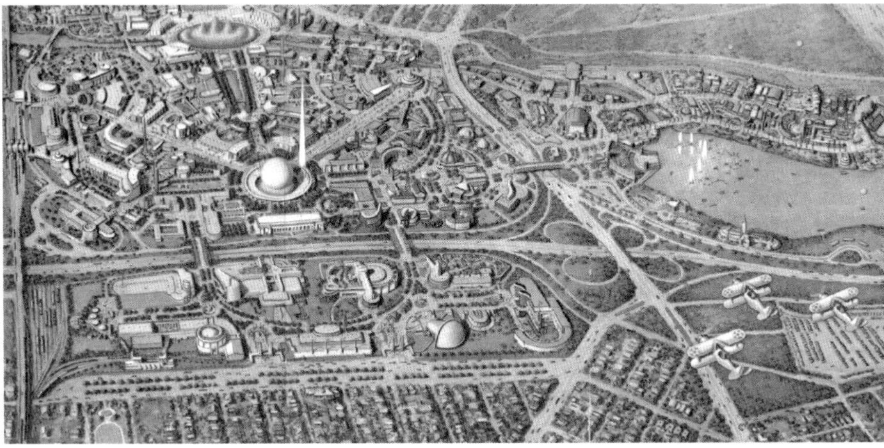

A map of the 1939 World's Fair. *Author's collection.*

the future would look like. To see an aerial view of the fairgrounds is to look at a small city filled with all kinds of buildings and plazas.

The focal point of the fair, the theme of which was "The World of Tomorrow," was the "Theme Center," consisting of a 610-foot-high obelisk-like tower called the Trylon and a 200-foot-diameter globe-like Perisphere, which sat together. According to the official guidebook, the Perisphere was eighteen stories high and its interior was twice the size of Radio City Music Hall. Inside was a display called Democracity, a miniature model of a futuristic city of one million people.

More than 250,000 rivets were used to create the Perisphere, which was made of six thousand pieces weighing between a few pounds and eighteen tons each. These were not intended to be permanent; the Perisphere, for example, was covered with two half-inch-thick layers of damp-proofed gypsum board nailed to wooden pieces that were in turn screwed into the steel system. The whole thing was painted white. Other buildings received the same gypsum treatment, with applied stucco for texture and a permanent appearance.

The 1939–40 New York World's Fair opened on April 30, 1939 (by design on the 150th anniversary of George Washington's inauguration in New York City), and closed on October 27, 1940. President Franklin Roosevelt said of the fair: "The New York World's Fair is a challenge to all Americans who believe in the destiny of this nation....[I]t will be a memorable and historic Fair, one that will influence our national life for many years to come."

At a glance, the statistics would seem to indicate a success, with twenty-five million visitors in the first season alone. In actuality, it would have taken fifty million visitors that first season in order to pay back the investors. Though the fair actually made a profit in its second year, with its twenty million visitors, that did not make up for the losses it suffered the first year.

It is fascinating to me that within a year or so, the entire world's fair complex was dismantled, including the Trylon and Perisphere, the very symbols of the '39 fair. They were taken completely apart, their steel going to the war effort. The pair of iconic structures live on forever in their depiction on countless postcards, dishes, paperweights and other knickknacks. The exceptions were very few: the Queens Museum building is the only building left from 1939, originally erected to house the New York City pavilion but intended all along to be a "permanent recreation building" and so constructed accordingly, as opposed to the temporary and flimsier materials of the rest of the fair. That, and the time capsule that was buried in 1939, are really the only tangible remnants of the first New York World's Fair. (The latter is unseen, fifty feet below the ground, though there is a marker to denote where it was buried.) Well, Meadow and Willow Lakes, man-made water bodies created for the fair, are still there, too, but it was easy enough just to leave them be. The Billy Rose Aquacade, one of the 1939 fair's star attractions and part of the New York State Pavilion, was used for a few decades and actually survived into the 1990s, when it was demolished after years of sitting abandoned and forlorn.

You'd think that, given the fair's financial state as the closing day approached, the investors and the local government would have discussed a way to keep at least some of these exhibits running past the closing date and make a little more money. But, nope, that never happened. Just a few years after the last guests passed through the gates, you could walk around the site, and it was like the 1939 World's Fair had never happened. (The site was slated to become a city park, which it did, after World War II.) The New York City Pavilion building did have one important historical function; it served as the temporary headquarters for the United Nations General Assembly. A proposal by Robert Moses to have the UN permanently located in Flushing Meadows was rejected.

Fittingly, the vintage New York City pavilion building in its current role as the Queens Museum actually houses many relics and souvenirs from the '39 fair, preserved for all to see.

WORLD'S FAIR REDUX

Unlike its predecessor, the 1964–65 New York World's Fair left us a number of remnants. If you grew up in Queens, and especially if you drove on the Grand Central Parkway or the LIE often, you had a reminder of the 1964 fair every time you passed through. To me, the welcome sight of the New York Pavilion meant I was almost home after a sometimes very (very) late night working on the newspaper at college on Long Island. But back then, though I knew what I was looking at, I didn't really know. I didn't really know the whole story. I didn't know the hidden history. But I do now, and so will you.

The 1964–65 New York World's Fair opened on April 22, 1964. There had been plans for a massive "stall-in" on April 22 by the Brooklyn chapter of the Congress of Racial Equality. The bizarre idea was for motorists to purposely run out of gas on the highways leading to the fair and clog the roads so nobody could get there. Though it never happened, the very threat of it, along with inclement weather and other protests, cut the opening day attendance from an expected 250,000 to 92,000. There were actually demonstrators inside the fair, and they heckled during President Lyndon Johnson's speech at the Federal Pavilion.

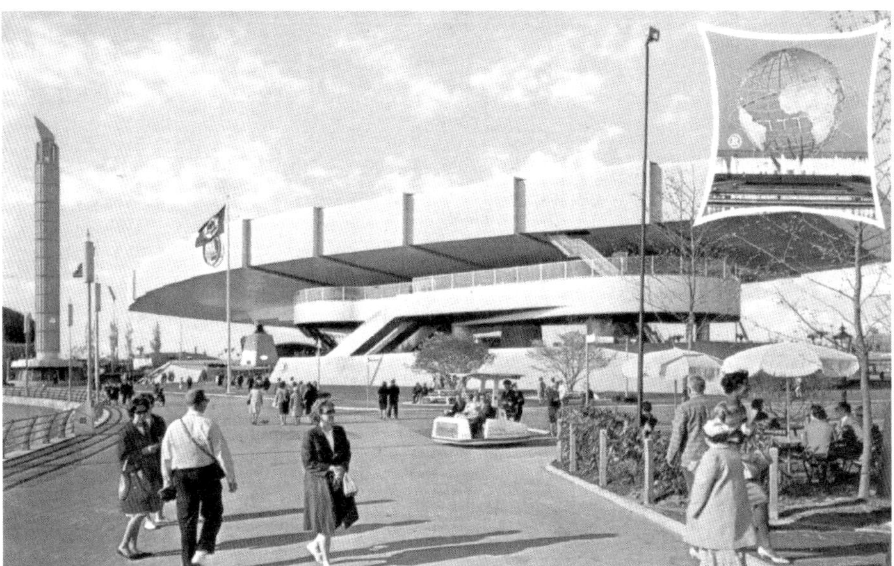

The Bell Telephone Pavilion at the 1964 World's Fair. *Author's collection.*

Of course, the '64 fair was meant to outdo the '39 event. If the 1939 fair was futuristic, the 1964 fair was even more ambitiously forward thinking. To put it into perspective, the whole thing looked like the set of *The Jetsons*. Many of the buildings and pavilions were saucer-shaped, soaring, light and aerodynamic. There were plenty of domes and arches. The centerpiece of all this modernity was the 900,000-pound steel Unisphere (called "the largest earth model in history" and built by U.S. Steel), which replaced the 1939 Perisphere on the same foundations. The Johnson Wax Pavilion, for example, featured a gold disk that it called "the Golden Rondelle" and that hovered 24 feet above the ground supported by six space-age columns that broadened into triangles and arch and met at the top. Coca-Cola had a 120-foot-high tower with a 610-bell carillon, the world's largest.

Even some of the lesser known and less exciting exhibitors had impressive future-minded structures; take SKF, a ball-bearing manufacturer that featured a circular roof that rose from its apex as an 82-foot-high needle. Futuristic sometimes met absurd; when trying to describe the displays, the results could be amusing. How about Schaefer Beer, whose pavilion was described as "roofed with air-filled plastic discs that look like huge pillows." There was IBM, whose pavilion featured a "startling white egg-shaped theater 90 feet high." And the award for best pavilion name goes to the "Festival of Gas," which was assembled by the gas industry to highlight… gas. As advanced as the fair was intended to be, some of the ads for exhibitors seem dated as times have changed. For example, "Meet me under the smoke rings at General Cigar's Hall of Magic!"

Despite all the modernity, the official sales pitch for the fair by Robert Moses, president of the World's Fair Corporation, was not modernity. He instead stressed its diversity and timelessness. This was the message he included in the official guidebook:

> *The Fair aims to be universal, to have something for everyone. What is it you want? Vast forces dormant in nuggets of imprisoned sunlight? Machines that fly, think, transport, fashion and do man's work? Spices, perfumes, ivory, apes and peacocks? Dead Sea Scrolls? Images divine and graven? Painted lilies and refined gold? The products of philosophy, which is the guide of life, and knowledge, which is power? We have them all. Study the fair. Come often. When you get here, don't rush. Be wise. Space your visits, save your arches, spare your muscles, use your head; patronize buses, rolling stock, rides, ramps and escalators; spot the oases and cultivate repose in the midst of multifarious activities.*

One thing was certain. This fair was enormous. There were eighty countries exhibiting, along with twenty-four states and New York City. The exhibits were extensive and immersive. For example, Belgium offered a reproduction of a Belgian village with one hundred houses, a church, a city hall, a canal and a bridge. The fairgrounds had 1,400 public telephones with "new" Touch Tone dialing, 60 mailboxes, 2,500 public lockers, 3,500 benches and parking lots with spaces for 20,000 cars. The 1964 season attracted 27,000,000 paying visitors, and there were 30,000 people employed during the fair.

Yet for all its vastness, most of the fair's structures, no matter how futuristic or ingenious, suffered the same fate as their earlier counterparts: dismantled, leaving no trace behind. It is hard to believe as you walk through Flushing Meadows–Corona Park that this used to be the site of hundreds of impressive buildings. A total of 250,000 tons of steel were used to create the world's fair, but just a small fraction of that is left behind. Also gone now is Shea Stadium, which opened next door, the same year as the fair.

Come with me and explore the remains. Some are very obvious and others practically hidden. The Unisphere still stands in all its glory and remains a focal point of the park. Other remaining structures include the undulating concrete and glass Hall of Science, which was fully opened for the '65 fair season, and the badly decayed one-hundred-foot-high New York State Pavilion (designed by famous architect Philip Johnson) with its three towers and iconic elliptical ring. The roof of the ring was made from colorful fiberglass, but it was deemed unstable and removed in the 1970s. The structure is slated to get a $14 million renovation that will help stabilize and preserve it for future generations to behold (and to drive by on the highway).

There is also the imposing 120-foot-high Terrace on the Park building, which was originally the heliport for the fair. The profile of the building is a *T* for transportation. The building's roof, now used as a scenic lookout for catered weddings, was the 175-foot- by 200-foot landing pad. For $6.50, you could take off in a twin-engine Sikorsky S-61 helicopter and fly over the fair and "see [the] location of all exhibits, all points of interest."

The World's Fair Marina is still there, too. Built on Flushing Bay as a "boat basin" in 1939 and then expanded for 1964, it was intended to become permanent. More than two hundred million cubic yards of silt were removed from the bay during construction of the '64 fair to create the new and expanded version. It originally had 800 slips, down to about 250 now because of neglect and the silting in of some of the area.

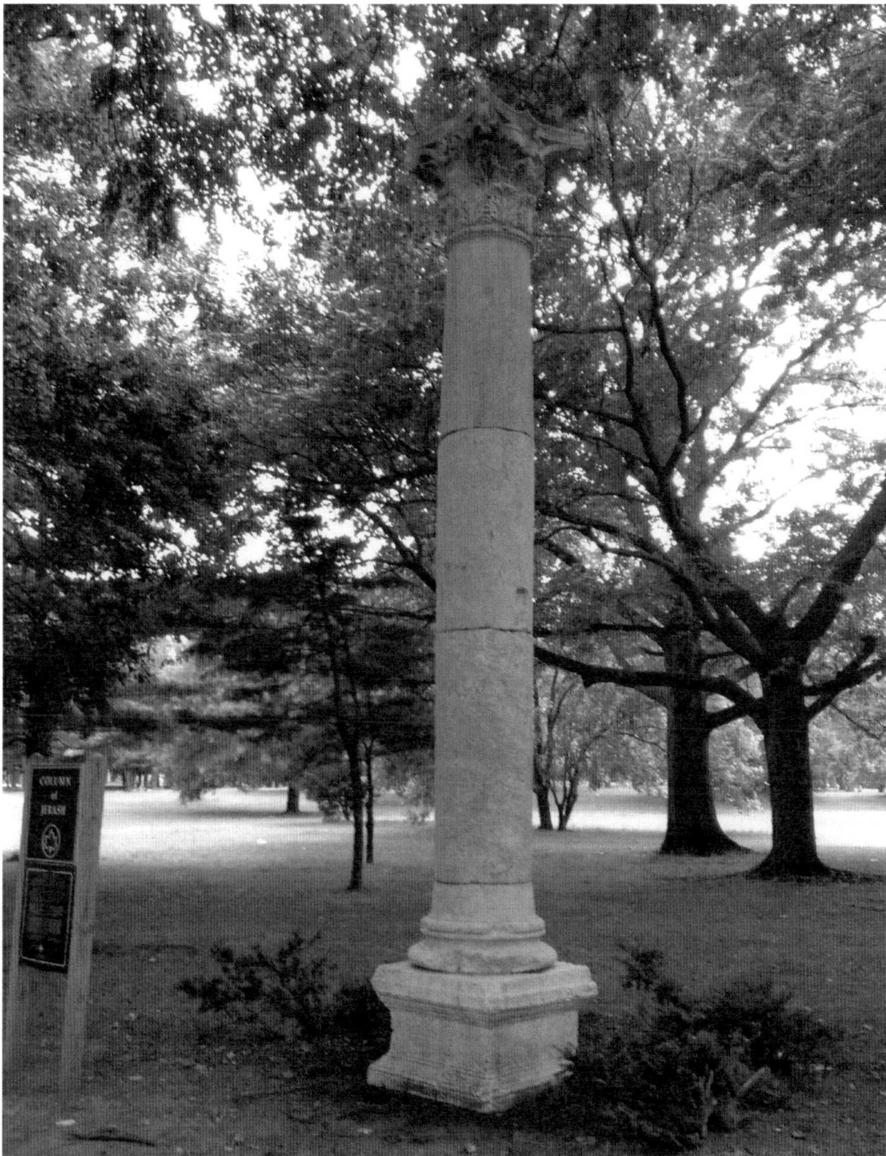

The Column of Jerash, a gift from the king of Jordan to the 1964 World's Fair, still stands in Flushing Meadows–Corona Park. *Author's collection.*

Walk around near the Unisphere, trace the nearby paths (which are original to the fair), and you will find treasures from the 1964 fair, such as several sculptures. There is the Column of Jerash, which was given to the world's fair and New York City by the king of Jordan. This valuable gift had been erected by the Romans in Jordan in AD 120 and now resides permanently in Flushing Meadows–Corona Park. The statue of George Washington is a bronze replica (1967) of a plaster version that stood at the Masonic Pavilion at the fair.

What else is left? There are fountains and reflecting pools that are also original, as well as even more mundane artifacts such as drinking fountains. Going to the park and looking for remnants of '64 can make for a fun day, a sort of world's fair treasure hunt.

Creedmoor Psychiatric Hospital

In 1909, the State Lunacy Commission (yes, it really was called that) decided that the former Creedmoor rifle range would be the perfect site for a mental hospital. It was a lot of open land and would be a good place to erect a complex of buildings. The real estate agents who had wanted to swoop in and buy the Creedmoor land quickly concocted another scheme, to buy options on farmland in Greenville (Greenvale, Nassau County), and they succeeded in obtaining options on about nine hundred acres of land at a price of about $1,500 per acre, arguing that this would be preferable, as it would allow the mental patients more room to exercise and work outdoors. Arguments were also made that the Creedmoor land was too valuable to be used as a mental hospital, so the governor next signed a bill that would allow the lunacy commission the power to exchange the Creedmoor site for some other site on Long Island.

A March 1909 newspaper headline proclaimed "Governor Said to Have Been Tricked by Local Politicians into Giving Up Creedmoor Range Location." This plan was met with opposition from some of the area's wealthiest citizens, whose estates were as close as a half mile away. Mrs. Clarence Mackay of Harbor Hill enlisted the aid of the Long Island Farmers' Club, which held a meeting in protest of the Long Island option. Residents declared that land values would drop by millions if the hospital was allowed to be built in Greenvale.

The Long Island plan fell through, and nothing was done for several years, despite the need for a new facility. In 1910, there were thirty-one thousand "insane" in the state and not enough room to house them. Ironically and tragically, it was after the range was abandoned that the most serious injury occurred; in 1912, a scene depicting a Civil War battle was staged at the old range and filmed by a motion picture company. The scene utilized four hundred off-duty soldiers from Fort Hamilton in Brooklyn. One of the men on set had a bag of explosives that he was to toss into the air every so often for effect. Everything went fine until a nearby boy threw a lit cigarette into the bag, causing an explosion that left the man in critical condition.

That same year, a "farm colony" of the Brooklyn State Hospital was finally opened at Creedmoor using the old rifle range buildings. In 1918, the State Hospital Development Commission reported to the state legislature that the Brooklyn State Hospital was badly overcrowded and that a new state hospital be built at Creedmoor, to accommodate 3,000 patients. By this time, there were already 150 patients being housed in the old barracks of the National Guard on the site of the former rifle range. The huge amount of $3 million was set aside for the new hospital, but at first there was a dispute over the intent of its use. The state wanted to use it to house ordinary patients, but the U.S. House of Representatives authorized the Treasury Department to take over and build a hospital exclusively for ex-servicemen.

The state won, and construction finally began. New buildings were constructed beginning in the 1920s to create a proper facility for housing mentally ill patients. By 1926, there were already calls for expanding the hospital property from 265 acres to 465 acres. By 1929, there were more than one thousand patients on the campus, and by 1933, more than three thousand. By 1943, there were sixty-seven buildings on the campus of 327 acres.

Creedmoor was not without problems. Through the years, there were allegations of mistreatment of patients. In 1935, a young male patient died in Creedmoor; an autopsy revealed that his death had been caused by a blow to the abdomen. A few weeks later, a twenty-eight-year-old woman died at Creedmoor; upon examination, the cause was revealed to be that her skull was crushed by a heavy, blunt instrument. That same year, an eighteen-year-old girl died from burns and shock after being in a tub of scalding hot water.

By 1943, there were 4,500 patients at Creedmoor and growing concerns about conditions there. There were many rumors floating around, so that year, a New York state senator from Kew Gardens visited Creedmoor incognito, in raggy clothes, and spent three hours there. The conditions he found were so abysmal that he immediately filed a report with Governor Thomas Dewey. The governor in turn ordered an investigation into conditions at Creedmoor. An epidemic of amoebic dysentery had been raging at the hospital. In fact, between 1938 and 1943, there were 103 cases of the disease with eleven fatalities. At the time of the 1943 investigation, there were 53 active cases and 32 carriers in the hospital, 37 of whom were food handlers. It was such a big deal at the time that in one *Long Island Daily Press* edition, the main front-page headline was "Rommel Retreats to Sea," followed by a smaller headline, "Epidemic Sweeps through Creedmoor Hospital." The investigation resulted in a shake-up at the hospital.

The most famous patient at Creedmoor was the beloved folk singer Woody Guthrie, who was briefly a resident during the tail end of his fifteen-year battle with the mentally and physically debilitating Huntington's disease. He died there in 1967.

With the advent of medication to treat mental illness in the 1950s, the population of Creedmoor began to decline as fewer people required institutionalization. Many of the original buildings fell into disuse over

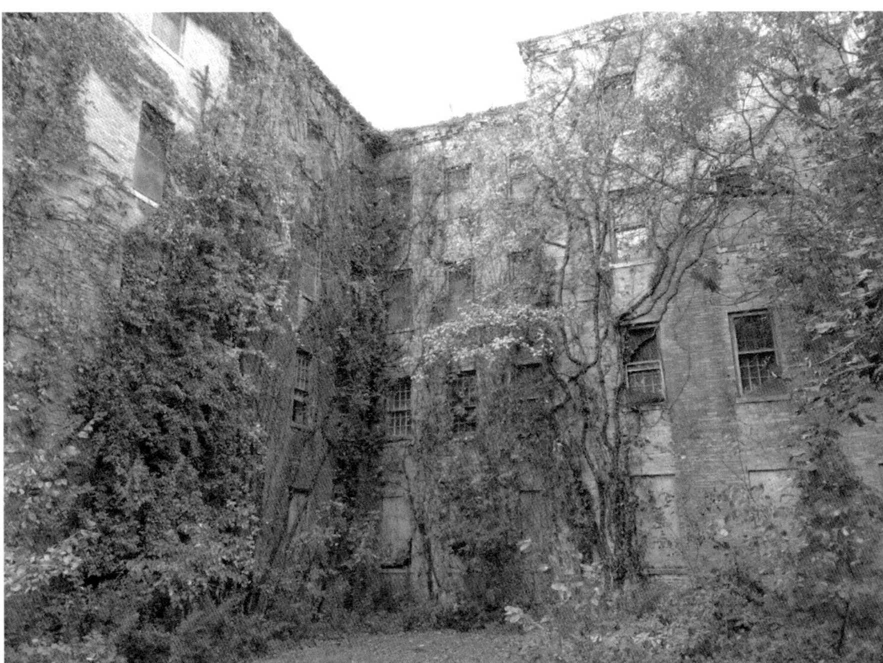

Many of the buildings on the old Creedmoor Psychiatric campus are abandoned. *Author's collection.*

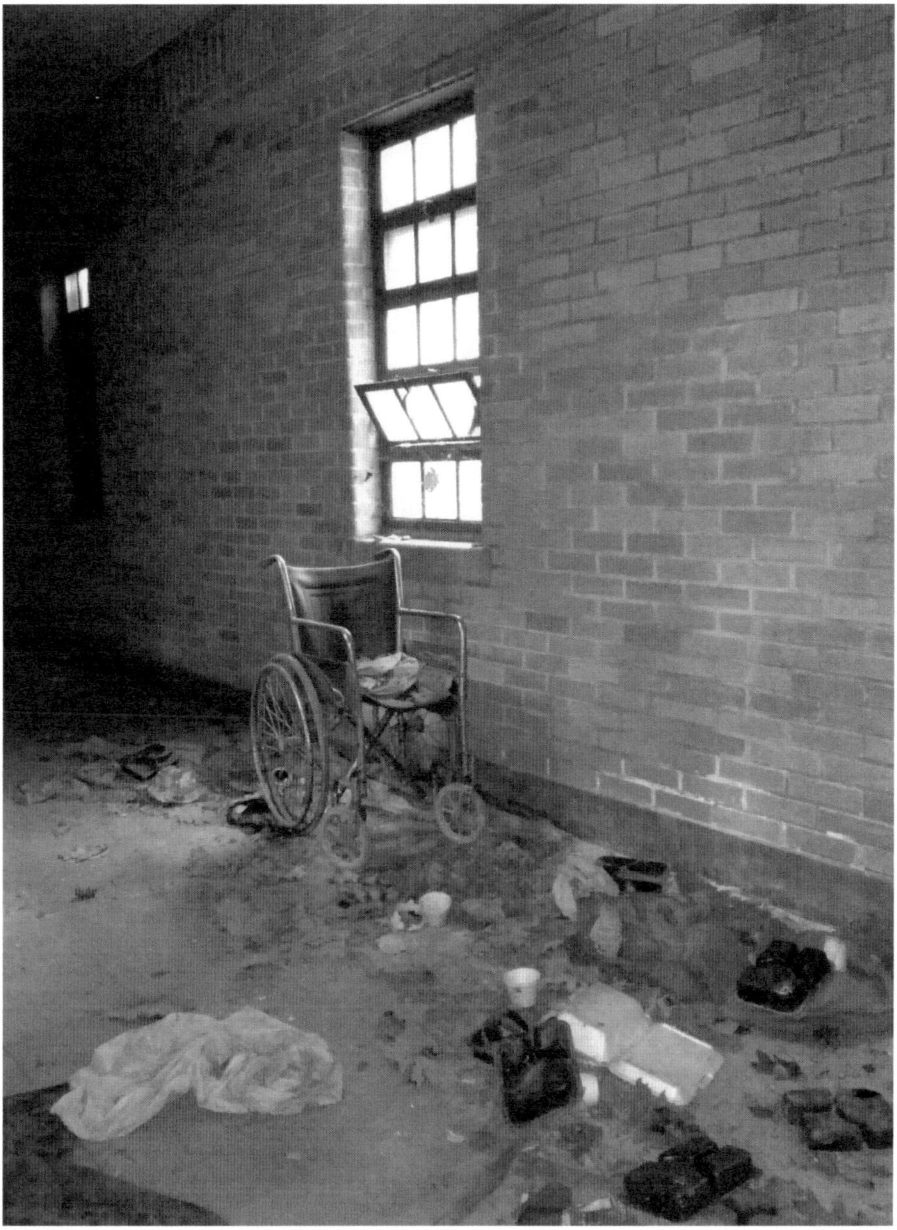

Inside the abandoned Creedmoor buildings are eerie scenes. *Author's collection.*

the years. Though the Creedmoor Psychiatric Center still exists today, its patients are housed in a massive high-rise building (clearly visible from the Grand Central Parkway) that was erected in 1959.

As for the old Creedmoor campus, it is a fascinating and eerie place—not because it is abandoned, but because it is partially abandoned. Many of the old buildings are being reused by state agencies such as the New York State Dormitory Authority, but they sit adjacent to or across from completely abandoned ones. Wandering around the Creedmoor campus (it's open to the public—the automobile entrance is on Winchester Boulevard, but there is a way for pedestrians to get in from Hillside Avenue, too) makes for a thoroughly creepy and rewarding experience. There has been much buzz about the infamous Building 25 (just one of many abandoned buildings), which has been a favorite with urban explorers in recent years. One of the days I wandered around Building 25, I heard footsteps behind me and tensed up, but it was just some kids who were also there to explore.

Though some enjoy getting inside the building, I was satisfied just to peek through one of the broken windows and see the spine-tingling sight of an abandoned wheelchair sitting there. For me, the most eerie scenes can be found on the exterior—from the ivy-covered walls to the partly obscured carved stone details at the building entrances. One minute you're among the neatly parked cars of state employees who are working in a refurbished building nearby, and the next you are walking amid an overgrown, abandoned landscape that is hauntingly silent.

A LITTLE PAINT REVEALS HIDDEN HISTORY

Some hidden history is hidden literally in plain sight. There are plenty of things New Yorkers pass on a daily basis without even realizing their age or significance. And when I was walking in Woodside one day, it hit me. Hard. Standing in front of me was one of those ubiquitous fire call boxes that are all over the city—yes, those red structures we think nothing of. But this one had been recently painted, and boy was it beautiful! It had been restored to a brilliance that made its vintage beauty stand out. Suddenly I was seeing a fire call box again for the first time after having walked past similar ones for years and years. I found myself standing in front of it, taking photos and admiring the details. It turns out that there's a security guard from Queens named John Colgan who has been restoring these call boxes by the dozens, lifting them from their rusty graffiti-filled existences and repainting them lustrous shades of red and gold. Not only did the restoration make the call box pop, it also made it look its age—much the way an old house actually looks older when it is restored; truly vintage would be the more accurate way to say it. According to Colgan, many of the oldest fire call boxes date to 1913, 1921 or 1932.

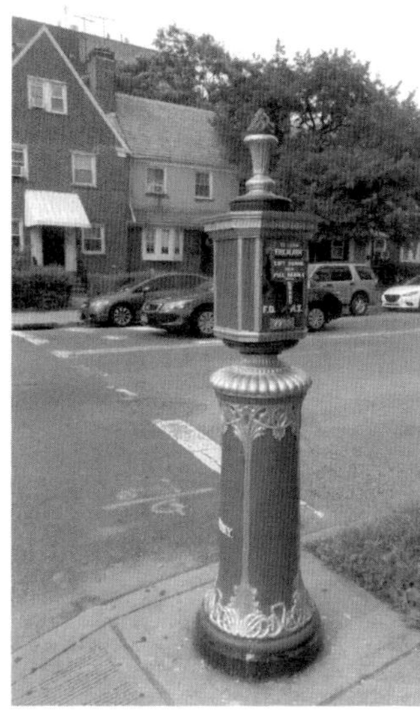

A recently restored fire call box. *Author's collection.*

A little more research revealed that there are about fifteen thousand of these call boxes throughout the city. Some are truly vintage, like the one shown here (in the vicinity of one hundred years old); others are more recent (but still pretty old), red with a domed top. Though in my newly opened eyes they are attractive and historic, they cost the city almost $7 million a year in maintenance, and the statistics tell the real story. Only about 3 percent of fires in the city are reported through call boxes, and 86 percent of the fire department calls that are made using the boxes are actually false alarms. When the City of New York wanted to get rid of these call boxes in 2011, arguing that they were obsolete with the prevalence of cell phones, a deaf-rights group sued, and a judge sided with the group, saying the boxes had to stay. And stay they will until someone goes through a lot of trouble to remove them—the oldest of these weigh about nine hundred pounds each!

OCTAGON BE GONE!

In my book *Hidden History of Long Island*, I talk about an octagonal building with an interesting history, and as it turns out, I am featuring one here, since there is an octagonal beauty in Queens that fits the bill. As I drove north on Woodhaven Boulevard one day, the attractive building on the corner of Woodhaven Boulevard and Park Lane South (formerly Ashland Street) caught my eye. I pulled over to take a closer look at the Beaux-Arts building that stands on the southeastern corner of Forest Park. As I approached, I saw that the lettering on the façade read "Fire Alarm Telegraph Station" and was intrigued. I knew I had to do a little digging to figure out what that meant. In the process, I uncovered the interesting story of how the building came to be.

The building was erected to serve as a command center for receiving fire calls from fire boxes throughout Queens. The previous location was for years crammed into the basement of the old wooden Jamaica Town Hall, and it was badly outdated, containing only twenty circuits, not nearly enough to handle the planned increase in call boxes to make Queens more fire-safe. The goal of a new building was to allow greater speed and efficiency in dispatching fire trucks when an alarm went out. Incoming signals from fire-alarm boxes would be received within, and the fire companies to be called out would be immediately signaled from the operating room.

The original plans for the building were created by the city's public works architects and approved around 1924. By this time, new fire alarm telegraph buildings had been opened in Manhattan (1922) and the Bronx

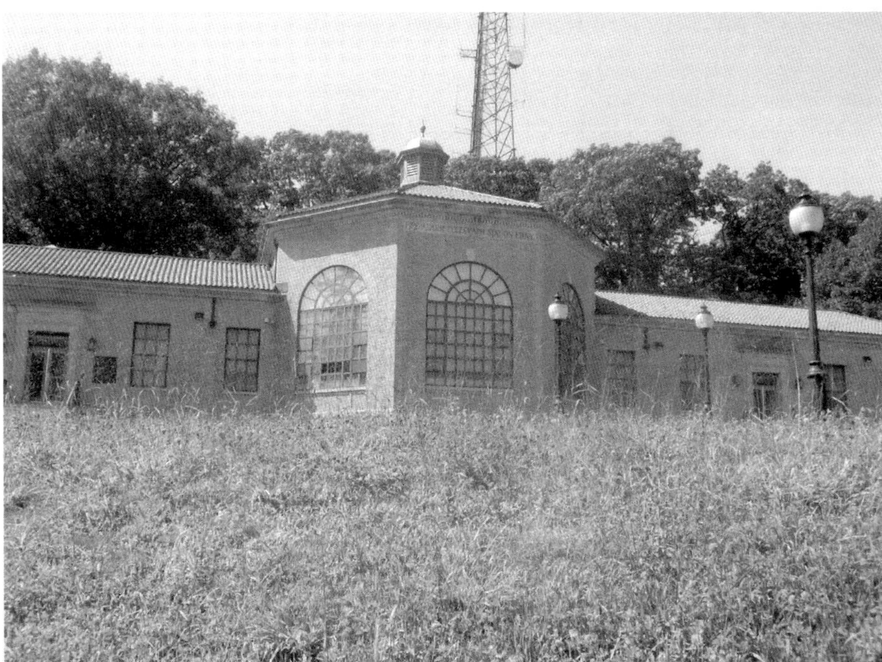

The Woodhaven Fire Command Station met with opposition at first but was eventually embraced by the community. *Author's collection.*

and Brooklyn (1923). It was Queens' turn. The octagonal, buff-colored, brick, one-story building was set to be constructed at Myrtle Avenue and 109th Street in Richmond Hill when a real estate developer led the successful charge against that location. Instead, a site on the edge of Forest Park in Woodhaven was chosen.

In early October 1925, the contractor broke ground at the Woodhaven site, and the local residents held a protest meeting at the American Legion clubhouse. The community was worried the fire alarm building's design would not be in keeping with the architecture of Forest Park. One suggestion was to place it deeper within the park, in a more hidden location. An editorial in the local *Leader-Observer* newspaper explained, "If a fire alarm telegraph station is distasteful to residents of Richmond Hill, there is no reason why Woodhaven should be forced to accommodate it, particularly in one of the most attractive sections of Forest Park….City parks are for recreation purposes and should not be desecrated by unsightly buildings."

The citizens of Woodhaven decided to send a delegation of five prominent residents to meet with Queens Borough President Maurice Connolly and Public Works Commissioner Michael Shugrue to try to dissuade them from using the Forest Park site. When the delegation got to Connolly's office, he was not around, so they met with Shugrue, who promised to do what he could to prevent the building from being constructed. Soon after, the delegation received a letter from the borough president that read, "I am glad to inform you that the Fire Commissioner promised me that he would hold up all further work upon the construction of this building, and that in the meantime he would endeavor to secure a site which would be free from objection."

Then came Election Day, and Connolly won reelection and then went off to Bermuda. At a board of estimate meeting on November 20, the site was mentioned and quickly approved, even though it was not on the meeting agenda for the day. Work started at the site the very next day. The residents of Woodhaven were taken by surprise; they were sure they had won their fight to get the building moved. When they explored their options, they discovered that an injunction would be too costly to obtain and gave up their fight. The *Leader-Observer* called out Connolly for this post-election "brazen disregard for the welfare and wishes of the citizens of the borough he is supposed to represent."

By 1926, there were signs that the locals were coming around. An article in the *Jamaica Daily Farmer* spun the building in a different light: "A civic structure of real beauty will grace this corner then. It will be set well back from the street, on the crest of a terraced and landscaped slope. Steps will lead from the sidewalk through the gardens in a semicircle to doors in the two wings which will branch out from each side of the center of the building, topped by a handsome dome and cupula. Trees, shrubs and lawns will add to the attractiveness of the structure."

By June 1927, the building and landscaping were seemingly complete, but then someone realized that telegraph cables had to be laid, so the surrounding streets were dug up for weeks, once again riling up the neighbors. Even with that work done, untold delays continued, and it was almost another year and a half before the building finally opened. The building had one hundred new box circuits to provide the capacity for two thousand extra call boxes in Queens. There was a battery room, a generating room and an operating room that was itself three times the size of the entire old fire telegraph station in Jamaica. The building also had a washroom, telephone wire room, mess hall, the commanding officer's office and a locker room/workshop.

When opening ceremonies were finally held for the $135,000 building in November 1928 in front of a crowd of five hundred people, it was proclaimed the "best fire headquarters in N.Y" by the *Jamaica Long Island Daily Press*, which also called it "one of the greatest if not the greatest of its kind in the country." The fire commissioner was even bolder in his assessment of the facility; in his opening day speech, he said it was the finest of its type in the world and could last for one hundred years if it had to. A representative of the local chamber of commerce said on this occasion that they were proud to have the building, a marked change from a few years prior.

The idea of a central command fire station still makes sense, and the building is still in use today.

Remnants of Industrial Glory

Though Long Island City was formed in 1870 as a conglomeration of local communities along the East River in Queens, after Queens became part of New York City in 1898, Long Island City was no longer a "city" so to speak; no longer did it elect its own mayor. Some of the once-separate communities that had joined together to become Long Island City lost their identities (Ravenswood and Dutch Kills, for example), but others retained theirs and do to this day (Astoria and Sunnyside). But Long Island

City itself did not disappear with the consolidation of Queens into New York City. No, Long Island City maintained a separate identity, in part because it was already by then such an important manufacturing center, a place name that had significance.

As I mentioned in an earlier section, its frontage along both the East River and Newtown Creek drew many heavy industries to Long Island City. But the proximity to water was not the only reason for its popularity with industry. By the 1890s, Long Island City was the railroad center of the borough, with Long Island Railroad yards located there. The Pennsylvania Railroad opened Sunnyside Yard in Long Island City in 1910, another factor that aided in growth. Rail spurs off the tracks meant that train cars could be loaded and unloaded practically at the back door of many factories.

Further still, word of upcoming transportation improvements such as a planned bridge over the East River and a tunnel to Long Island City from Manhattan was a boon to speculators. A report in the *New York Times* in March 1906 said that "even six months ago it was almost impossible to get anyone to consider buying in Long Island City. Since that time, almost $10,000,000 worth of property there has changed hands."

In 1909, the Queensboro Bridge (originally known as the Blackwell's Island Bridge) finally opened, providing an easy and direct link between Manhattan and Long Island City. This was a huge boon to Long Island City, and after the bridge opened, land prices increased by as much as 1,000 percent. Originally a toll bridge, the city abolished its tolls in 1911, making Queens an even more popular destination for businesses. In 1910, the Long Island Rail Road opened tunnels into Queens that passed through Long Island City, and in 1915, when the subway first extended into Queens, there was a celebration attended by thousands of people. Many local manufacturers gave their employees a half day off so they could attend.

Between 1909 and 1913, more than three hundred offices, factories and warehouses opened in Long Island City. By 1913, there were twenty thousand people employed there. Thanks to Long Island City's growth, by 1909, Queens was ranked seventh in the nation among industrial centers. Now the kind of businesses that were moving to Long Island City were not just noxious and toxic ones such as oil works and varnish factories. Manufacturers of consumer products were setting up shop, and they were not in waterfront factories, they were in attractive buildings located along main roads in Long Island City such as Vernon Boulevard and Thomson

Avenue. By 1913, you could find the Steinway Piano Factory, the National Enameling and Stamping Company and the Loose Wiles Biscuit Factory, which erected a ten-story building and employed two thousand people to make more than five hundred kinds of cakes and crackers, the largest biscuit manufacturing plant in the country.

The American Chicle Company opened a factory at 30-30 Thomson Avenue in 1919 (a good year for Long Island City; more than eighty new factories opened there in 1919 alone). Name not sounding familiar? Well, they are better known to most as the makers of Chiclets gum. The raw chicle was stored on the roof, where it could be sprayed to keep it moist. The company also made Dentyne, and Chiclets and Dentyne signs used to grace the top of the building. A 1919 American Chicle advertisement in a local newspaper sought "girls and women" to "learn to operate machines, wrapping chewing gum, clean, interesting work." The starting salary for trainees was twelve dollars a week with a one-dollar attendance bonus,

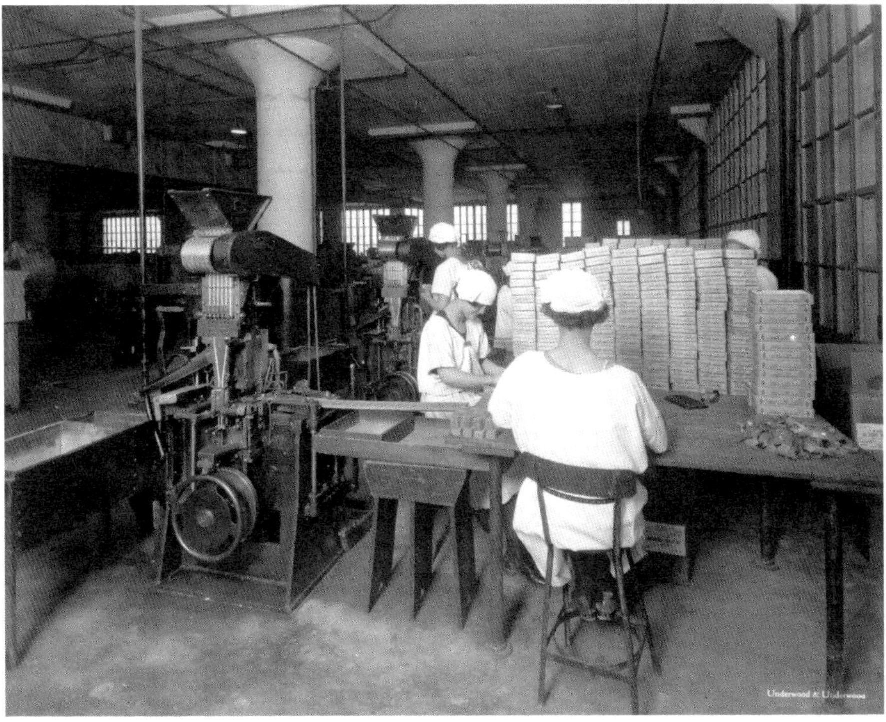

American Chicle Company workers in the Long Island City factory, 1923. *Library of Congress.*

with experienced operators making between eighteen dollars and twenty-five dollars a week. Local factory teams played lunchtime volleyball on the roof of the Chicle building and other factory buildings. American Chicle took chewing gum research seriously. By 1950, it had a director of research, a chief chemist, five chemists, two engineers and a one-thousand-volume library.

The bridge across the East River helped the automobile industry become one of the biggest in Long Island City. There were numerous factories, showrooms and service stations that attracted motorists from all across the tri-state region. As of 1914, 2,500 men were employed in Long Island City's automotive service industry. The Harrolds Motor Car Company, the local distributors of Pierce-Arrow cars, had a four-story building that could accommodate five hundred cars at a time located on Thirty-Eighth Avenue (the building is still there). The Galvin Building, just south of the Queensboro Bridge, housed three automotive service stations—Renault, Maxwell and Benz. The General Vehicle Company manufactured seventy-five electric-powered Mercedes trucks per month from its five-building plant in Long Island City.

The eight-story Packard service building on Queens Boulevard not only handled repairs to about sixty automobiles per day, it also provided storage space for Packard owners who might bring their hardtop cars in to storage for the summer (when driving such small-windowed, non–air conditioned, dark-painted vehicles would be a very hot experience) and their open touring cars in for the winter.

The Ford Motor Company had a factory that expanded from four stories to nine stories within a few years of opening in 1911. In 1913, the Queens Ford plant was turning out 25 automobiles per day (the number rose to 50 by 1914) from parts that were shipped from Detroit and assembled in Long Island City. This approach actually was ingenious and saved Ford a bundle of cash. Shipping fully assembled automobiles for New York–area customers would have cost far more. A shipment of 350 cars (in parts) occupied 21 freight cars, versus 116 freight cars it would take to ship the finished cars to New York.

Aside from whole cars, there were also tire service and manufacturing buildings owned by Goodyear (Jackson Avenue and Honeywell Street) and the Akron Tire Company (Honeywell Street and Skillman Avenue), as well as a wheel manufacturer that made fifty thousand wheels per year.

In 1928, it was said that of the 2,000 industries in Queens, 1,500 of them were located in Long Island City. Aside from factories, there were

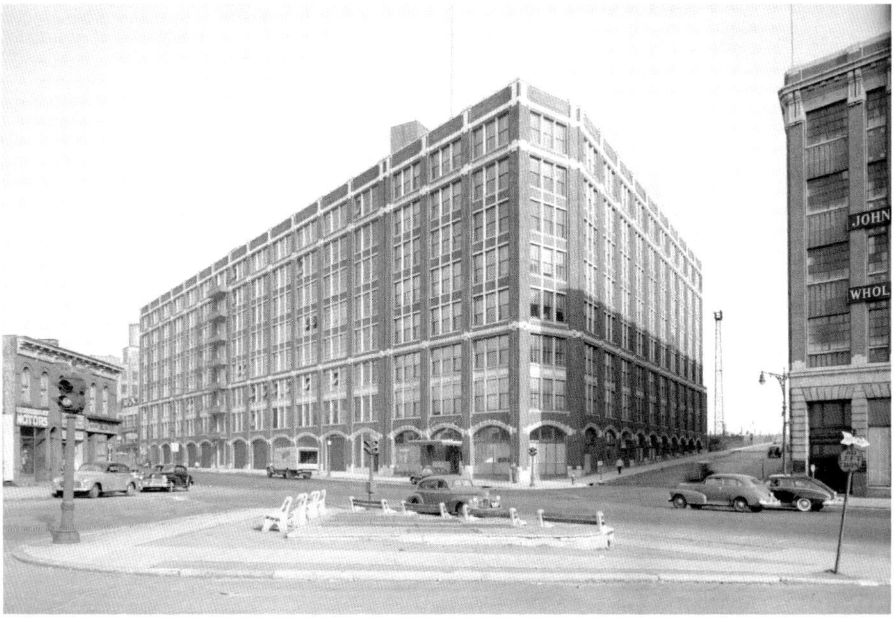

The E.R. Squibb & Son building in Long Island City, 1948. *Library of Congress.*

plenty of warehouses, where large department stores such as Macy's and Bloomingdales could store inventory. The National Sugar Company refining plant, which had opened around the turn of the twentieth century, was by 1931 on a twenty-seven-acre site and could refine four million pounds of sugar per day.

As late as 1967, Long Island City still contained 65 percent of the city's industrial plants, but things were going downhill fast. Companies were closing or relocating. Long Island City began to undergo a transformation in the 1980s and came back to life. While some of the old factory buildings no longer exist, many do and are quite aesthetically pleasing, with some nice architectural touches ranging from Gothic to Art Deco. Some are still factories and warehouses, while others have been repurposed. The old is mingled with the new; in 1989, the 658-foot-high Citicorp Building—a startlingly tall building that seemed like a forlorn outcast from Manhattan's skyline—was erected on Courthouse Square.

The old five- and ten-story factory and warehouse buildings were purchased by new owners and repurposed. LaGuardia Community College is housed in the International Design Center building, whose red rooftop "IDCNY" sign is a familiar sight to Long Island Railroad and 7-line subway users who pass by every day. The structure used to be the Loose Wiles Biscuit Company building (aka, the Sunshine Bakery). The Pierce-Arrow building had a string of owners after Pierce-Arrow went bankrupt in the 1930s, most recently being used by Studio 34, a community of artists. The Chiclet factory closed in 1981 and later became the headquarters for the New York City School Construction Authority and the Department of Design and Construction.

One of the best-known Long Island City icons was not a building but a sign that dated to the 1950s. Originally the Speed Fastener Company, Swingline started in 1925 and was located on Northern Boulevard before moving to a new and bigger factory at 32-01 Queens Boulevard in 1951. The giant 110-foot-long neon Swingline Stapler sign on the roof (circa 1952) was a Queens landmark for almost fifty years. After the factory closed in 1998, the sign came down…but the building is still there.

Chapter 7
Final Resting Places

The living population of Queens is far outnumbered by the population that lies six feet beneath its surface. I well recall all the cemeteries that I encountered as a kid growing up in Queens. There were two venerable burying grounds in my hometown of Elmhurst, those of the old Dutch Reformed Church and St. James Episcopal Church. There was peaceful Maple Grove on Queens Boulevard in Kew Gardens, where my grandfather was buried. There was also Calvary Cemetery, along Queens Boulevard in Woodside, hidden and mysterious behind its stone wall. And there were the cemeteries I used to pass on frequent trips to the old TSS department store at the Metro Mall in Middle Village: Mount Olivet Cemetery and the Lutheran Cemetery. And I remember my grandmother describing the headstone in St. Michael's in Astoria that marked the spot where her grandparents were interred and how it had fallen over.

The earliest cemeteries in Queens were churchyards, town burying grounds and private family cemeteries. As the nineteenth century progressed, Manhattan's population was growing rapidly, and more space was needed to bury the dead. In 1847, New York State's Rural Cemetery Act was passed, allowing nonprofit organizations to establish commercial cemeteries and benefit from the selling of plots. Because of this act, large, sprawling cemeteries began to spring up on open land in western Queens, the first of which was Calvary Cemetery, created in 1848. The massive Calvary has three million burials, the most of any cemetery in the entire

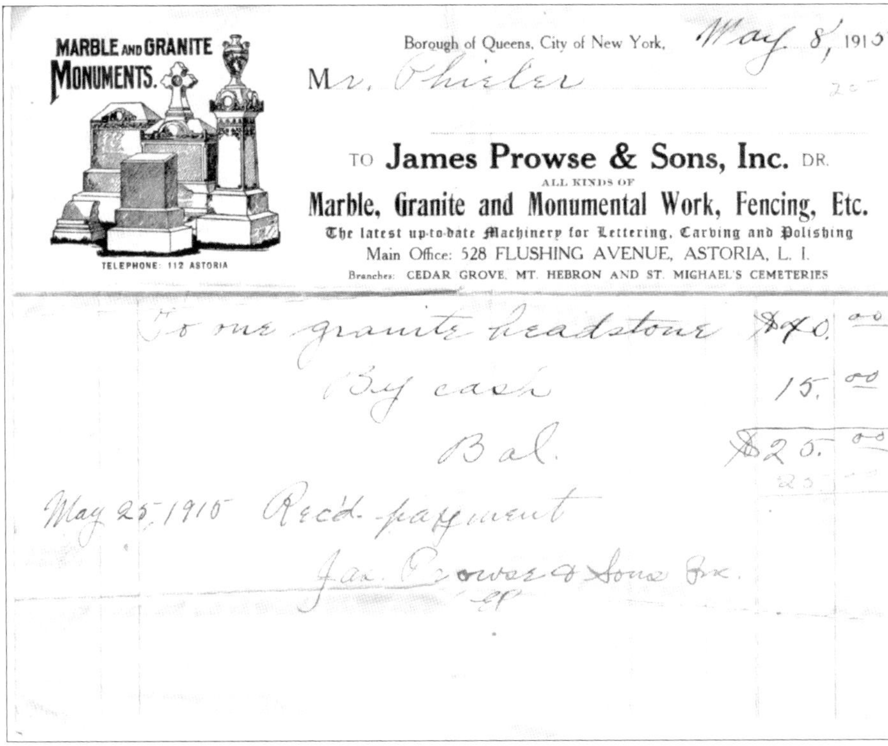

MARBLE AND GRANITE MONUMENTS.

TELEPHONE: 112 ASTORIA

Borough of Queens, City of New York, May 8, 1915

Mr. Phisler

TO James Prowse & Sons, Inc. DR.

ALL KINDS OF

Marble, Granite and Monumental Work, Fencing, Etc.

The latest up-to-date Machinery for Lettering, Carving and Polishing

Main Office: 528 FLUSHING AVENUE, ASTORIA, L. I.

Branches: CEDAR GROVE, MT. HEBRON AND ST. MICHAEL'S CEMETERIES

To one granite headstone	$40.00
By cash	15.00
Bal.	$25.00

May 25, 1915 Rec'd. payment

Jas. Prowse & Sons Inc.

A receipt for a granite headstone from an Astoria memorial company, 1915. *Author's collection.*

country. The Lutheran Cemetery in Middle Village and St. Michael's in Astoria followed in 1852, as did many others in the decades after. In this chapter, we'll explore the hidden history behind some of Queens' many cemeteries.

PROSPECT CEMETERY

The oldest cemetery in Queens was for decades also the most neglected. Located in the heart of old Jamaica village, Prospect Cemetery was founded in 1665 as the town burial ground. The first mention of it was in a record of the November 5, 1668 Jamaica town meeting, where it was agreed that John Wascot was to build a fence around the burial ground and would be paid four pounds for his efforts if he got it done by March of the following year.

Located just south of the Long Island Rail Road tracks, the Prospect Cemetery sits adjacent to the remains of St. Monica's Church and the York College campus. The earliest surviving stone dates to 1709. The names in the cemetery are like a roadmap to Jamaica's history—literally. The Sutphins, Van Wycks and Merricks all have roads in Jamaica named after them. Among those buried there are Elias Baylis, chairman of the Jamaica Revolutionary Committee; Amos Denton, another member of the committee; and his son Amos, a Revolutionary War soldier. More than fifty Revolutionary War soldiers are buried in the cemetery. Also in Prospect is Egbert Benson (1746–1833), who was New York State's first attorney general and also a New York State Supreme Court justice. He represented New York in the Continental Congress and was elected to the first U.S. Congress in 1789.

The most visually impressive feature of the cemetery did not even exist until the mid-nineteenth century. In 1856, Nicholas Ludlam, a longtime Jamaica resident, purchased three acres of land to enlarge the cemetery to what was then Prospect Street (now 159th Street). He built a Romanesque Revival stone chapel with two stained-glass rose windows (at a cost of about

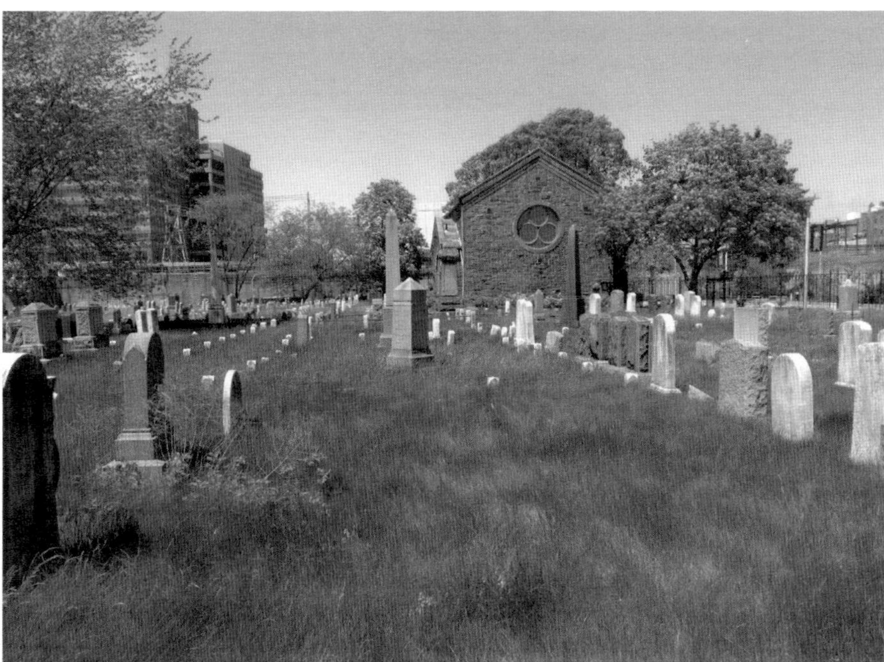

The Prospect Cemetery is the oldest in Queens, but for years it was badly neglected. *Author's collection.*

$4,000) on the eastern edge of the cemetery in remembrance of his three deceased daughters. His intent was not purely personal; the Chapel of the Sisters was to be used as a place of reflection and commemoration for any Prospect Cemetery funeral.

By the twentieth century, the cemetery was already overgrown and showing signs of neglect. A 1910 book about the cemetery said, "It is sad to record that many old stones have been used to form a walk and new graves are being made over the old ones."

Prospect Cemetery was designated as a New York City Landmark in 1977. The last burial at Prospect was in 1988, and conditions continued to get worse. A *Queens Courier* heading in 1988 said it with a pun: "Historic Graveyard in Mortifying Shape." By the turn of the twenty-first century, Prospect Cemetery had become completely overgrown, and three thousand of its gravestones had been damaged by the elements or vandalism. In 1999, the Landmarks Conservancy of New York began a fifteen-year project to give the cemetery some love and restore the beautiful stone Chapel of the Sisters (at a cost of $700,000).

GRACE CEMETERY

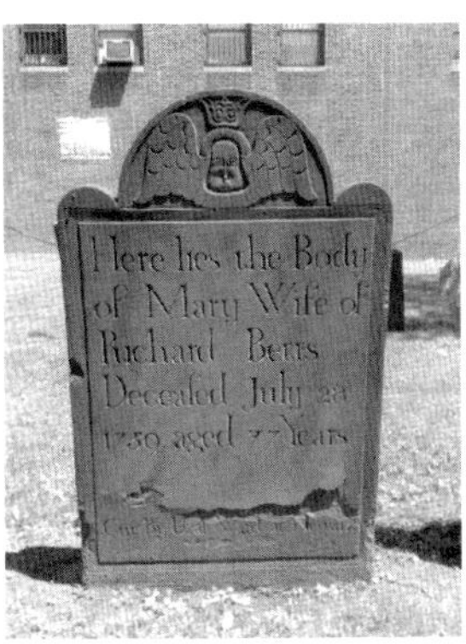

The Grace Church Cemetery has numerous stones dating to the eighteenth century. *Author's collection.*

One of New York City's oldest cemeteries is tucked away in the heart of downtown Jamaica, next to the 1862 Gothic-style Grace Episcopal Church on Jamaica Avenue (the third iteration of that church on the site). As a rule, never let the date of a church fool you as to the age of its associated cemetery. Fires were common in those days, and many churches were rebuilt a few times while the original ancient cemetery remained intact.

Wander through the cemetery, and you are instantly transported back in time. Rufus King, signer of the Constitution and Jamaica resident (he lived across the street, and his home still stands today), is buried at Grace Cemetery, as is his son John Alsop King, governor of New York from 1857 to 1859. Other important New Yorkers

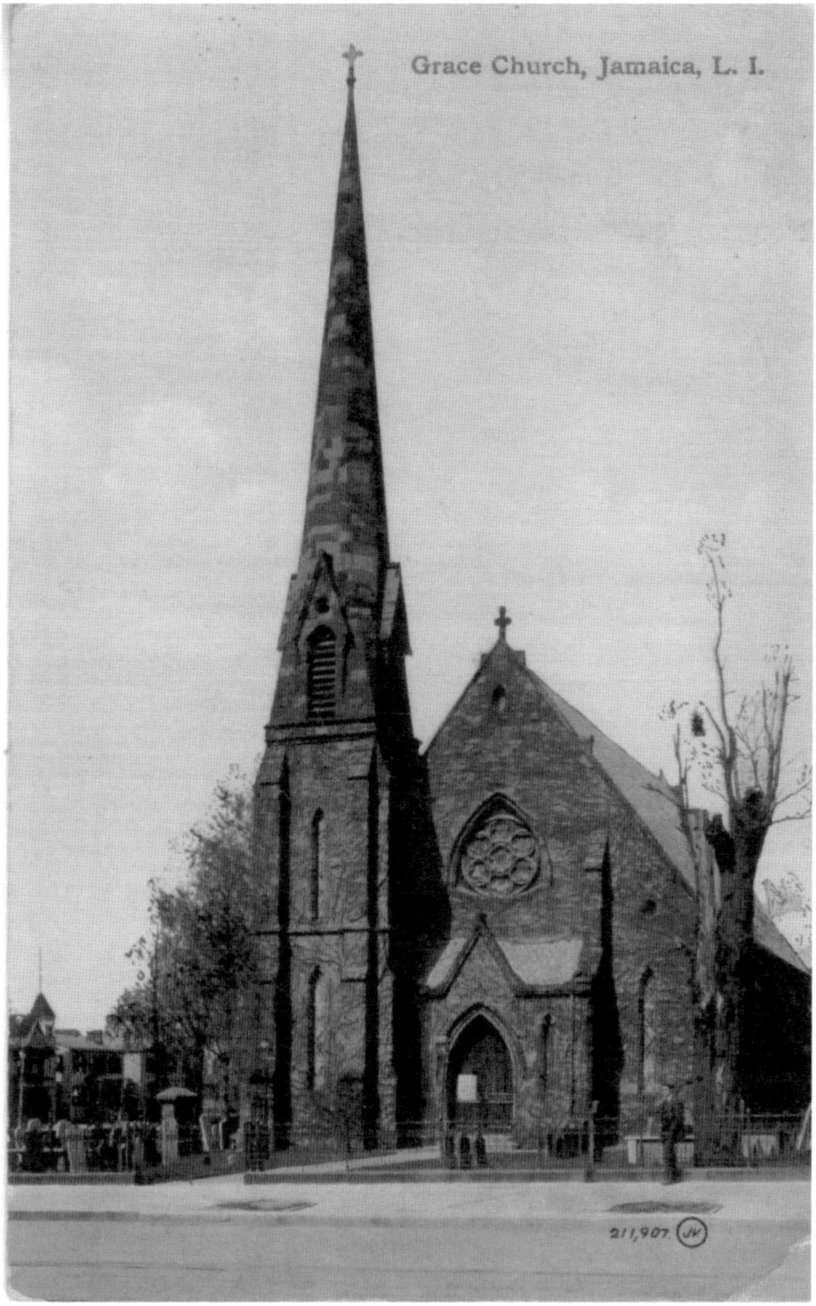

An early twentieth-century postcard showing Grace Church and cemetery in Jamaica. *Author's collection.*

are here, too, such as Cadwallader Colden, mayor of New York City from 1818 to 1821. The gravestones date from the early eighteenth century to the twentieth century, with the older ones toward the front of the church. Many are faded and hard to read, but there are several fine examples of eighteenth-century stones, with a variety of cherub heads. Some stones have poems. Here are three I found when I visited:

> *1738: External bliss shall innocence enjoy, & endless pleasures which can never cloy / while here entombed a virtuous youth doth rest / in certain hoped of being completely blessed.*
>
> *1749: Into thy courts O Lord she fled / Through the dark mansions of the dead / Within thy palace now she's fixt / In joys celestial and unmixed.*
>
> *1780: Thy Christian race is run / a glorious prize she now has won / with angelic host she's fix'd / In joys celestial and unmixed.*

THREE MOORE CEMETERIES

The Moore family of Newtown was one of the most prominent in Queens between the seventeenth and nineteenth centuries. Not only were the Moores credited with growing the first Newtown Pippin, a world-famous apple that was favored by Benjamin Franklin, George Washington and Thomas Jefferson (and currently used to make the juice in Martinelli brand apple juice), but one of their descendants was also none other than Clement Clarke Moore, the author of the Christmas poem.

There are at least three cemeteries in Queens associated with the family. Two of them are in Elmhurst and retain no sign of the original headstones: one is on the site of the Newtown Playground across from the Queens Center Mall, and the other is on the site of the Moore Homestead Playground along Broadway, which is where the Moore house stood from the 1660s until 1929, when subway construction on the IND line led to its demolition.

The third Moore cemetery is still extant and is a true hidden treasure. In fact, when I was looking for it, I passed right by before I doubled back and found it. It was supposed to be there, I told myself as I looked at my map. Where was it? And then I saw it. What looks like an abandoned shady, shrubby lot behind a chain-link fence is in reality the Moore-Jackson Cemetery, a time machine to the 1700s.

Located at 31-30 to 31-36 Fifty-Fourth Street in Woodside (between Thirty-First and Thirty-Second Avenues and Fifty-Fourth Street and Fifty-First Street—which was known as Bowery Bay Road back then), the site's usage dates to the 1680s, when Samuel Moore built a house on the Moore property (which at the time was huge and extended to the East River). The cemetery at this location dates to 1733 and survived even after the other parts of the Moore property were sold. The farmhouse did not survive (it was demolished in 1901), but the cemetery and some gravestones are still there (forgotten by the early twentieth century and rediscovered in 1919). The site was declared a New York City Landmark in 1997 so is protected from destruction. It is currently owned by the Queens Historical Society.

There are currently fifteen headstones in the cemetery, some legible and others not so much (though a nineteenth-century survey found forty-six of them and a 1919 survey found forty-two). There have been a few attempts

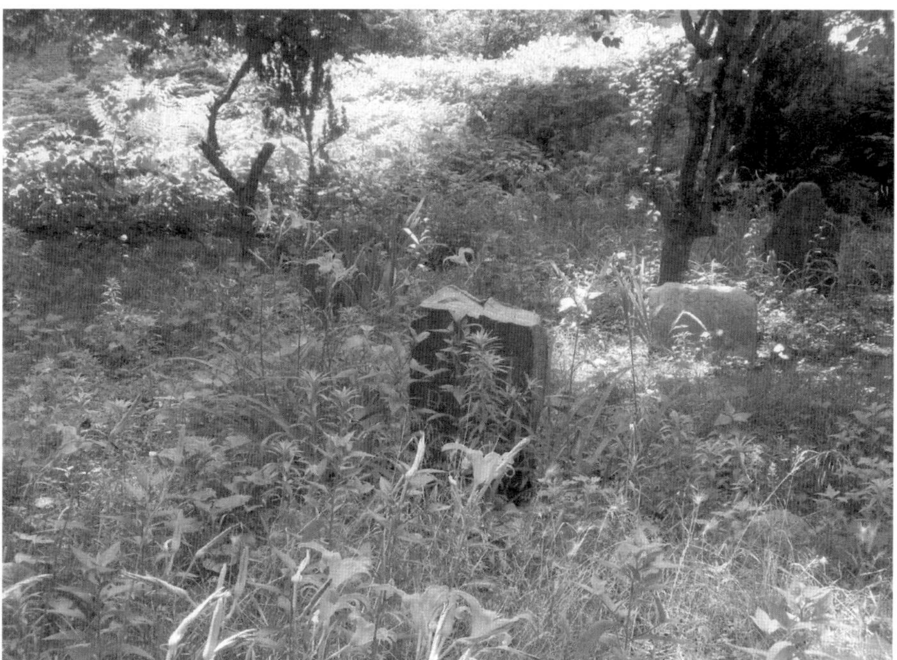

The Moore-Jackson Cemetery in Woodside. *Author's collection.*

at restoration and cleanup, including in 1936, when a WPA project stripped away all the undergrowth, leaving a very bare-looking cemetery. What you see today does not represent the actual arrangement of the original stones. The remaining stones have been re-erected and placed on a forty- by fifty-foot plot facing Fifty-Fourth Street. It makes for a fascinating and eerie reminder of the colonial past in the middle of a crowded residential neighborhood.

Another interesting fact about this property is that Samuel Moore's son Nathaniel was a Loyalist during the Revolution, and British general Henry Clinton used the Moore house as his headquarters for a couple of weeks. It was from there that he planned the attack on Manhattan.

LAWRENCE CEMETERY

One of the oldest cemeteries in New York City is tucked away in the northern reaches of Astoria, between Thirty-Fifth and Thirty-Sixth Streets on Twentieth Road, which itself is a vestige—a curving thoroughfare that breaks out of the grid around it. The road is a remnant of the old Bowery Bay Road from colonial times, as is the cemetery. Set aside in 1654 by Major Thomas Lawrence, who had recently emigrated from England, the private walled cemetery has about one hundred burials, all of them members of the Lawrence family, starting in 1703 with Thomas Lawrence himself. There is another Lawrence family cemetery in Bayside, the first burial in which took place in 1832 and that is owned by the Bayside Historical Society

James Sheehan, who was eighty-eight at the time of this writing, has been caring for the cemetery for sixty-one years. At the time he began watching over the cemetery, the property belonged to his father-in-law, given to him by Ruth Lawrence (1866–1956), the second-to-last last in the Lawrence family line of inheritance (more about that later; she is buried in the cemetery). "I don't know what the reasoning was, but I was attracted to the place," says Sheehan of those early days when he began to take care of the place. He started cutting down the dead trees that made the cemetery seem unkempt, which bothered him greatly. "For some reason, unbeknownst to me, I took a big shine to it. I started taking care of it out of respect for my father-in-law." When his father-in-law died in 1963, the house went to his wife and the cemetery with it.

When Ruth Lawrence's nephew Oliver, who would have inherited it all but had been cut out of her will, approached Sheehan and asked if he could

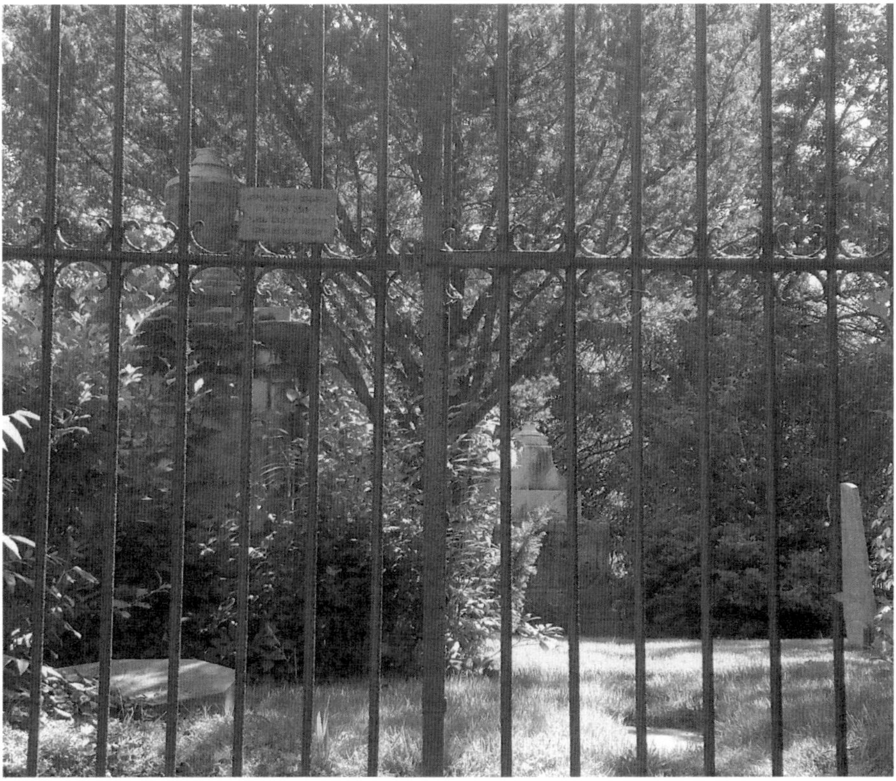

The Lawrence Cemetery in Astoria. *Author's collection.*

be buried in the cemetery, Sheehan agreed; after all, Oliver's parents were there, too. And so it was that in 1975, Oliver Lawrence, a World War I and II veteran and the last to bear the Lawrence name and the last to be buried in the cemetery, was laid to rest there.

The cemetery may be closed to the general public, but Sheehan gets special-request visitors from all over who come to see the final resting place of their family members or who are just serious history buffs. When I spoke to him, he mentioned receiving visitors from Connecticut, Arizona and California.

As he learned of the illustrious history of the Lawrence family, Sheehan gained even more respect for the importance of the cemetery. One of the Lawrences (not buried here, but at Trinity Church Cemetery) was Jonathan Lawrence, the one who uttered the famous words "Don't give up the ship" during the War of 1812 as he lay mortally wounded on his ship, which had been attacked by the British. Other Lawrence family members who actually are buried here include Abraham Lawrence Riker, justice of the New York State Supreme Court; Isaac Lawrence, president of the United States Bank; Major Jonathan Lawrence, Revolutionary War veteran who helped General Washington obtain additional forces for the army and member of the New York Provincial Congress; and Brigadier General Albert Gallatin Lawrence, a Civil War hero. The Lawrences intermarried with other famous Queens families, and the names on the stones reflect that heritage: Riker, Suydam, Rapelye.

Thanks to Sheehan's efforts, the half-acre cemetery was designated as a New York City Landmark in 1966. (Its Bayside counterpart was designated in 1967.) The landmarks commission's report noted that "it serves as the last resting place of many notable citizens of a famous family that has always maintained a leading position in the annals of our history." Sheehan is constantly trying to get additional recognition and grant money to ensure the cemetery is properly maintained. Sheehan takes his cemetery upkeep responsibilities seriously. Even with the plot of land being closed to the public and off limits to potential vandals, the place requires serious upkeep to prevent nature from taking over and to fight the ravages of time. When I spoke to him one summer day, he was nursing a case of poison ivy he got while out among the gravestones, wondering about the stability of the wall enclosing the burial ground.

To walk past this Queens treasure is to contemplate life and death and celebrate three centuries of Queens history. All other glimpses of the neighborhood's colonial history have vanished; even the adjoining home that used to belong to Ruth Lawrence dates only to 1925. It is ironic that markers that remind us of the transient nature of life are often what remain with us the longest.

Remsen Cemetery

The Queens community of Rego Park has changed dramatically from the settlement that was known as Whitepot centuries ago. Every last vestige of the distant past has since been demolished save for two remnants—one of which is a street called Trotting Course Lane, which may be one of the more archaic and bizarre New York City street names out there. As the name might indicate, the street dates to the nineteenth century, when people used it for, pardon the pun, horsing around. Trotting Course Lane used to extend much farther; what is left now is just a small segment of the road that used to exist.

The second and more interesting vestige of the past dates to the eighteenth century and is tucked away, just off Trotting Course Lane, hidden in plain sight within a small triangle of greenery just steps from homes and streets and a Home Depot—the Remsen Family Cemetery.

The Remsen family, of German origins and originally called Van Der Beek, settled on Long Island in the late seventeenth century. One branch of the Remsens settled in what was known as Hempstead Swamp, then part of the sprawling Town of Newtown, and now the Rego Park and Forest Hills area. A member of that family, Jeromus Remsen, fought in the French and Indian War in 1757 and was active in local Newtown politics. When the colonies declared their independence, Remsen was one of the minority in Newtown, and in Queens County in general, who was not loyal to the king. He was a "Whig," as the Patriots were known, and his army experience made him the perfect choice to lead a regiment of militia soldiers. Remsen

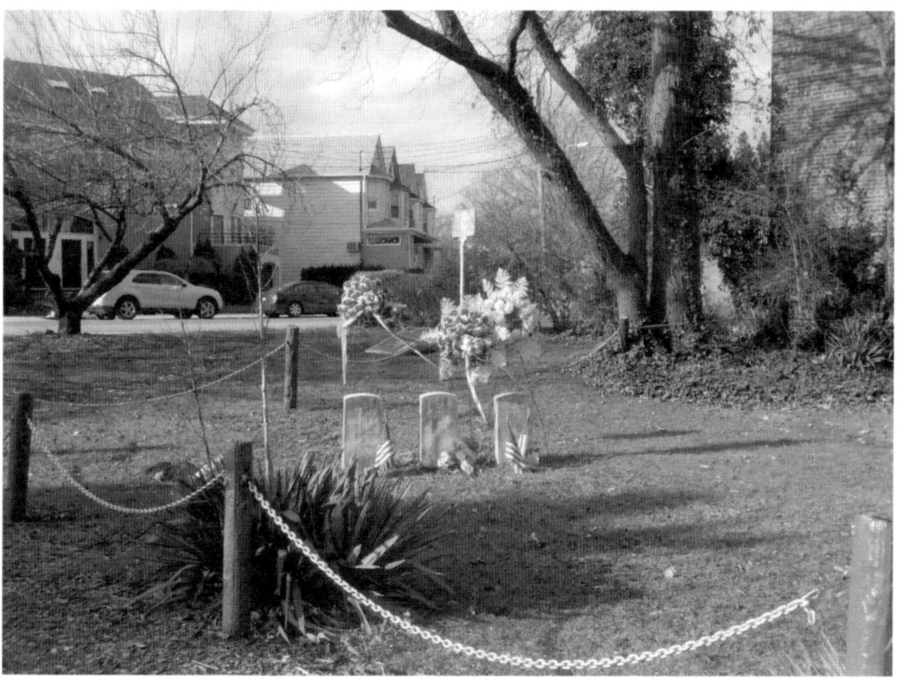

The Remsen Cemetery in Rego Park. *Author's collection.*

became a colonel and gathered a small group of men under his command in the summer of 1776 as the British massed on Staten Island preparing to attack. After the Americans were routed, he retreated to New Jersey and remained there until after the war.

Jeromus Remsen died in 1790. He and at least seven of his family members (including his brother Major Abraham Remsen, also a veteran of the Revolutionary War) are buried in this little cemetery. Much of the Remsen property was sold in the nineteenth century, and the house itself was demolished in 1925. Sadly, a period of vandalism and neglect followed this. Some years later, an American Legion post bought the cemetery property, but its plans to build were halted due to the graves.

The cemetery, which became a New York City Landmark in 1981, is now owned by the City of New York and maintained by the parks department. Because many of the original markers were destroyed over the years, new ones were erected in 1980 to honor those buried on the site, hidden in plain sight in a busy neighborhood. The day I visited, I was moved by the patriotic solemnity of the site and by the sheer fact of its existence against all odds. I could feel a definite connection to the past as well as a sense of relief at the secure future of this important little burial ground.

CEMETERY IN A PARK

Also in the area of the Remsen Cemetery, in fact just a few minutes away to the southwest, is another preserved small family cemetery. This one is located near the northwestern corner of Juniper Valley Park in Middle Village (much of which was swampy land in the 1700s), on North Sixty-Third Street near Eighty-First Street. The Pullis Farm Cemetery (seven graves) was begun in 1846 on what was then the thirty-two-acre farm of Thomas Pullis, to bury a child. Thomas Pullis (born 1778) was buried there in 1854. His will prohibited the sale of the cemetery, and so it still stands today. The park was created in 1938 and incorporated the cemetery, while the rest of the farmland was sold off. Part of the property went to the St. Margaret's Parish, which built a Catholic church in 1860 on what was called Pullis Road (now Seventy-Ninth Street).

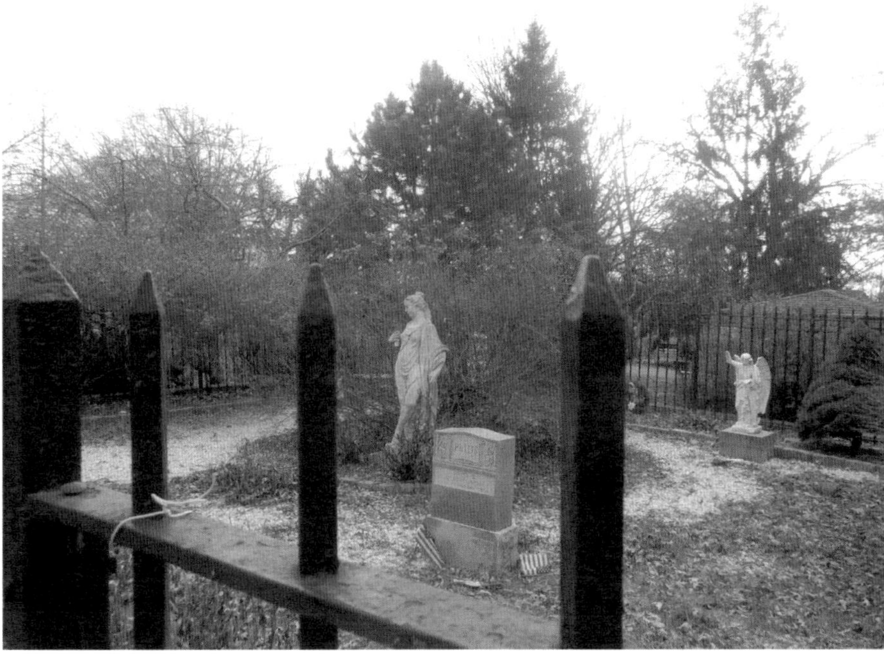

The Pullis Cemetery is located within Juniper Valley Park. *Author's collection.*

THE OLDE TOWNE BURIAL GROUND OF FLUSHING

This cemetery, located on Forty-Sixth Avenue directly across the street from, and dwarfed by, the Flushing Cemetery, has an interesting history. It was formed in 1840 when the Town of Flushing purchased land from the Bowne family to create a cemetery for a public burial ground to house victims of a cholera epidemic. The cemetery, originally known as "Paupers' Burial Ground," was in use for a dozen or so years and then again starting in 1881, when it was used as a burial site for African Americans and Native Americans. By the time it was closed in 1898, there were between five hundred and one thousand burials in the cemetery. The Queens Department of Parks acquired the property in 1914. The four remaining headstones, marking burials of members of the local African American Bunn family, were removed by the parks department.

In 1930, local resident and tree conservationist Everett Marin wrote to the parks commissioner, saying the place was "probably the most unsightly and useless of all the park sites in Queens. It would be greatly appreciated by many in Flushing if the lot could be cleared of brush and graded." In 1931, it was renamed Martin's Field in his honor. In 1936, the Works Progress Administration (WPA) converted part of the site into a playground with a wading pool, baseball field and swings. In the process, the historic significance of the park was downplayed. It was only recently that the city placed more emphasis on the cemetery as a hallowed ground. A 2006 project relocated the playground and placed it on special foundations in order to not disturb the burials. The site was renamed the Olde Towne of Flushing Burial Ground in 2009. Some residents still want the city to display more reverence, including restoration of the four headstones, which are in the city's possession.

Selected Bibliography

Denton, Daniel. *A Brief Description of New York (Formerly Called New Netherlands)*. New York: William Gowans, 1670. Reprint, 1845.

Grasso, Dr. Joanne S. *The American Revolution in Long Island.* Charleston, SC: The History Press, 2016.

Kroplick, Howard, and Al Velocci. *The Long Island Motor Parkway.* Charleston, SC: Arcadia Publishing, 2008.

Official Guide Book of the 1939 World's Fair. New York: Exposition Publications, 1939.

Official Guide New York World's Fair 1964/1965. New York: Time Incorporated, 1964.

Onderdonk, Henry. *Queens County in Olden Times: A Supplement to the Several Histories Thereof.* Jamaica, NY: Charles Welling, 1865.

Panchyk, Richard. *Hidden History of Long Island.* Charleston, SC: The History Press, 2016.

Riker, James. *The Annals of Newtown, in Queens County, New-York.* New York: D. Fanshaw, 1852.

Seyfried, Vincent, and William Asadorian. *Old Queens, N.Y. in Early Photographs.* Mineola, NY: Dover, 1991.

Walsh, Kevin, and the Greater Astoria Historical Society. *Forgotten Queens.* Charleston, SC: Arcadia Publishing, 2013.

I have consulted numerous period newspaper articles while writing this book. Some of the newspapers I have consulted include the *Newtown Register*, the *Daily Star*, *Long Island Daily Press*, *Long Island Star-Journal*, *New York Times*, *New York Sun* and *Brooklyn Daily Eagle*. Fultonhistory.com is a great resource for searching for historical articles about Queens.

Index

Y

About the Author

Richard Panchyk knew he wanted to be a writer by the time he was seven years old. He sold his first "book," a four-page handwritten trivia booklet written on a folded piece of loose-leaf paper in runny blue ink, to a third-grade classmate for a nickel. A proud native of Elmhurst, Queens, Richard attended Stuyvesant High School in Manhattan, where a class on New York ignited his interest in the area's fascinating history. He has published a total of thirty-three books, including nine titles on New York City and five on Long Island. He published his first book with The History Press in 2007.

Visit us at
www.historypress.com